KIN CARE AND THE AMERICAN CORPORATION

Solving the Work/Family Dilemma

KIN CARE AND THE AMERICAN CORPORATION
Solving the Work/Family Dilemma

DAYLE M. SMITH

Business One Irwin
Homewood, Illinois 60430

Sponsoring editor: Jeffrey A. Krames
Project editor: Rebecca Dodson
Production manager: Irene H. Sotiroff
Jacket Designer: Renee Klyczak-Nordstrom
Compositor: Bi-Comp, Inc.
Typeface: 11/13 Palatino
Printer: Arcata/Fairfield

Library of Congress Cataloging-in-Publication Data

Smith, Dayle M.
    Kin care and the American corporation: solving the work/family dilemma/by Dayle M. Smith.
      p.   cm.
    Includes bibliographical references.
    ISBN 1-55623-449-X
    1. Employer–supported day care—United States.   2. Work and family—United States.   I. Title.
HF5549.5.D39S65   1991
331.25—dc20   90–25446

Printed in the United States of America
1 2 3 4 5 6 7 8 9 0 AGF 8 7 6 5 4 3 2 1

To my family, with love

Foreword

I n 1925 when President Calvin Coolidge told the Society of
American Newspaper Editors that "the business of America is
business," it was almost surely understood by those in attendance to embrace a no-nonsense, practical business environment
where managers briskly and efficiently directed work processes,
and employees loyally and dutifully carried out their assigned
tasks. All this was to be accomplished devoid of such distracting
and attention-robbing concerns as personal matters or family considerations.

And Silent Cal was, at least, conceptually right. To a large
extent, the business of America is still business, and profit must
be paramount. What has clearly changed, however, is the very
fabric of this country's labor demographics. The figures are stag-
gering: for example, there are more single-parent families than
ever before. Twenty percent of American children—over 12 million—live in single-parent households. Not only single-parent
households, but *all* households with children have and will have
substantially more working mothers. However, that's not the rev-
olutionary change. In 1947 only 18 percent of mothers worked
outside the home: today almost *two-thirds* of mothers are in the
out-of-home work force. Statistics recently released indicate that
two-thirds of children under age five have mothers in the out-of-
home work force.

This country, the most amazing economic and social success in the history of the world, has simply evolved to the point where corporate concerns and corporate objectives can only be achieved by the manifest recognition of the business necessity for corporate involvement in child and elder care issues.

Our company, Dominion Bankshares Corporation, was the second banking organization in the country to offer an on-site day care center and the first to offer infant care. I tell you now that day care was not an easy decision for us to make. I am mildly ashamed that it took us five years to make that commitment and a little sheepish about that because the need for child care was no less nine years ago for parents who work for us than it is now.

There were corporate skeptics. And the skeptics were right to urge caution. As a business, Dominion is not a child-care center. Dominion is a commercial banking corporation with a reputation for excellence and for quality service and quality assets and profitability. But as I assured our Officers and Board of Directors, there were no altruistic motivations in this decision. We do everything we do with the objective of profit. And we were firmly convinced that our child-care efforts would ultimately lead to more profits. We are not ashamed of that. That's the way the world works. We simply know we must pursue those pragmatic goals of professional excellence and profitability through people dedicated to Dominion and its way of doing business.

Corporate-sponsored day care centers for children are good sense and good business. Consider that children in day care will be workers and stockholders and customers in years to come. Business needs to be concerned that their values be formed in healthy, stimulating, safe, and intellectually nurturing environments. If child development centers prevent drug abuse or crime or poverty the social progress will, in the long run, keep our taxes lower, and that will translate into higher profits for business. And more positively, if young minds are stimulated and children develop basic values and are best prepared for education, business will be developing productive, imaginative, valuable citizens.

Businesses are rooted—and prosper or decline—in the social and economic climates of their time. One must wonder at times about our society's priorities. We have more latchkey children than Dickensian London, yet too often we have chosen to squan-

der the time needed to develop quality dependent care arrangements.

I can affirm that our on-site Child Development Center has
made a huge difference to the Dominion employees it has served.
It has reduced absenteeism, tardiness, and turnover. It has saved
us training dollars, salaries, and overtime. It has enabled careers
and families.

Our Center serves the children of both male and female employees. But its first champions were women. Women seriously
committed to this company and its future and, cared for as children themselves, would have no less for their own children.
Years and years ago, we first looked to these women to respond
to a call to career building and leadership. They determined to
succeed at Dominion not by "becoming men," but by changing
the institution.

We have all learned and benefited. Men. Women. Families.
The company. And, of course, the children.

WARNER N. DALHOUSE
Chairman of the Board and Chief Executive Officer
Dominion Bankshares Corporation
Roanoke, Virginia

Preface

T his book is addressed to working parents and the companies they work for. As such, it is filled with very personal family stories. It's only fair that I share mine as well.

I am a working mother. My 22-month-old daughter, Lauren, is now playing . . . no, that's not true. I don't know what my baby is doing right now, some 14 miles away from me, in the care of Jeannette, a 50-year-old woman I trust, a woman I can't afford. Long waiting lists exist in the few day care centers in my area. There are no openings for a year or more.

I picture Lauren playing happily with Jeannette. I can't let myself picture her hurt, frightened, or lonely while I'm away from her at work. I don't call Jeannette often during the day. I tell myself everything is probably fine.

Do I have to work? That's a painful question to answer. Much as I love my daughter, I like the person I am at work. I like to put my education and my talents to use outside my home as well as inside it. I have to work, for myself.

Then there's the money. My husband and I earn modest salaries, of which 15 percent goes to child care. Together, we can just afford to live within a 30-minute drive of our jobs in Washington, D.C. Living on one salary would require us to move, not only away from Washington, but probably away from any other major urban center. We don't kid ourselves that Chicago or Seattle or

Los Angeles would be more affordable than Washington. Small-town life isn't an option; our jobs don't exist there. I have to work, for us.

My parents and my husband's parents are living. We love them, and in the next decade reasonably expect to be caring for one or more of them in our home. In their later years, they too may require a Jeannette for day care. They may well need us most just as Lauren begins college.

Finally (why does it come to mind last?), there's our marriage. Like sepia lovers in an old cameo, we're still there, looking at each other, looking for each other. We've never doubted how very good we are together, or can be. Our dreams for our 30s, 40s, and beyond don't center on care-giving for children or parents. It may look sappy and silly set here in print, but we really like to get away on a country drive, to play tennis for more than 45 minutes (remember the baby-sitter!), to sleep in on an occasional Saturday, to say yes to civic involvement, to have the energy, passion, and time for each other that we had in our dating days. We like all that stuff, and we want it.

Put another way, we want to be good: good parents, good friends, good lovers, good children, good employees, good citizens, good neighbors.

But somehow, for us and for many other working parents, it's all slipping. We're working at the expense of parenting, or parenting at the expense of work or marriage.

Enter the dream of kin care—a benevolent employer that provides a safe, nurturing environment for Lauren, or Grandma, just around the corner from my office. The dream continues: I pop in during the day to give a hug, maybe share a peanut butter and jelly sandwich. I keep this job *forever*, even without major raises, because it affords what I thought my salary should buy: quality of life. I tell others what a terrific company I work for. I manage family and career without losing myself.

Exit the dream. My employer, like 95 percent of American companies, has no direct form of kin care. When Lauren is sick, I stay home with her. To his credit, and his professional disadvantage, my husband takes turns with me. Nothing new or noble here, of course; it's a story familiar to every working parent.

The story of *Kin Care and the American Corporation* is really the story of possibilities. Like half-starry nights, bright experiments in kin care have glowed, and just as often faded, during the past decade. As the 1990s begin, thousands of companies are watching, listening, and waiting—watching the kin care attempts of their competitors, listening to the "must have" demands of employees with children, and waiting for congressional action.

Working parents are waiting as well. They are waiting for rising child-care costs, or the arrival of an elderly parent on the doorstep, to tip household budgeting from "difficult" to "impossible." They are waiting, often in quiet dread, for the call from a caregiver: "I won't be able to sit after tomorrow because. . . ." They are waiting for the inevitable sick spell that lasts more than a day or two—the fevers or upsets that demand a parent's care, in spite of crucial meetings, projects, and business trips. For single parents especially, the waiting can be depressing and frightening.

As I think about my daughter, now approaching her naptime (Will she cry for long in her crib? Did she eat a good lunch? Did Jeannette change her?), I recognize that this book will not yield a single "game plan" for meeting your needs and those of your children. Nor will this book emphasize family finances, corporate responsibility, or what singer Paul Simon called "the mother and child reunion."

This book is primarily about experiments—possibilities spawned by creative employees and insightful corporations for resolving the work/family dilemma. Selfishly, I want one of those experiments to build a fire under my employer, to rescue me from many of the working parent's headaches and heartaches. More generally, I want to help other parents, corporate decision makers, and government planners answer these questions of the 1990s: Who will take care of the kids? Who will help us care for our parents? How do we manage work and family?

But now I have to phone home.

DAYLE M. SMITH

Acknowledgments

M any people helped make this book possible, including the hundreds of corporate employees who shared their experiences; the managers and corporate spokespersons who spent time describing their programs and discussing the challenges of balancing work and family; the parents and caregivers who shared their perspectives; the children and elders who spoke with me about what it means to receive care; and my friends and relatives who understood what writing a book means.

I want to thank the Graduate School at Georgetown University, along with Dean Bob Parker and Associate Dean Ali Fekrat, for supporting this research endeavor. My colleagues at Georgetown all, in some way, contributed to my thinking and helped encourage me in this project. Special thanks to Bob Bies, Elizabeth Cooper–Martin, Mary Culnan, Karen Gaertner, Bill Gardner, Doug McCabe, Stan Nollen, Dennis Quinn, and Annette Shelby. Thanks also go to my friends who shared their experiences and ideas with me: Patti Allman, Jeanne and Don DiAmicis, Wendy Feldman, Cate and Lew Fernandez, Shelly and Gary Rothschild, Caren Siehl, Lisa Beatty, and Carolyn Walsh.

Special thanks to my research assistants Arthur Bell, Sr., Dorothy Bell, Susan Frank, Kye Johanning, Antonio Peña, and C. Whitney Mandel. For assistance in correspondence, manuscript preparation, and other research support, I want to thank Emmy

Curtis, Virginia Flavin, Al Razick, and Dorothy Sykes in Faculty Services.

I especially appreciated the time, effort, and enthusiasm of Scott Mies, Director of the Fel–Pro Daycare Center, President Paul Lehman, and Vice President of Human Resources Bob O'Keefe, all of whom gave me special insights. Corey Gold, Director of the Children's Center at Baptist Hospital in Miami; Steve Zwolak, Director of MCCARE at McDonnell Douglas; Phil Sharkey, Senior Vice President at American Bankers Insurance Group; Warner Dalhouse, CEO of Dominion Bankshares; and Bill McCullough, Senior Vice President at US Sprint also deserve thanks for sharing their perspectives, concerns, and hopes for corporate kin care.

Other professionals so helpful in the research process include Emily Baker, The Conference Board; Ed Coates, Bureau of Labor Statistics; Gail Bjorklund of the Fairfax County Employer Child Care Council; Barbara Dykes and Sherry Sheridan of Play & Learn Corporation; Dave Gleason and Dianne Huggins, of Corporate Child Care, Inc.; Sarah Ann Gomez and Jim Smith, IBM; Rosalyn Karll, Administrative Director and Founder of BASE; Martin O'Connell, Bureau of the Census; Carol Anne Rudolph of Child Care Management Resources; Margery Scher of Fried & Scher, Inc.; Carol Statuto, Minority Deputy Staff Director for the Select Committee on Children, Youth and Families, U.S. House of Representatives; and Theresa Steitz, The Partnership Group, Inc.

The wealth of information provided by so many people in over 100 companies throughout the country truly enriched this book. I do want to extend extra thanks to the following individuals who were so helpful: Laura Avakian, Beth Israel Hospital, Boston; Madeline Baker, Lincoln National; Melvin Benjamin, Johnson & Johnson; Allen Bergerson, Kodak; John Bradley, J.P. Morgan; Deborah Burke, EG & G; JoAnne Brandes, S.C. Johnson & Son; Joyce Bustinduy, Levi Strauss; Pat Calloway, EDS; Alice Campbell, Baxter Healthcare; C. Gregory Cash, Northrop; Jane Cassi, Warner-Lambert; Cindy Chin, Calvert Group; Patsy Clemons, Baker Hughes; Kathleen Cucchiarella, PepsiCo; Jan Cuddington, Bell Atlantic; Marianne DeLuca, Pacific Telesis; Christopher Dona, Hasbro; Bruce Donatuti, Citicorp; Carolyn E. Dorais, Con Edison; Richard Dorazil, Motorola; Russell East, Exxon; Joan Engstrom, General Mills; Richard Erickson, J.C. Penney; Camille Emig, Anheuser-Busch; Janice Frazier-Scott, Federal Express;

Sheila Friedman, Hercules; J. David Furman, Dominion Bankshares; Elenor Gathany, Hershey Foods; Beverly George, McGraw-Hill; Missy Gegenheimer, McDermott Inc.; Emily Gilreath, Bureau of National Affairs; Julie Goldstein, Fannie Mae; Tracy Grantham, Household International; Debra Hall and Peter Jeff, Steelcase; Heidi Hawkins, Mobil Oil; Jacqueline Hempstead, Security Pacific; Deb Holt, US Sprint; George Johnson, Chrysler Motors; Donna Klein, Marriott; Mary Kramer, Sovran Bank; Adrienne Lallo, Hallmark; Brenda Lane, Ameritech; Karen Leibold, Stride Rite; Janet Louie, Charles Schwab; Sarah Mullady, Champion International; Rosemary Mans, Bank of America; Carla Mazotti, Tandem; Thomas Milligan, Merrill Lynch; Eugene Moore, Armstrong; Liz Needleman, UNUM; Robert Nash, Phillips Petroleum; Wendy Oden and Michael Mitchell, America West; Louise Perna and Judy Sonnett, Du Pont; Marte Pendley, Mervyns; Cynthia Perez, Manville; Laura Peterson, Cornerstone Child Care Centers; Nancy Platt, HBO; Judy Prutzman, Chevron; Terri Quinn, The Travelers; Beulah Richards, Cutler Ridge Elementary; Karol Rose, Time Warner; Judith Sanders, Grumman; Anthony Sapienza, Grieco Brothers; Michael Schmauderer, Zenith; Dan Scott, Burlington Northern Railroad; Joe Silberman, Leo Burnett; Diane Sikova, Upjohn; Margaret Stoltzfus, Lancaster Labs; Judith K. Stratman, Group 243; Art Strohmer, Merck; Peter Trikaminas, TIAA-CREF; Linda Vann, American Bankers; Lynn Warne, Honeywell; Marilyn Weisenberger, Syntex; R.V. Welty, Union Carbide; Annette Zalner, Kellogg; and Veronica Zollo, American Airlines.

Special thanks go to my editor, Jeffrey Krames, for his enthusiasm and support for the project and to Becky Dodson, my project editor, who was such a pleasure to work with for so many months. My copyeditor, Gene Zucker, deserves special credit as well. His editing was instrumental in helping me turn a manuscript into a book. Thanks also to the excellent staff at Business One Irwin—to May Stern and Michelle Krueger for their contributions and to the many others who worked on the book.

Throughout the writing of the book, Jeannette Connell was a wonderful caregiver to my daughter Lauren. She helped me manage the balance between family and work.

Finally, I want to thank my family—husband Art, baby daughter Lauren, Art, Jr.—along with my parents, Owen and Hinda Smith, for all their love, support, and inspiration.

Contents

KIN CARE PROGRAMS IN CORPORATE AMERICA

Chapter One

To Market, to Market

KIN CARE IN A GLOBAL ECONOMY

I t isn't unusual for working parents to get excited about the possibility of kin care at or through their workplace.

When Honeywell polled 1,200 salaried employees in 1986 (70 percent men, 30 percent women) regarding work/family issues, an overwhelming majority pointed to "routine care for children, adult children, and aging parents" as their major concern. One employee noted on the survey form, "I think employers such as Honeywell need to understand the changing roles in dual-career couples. When our children are sick or require emergency attention, I need to share those responsibilities with my wife, who is also employed full-time outside the home. Too often, people and companies perceive those responsibilities to be the sole responsibility of the wife/mother. I like my job very much, but my family is and will continue to be my first priority. When and if push comes to shove, my family comes first."

When Du Pont surveyed 4,000 of its employees in 1989, the company discovered that "25 percent of the men and about 50 percent of the women have considered seeking another employer who might offer more work or family flexibility," according to Du Pont personnel manager Benjamin D. Wilkinson. About half of all employees across industries, in the 1986 *Fortune* magazine Child

1

Care Study, favored on-site/near-site care centers, partial reimbursement from the company for child-care costs, or flextime to deal with child-care problems.[1]

"So?" a senator asked me bluntly two days after the Act for Better Child Care had passed the Senate Labor and Human Resources Committee. "*Wants* do not necessarily define true *needs*. The same workers would overwhelmingly say yes to the offer of a company car."

The senator's argument, expressed at length that day, was that working parents will *always* lobby for increased convenience or security.

Perhaps so. But the need for kin care through the workplace goes far beyond the "Make a Working Parent Happier" argument. How we care for our children and our elderly relatives directly impacts national competitiveness in the global marketplace. In short, kin care isn't a convenience issue—it may well become *the* survival issue for our country's business interests in the 1990s and beyond.

KIN CARE AND THE AMERICAN ABILITY TO COMPETE ABROAD

Even the cloudiest crystal ball spells out one clear tale for America in the 1990s: We will face trade wars as never before in our history. Our prime competitors for world markets, the Pacific Rim consortium and the now-solidifying European Economic Community, have spent the last decade building an economic and industrial infrastructure for the "Sold War" that is already replacing the Cold War.

Japan's success in seeding and feeding the efforts of its industrial giants has been much heralded (and often envied by American manufacturers). But less well known is the changing face of Japan's work force. The number of Japanese women returning to work has quadrupled in the last two decades—and this despite powerful cultural pressure for mothers to stay at home. By law, Japanese mothers are given 14 weeks of paid maternity leave. Some 23,000 licensed child-care centers and an even larger number of unlicensed centers have grown up to deal with the back-to-work phenomenon among Japanese mothers.

The nations of Western Europe, along with other industrialized nations, have taken even more significant action to strengthen their growing work force. Their rationale is straightforward: only by providing solutions to work/family conflicts can substantial numbers of new workers be brought into the labor force.

In France, for example, working parents can drop their three- to six-year-olds at free public preschools for day care and education. Infants of working parents are cared for through the crèche system, a network of infant-care centers located at the heart of industrial and commercial centers. Some 79,000 infants are cared for in 1,497 crèches, only 167 of which are private. Costs to the employee/parent run from $3.75 *a week* for occasional use to $90 a week for full-time care, with all other expenses (a total of $190 per child per week) paid for by the state. France also provides child-care centers called *haltes garderies* where preschoolers can play for a few hours at a time, and *nourrices,* nurses who care for other children and their own. In regions where these services are over-subscribed, the government provides subsidies of up to $340 per month for parents who hire in-home help with child care.

In Sweden, the full range of child-care options has been in place since 1980—mandatory paid leaves for parents of infants, heavily subsidized child-care centers and services, and an array of flextime work schedules to encourage part-time work for the care-giving parent. These programs, says University of Chicago economist Gary S. Becker, "have a huge effect on the labor force participation of married women. More than 80 percent of Sweden's married women with young children work."[2]

Denmark provides new parents with a maximum paid leave of six months, with the first three months reserved for the mother. Half of all Danish children under three and two thirds of those between the ages of three and five are enrolled in a public child-care facility. Fees paid by parents average around $125 per month per child. Where spaces are not available, as is often the case for infants, the government pays caregivers to watch two or three babies in their homes.

Even the Soviet Union, beset by economic woes in its efforts to participate as a powerful world trader, has maintained a strong child-care system. Mothers may take up to four months of paid maternity leave from their work, and additional leave at reduced pay through their child's first year. The government provides day-care centers for children from three months of age through the elementary school ages, though these centers vary widely in the quality of their services. In a snafu oddly suggestive of many American mothers' day in, day out child-care conflicts, the Soviet government recently confronted 90,000 angry mothers in Turkmenia who were on unofficial strike because they lacked adequate day-care facilities.

THE UNITED STATES AND WORKING WOMEN

The United States, by contrast, is the only industrialized nation that does not provide the right to maternity leave, much less a government-supported child-care system for working parents. A mother's right to keep her job for three months *without pay* after the birth of a child (the 1990 Family and Medical Leave Act) was vetoed by President Bush. Congresswoman Pat Schroeder puts the matter bluntly: "We're the only country where a woman can be fired for having a baby."[3]

Writing in *Working Mother*, Child Care Action Committee board members Vivian Cadden and Sheila Kamerman sum up the lonely position of the United States at the bottom of the family policy ladder: "All through Europe, indeed in most industrialized countries, working mothers are guaranteed paid leaves to stay home with their infants and then helped to return to work with a variety of government-sponsored fully or partially funded child-care arrangements. The principal difference between the American working mother and her counterpart in the rest of the industrialized world is that the American woman gets virtually no help. She's on her own."[4]

Table 1–1 demonstrates the stark contrast between U.S. child-care policies and those of other industrialized nations.

While women remain the primary caregivers for young children, the issue of child care in the United States is hardly a "women's issue," especially if that term implies that child-care solutions will benefit only women. A 1988 Du Pont study of 6,600 employees revealed that nearly half of the employees using or planning to use child care were men (see Figure 1–1). One third of the men surveyed said they were interested in part-time work

FIGURE 1–1
How Fathers Feel About Child Care

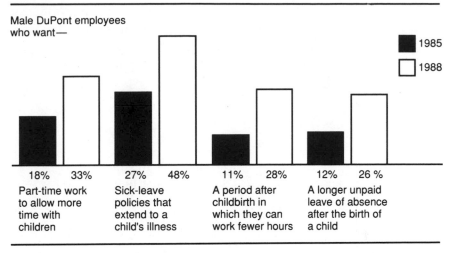

Male DuPont employees
who want—

■ 1985

□ 1988

18% 33%	27% 48%	11% 28%	12% 26 %
Part-time work to allow more time with children	Sick-leave policies that extend to a child's illness	A period after childbirth in which they can work fewer hours	A longer unpaid leave of absence after the birth of a child

Note: Based on surveys conducted by Du Pont of their employees in 1985 and 1988.
Source: The study and recommendations of the Du Pont Work and Family Committee are described in a new brochure, "Diversity—A Source of Strength," External Affairs, Du Pont Company, Wilmington, Delaware, 1989.

to accommodate child-care responsibilities, and half said they would like sick leave policies extended to cover time off to care for an ill child. Prior to the survey, the company thought "child care was still a female issue," says Faith Wohl, cochair of Du Pont's Corporate Work and Family Committee. "Clearly, that is no longer the case."

"Men feel cheated of time with their families too," says Linda Colvard Dorian, executive director of the National Federation of Business and Professional Women. "More men are asking for paternity leave and refusing job reassignments because of conflicts with the lives of their wives and children." Her point is underlined by a 1989 survey of 1,000 workers by Robert Half International. Nearly 8 out of 10 women *and* men said they would prefer a job that gave them adequate time for their families, even if that meant slower career advancement.[5]

TABLE 1-1
The Big Picture

Country	Percent of Women with Children under Six in Labor Force	Length of Paid Job-Protected Leave	Percent of Wage Replaced	Available to Fathers	Additional Benefits	Percent of Children under Three in Part- and Full-Time Care	Percent of Children Three–Six in Part- and Full-Time Care
Finland	75%	10½ months, including 1 month before birth	80%	Last 6 months	Job-protected leave until child is three, paid at lower level; four days annual paid sick-child leave	67% of two-year-olds and 33% of one-year-olds	70%
France	60	16 weeks, including 6 weeks before birth	90	No	Two-year unpaid parental leave for either parent; modest cash benefit for low-income families	45% of two-year-olds; 10–15% of under twos	97
West Germany	50	14 weeks, including 6 weeks before birth	90	No	18 months modest cash benefits	Under 5%	80
Hungary	80	24 weeks, including 4 weeks before birth	65–100%, depending on prior work history	No	For those who qualify, following 24 weeks, 75% of wages until child is 1½, then modest cash benefits; sick-child leave also	10–20%	85–90

Italy	45	5 months, including 2 months before birth	80%	Partly	One-year unpaid job-protected leave	5–10%	75
Sweden	80	15 months	One year at 90%; 3 months at low flat rate	Yes	3 additional months unpaid job-protected leave; right to work six-hour day until child is eight; sick-child leave	76% for all ages one–six	unknown
United States	57	No national policy	No national policy	No	Where paid disability leave is available, it must apply to pregnancy and maternity; about half of the states require unpaid job-protected leave	20%	70

Source: *Working Mother*, September 1990, p. 67.

THE RESULT: WILLING WORKERS STUCK AT HOME

What's wrong with a trained, talented woman or man opting to spend a month, a year, or a lifetime at home giving care to children? Absolutely nothing . . . unless that person *wants* to be working outside the home, but can't because of care-giving responsibilities. Fully 26 percent of mothers at home with preschool children said they would look for work if "reasonably priced child care were available," according to the U.S. Census Bureau.[6] Significantly, nonworking poor mothers and nonworking single-parent mothers ("nonworking" outside the home) were the most eager to join the work force: 36 percent of nonworking mothers in families with annual incomes below $15,000 and 45 percent of nonworking single, widowed, divorced, or separated mothers said they would seek work if they could find reasonably priced child care. In addition, 13 percent of *working* mothers with pre-schoolers said they would work more hours if additional or better child care were available.

This is the "hidden work force" willing to work—more than 2 million women, with a shadow contingent of men (probably more than we would guess), who are staying at home or working less than they wish to because of inadequate or unaffordable child care.

THE COMING LABOR SHORTAGE

The country needs its hidden work force now. From 1970 to 1985, the total number of American workers grew by 2.2 percent per year. Since 1985, the country has had difficulty sustaining even a 1 percent growth rate in its labor force each year, in large part due to the arrival (or nonarrival) in the labor force of the "baby-bust generation."

The phenomenon of the missing worker is summed up well by *American Demographics:* "The number of births affects the supply of workers decades hence: people born today will not become workers for at least 16 years, and perhaps 20 to 25 years. Right now and until the turn of the century, American business is stuck with a shrinking supply of entry-level workers because the small baby-bust generation, born from 1965 to 1976, will be going to work."[7]

Suddenly, every employer seems to be looking for this "only child generation." The signs posted in convenience stores, restaurants, supermarkets, and department stores tell the story: America is desperately seeking Susan or Sam—*any* warm body willing to work for hourly wages (often well above the minimum wage). But workers of the new generation are hard to find and even harder to keep employed. Roy Rogers, an East Coast fast-food chain, beats the bushes for employees by printing its job applications on the paper place mats served to customers.

The hiring problem has heated the toes of congressional representatives. Congressman Augustus Hawkins (D, CA) points out that the American work force needs special care and feeding: "Between now and the year 2000, women and minorities will constitute 85 percent of the new entrants into the labor force. We can't afford to lose them."[8]

Year by year, the worker shortage caused by the baby-bust generation will travel up the corporate personnel ladder, from entry-level positions to operations to management. With retirement ages dropping steadily in America, we will continue to face the need for educated, skilled workers at all levels of business and industry. A 1988 Bank Street College survey reported in *Fortune* concludes that "6 out of 10 companies are feeling the employee pinch already or expect to be scrounging for workers within the next five years."[9]

The country's best hope of filling these positions—some 21 million of them by the year 2000—lies in its hidden work force, the women who want to work outside the home in addition to playing their care-giving roles inside the home (see Figure 1–2).

THE NEED TO WORK

In 1990, "want to work" may be a polite euphemism in many families for "have to work." David Jordan, editor in chief of *Better Homes and Gardens*, tells of his own married daughter's struggle to combine work and family. "Sarah actually works at home on a computer, making ingenious arrangements for a few hours of day care and working into the night while her son is asleep. I appreci-

FIGURE 1–2
Labor Force Participation

If parents could find child care at a reasonable cost, women's labor force participation rates would rise.

(Actual and potential labor force participation rates for women aged 18 to 44 with children under five years of age, by selected characteristics)

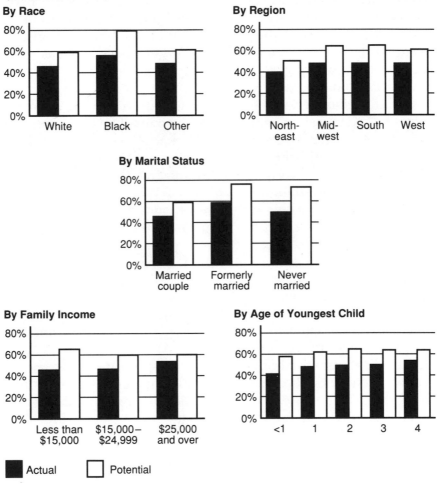

Source: Based on U.S. Dept. of Labor and Census Bureau Data.

ate Sarah's dedication to my grandson, Alex, and I sincerely applaud those parents who have cut back their standards of living so one parent can be home full-time with the kids. . . . However, I also think it's terrible that our young families have to work so hard just to keep afloat, and that working moms have to live with so much guilt and criticism."[10]

That point can be lost too easily: women like Sarah don't want to leave the kids behind for a career, nor do they want to give up all hopes for a career. Instead, they want a work life that fits well with care-giving responsibilities. So do the legions of women who now make up more than half of all MBA students, and who stand a good chance of becoming mothers with careers. In fact, no age group for women shows as large an increase in births as the 35 to 39 age range, up almost 400 percent since 1970.

These are the educated, talented women who are particularly at risk to the American work force unless workable child-care arrangements can be put in place. Given a forced, either/or choice between caring for a child and continuing a career, few mothers would opt for the job, as a 1987 Harris poll made clear. But given the option of meeting both care-giving responsibilities and career challenges, women who want to work won't hesitate to do so.

Janet Everwine, for example, is supervisor of employee services at Campbell Soup. "I wouldn't have been able to return to work if it hadn't been for the day care," she says. "I stayed home for a year and a half after my son Erik was born, but the day the [corporate daycare] center opened, I went back to work."

Figure 1–3 presents the findings of a poll for *Time* magazine reporting on work-life demands and care-giving responsibilities.

THE NATION SEEKS ITS HIDDEN WORK FORCE

Contemplate the implications of these forecasts, summed up in a recent issue of *Fortune:* two thirds of all employees hired between now and the year 2000 will be women, and 80 percent of that number will become pregnant.[11]

Portrayed visually in more detail this means that

- Six out of 10 women will be employed by 1995.

- There will be 20 million children under five by 1995.

FIGURE 1–3
A Woman's Place

In a poll for TIME by the firm Yankelovich Clancy Shulman*, 80% agreed with the statement that "many women today are having a hard time balancing the demands of raising children, marriage and work." Here are some of the findings:

More women are working outside of the home these days. Do you think this is good or bad for:

	Total		Women		Men	
	Good	Bad	Good	Bad	Good	Bad
Marriages	45%	36%	46%	34%	44%	39%
Children	24%	57%	26%	53%	22%	61%
The workplace	66%	12%	69%	10%	62%	15%
Women in general	72%	14%	70%	14%	73%	13%

In your view, most married women who work do so primarily:

	Total	Women	Men
Because they want to	19%	16%	23%
For economic reasons	66%	68%	64%

If one of you had to give up your job for some reason, whose job would it be?

	Total	Women	Men
Husband's	10%	11%	9%
Wife's	84%	84%	83%

Should business provide day care?

	Total	Women	Men
Yes	51%	56%	46%
No	39%	34%	46%

Should government do more to provide day care?

	Total	Women	Men
Yes	54%	56%	51%
No	43%	39%	48%

* The findings are based on a telephone survey of 1,014 adult Americans. The potential sampling error is plus or minus 3%.

Source: *Time*, June 22, 1987

- Two thirds of those children will have a working mother.

Figure 1–4 reports this significant trend of working mothers.

Is America ready, or getting ready, for this massive infusion of new talent and its accompanying work/family conflicts? The signs are hardly promising.

First, women entering the work force have suffered from the "hire-train-birth-quit-hire" cycle. Because the United States is the only industrialized nation without a policy of maternity leave, paid or unpaid, women in many companies despair of combining new child-care responsibilities with work. The result, writes Ronni Sandroff in *Working Woman*, is a "brain drain" for the company as well as "the cost not only of recruiting and training a new employee but also of lost productivity—a cost that Aetna Life & Casualty estimates at a whopping 93 percent of the employee's first-year salary."[12]

Second, women are made to bear inordinate physical and emotional burdens when they attempt to combine work and care-giving roles. In 1989, the *Harvard Business Review* reported on the work of Fran Sussner Rodgers and Charles Rodgers, principals of

FIGURE 1–4
Working Mothers of Children under Six

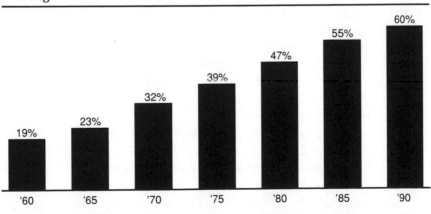

Source: Based on U.S. Dept. of Labor and Census Bureau Data, 1990.

Work/Family Directions, Inc. These researchers demonstrated in their study of two New England high-tech firms that "on average, working mothers put in an 84-hour workweek between their homes and their jobs; working fathers put in 72 hours; and married people with no children put in 50." Working mothers, the study concludes, "are working the equivalent of two full-time (at least 42 hours) jobs a week."[13]

The pressure takes its toll. In 1987, the National Center for Clinical Infant Programs (NCCIP) convened a "summit conference" of leading child-care researchers. One goal of the meeting, cohosted by the National Academy of Sciences and Institute of Medicine, was to discover areas of consensus regarding work/child-care issues. The "chief area of consensus" was the group's agreement "that both mothers and fathers of young children experience significant stress and loss of productivity when high-quality care for infants is not available and affordable, and when staying home to care for an infant is not economically feasible."

A female manager at Honeywell responded to that company's 1986 survey of work/family concerns with this cry for help: "Housekeeping is not the problem. It's being a chauffeur to the doctor, dentist, music lessons, confirmation classes, shopping, etc. I spend an average of three hours every day after work driving kids to and from places, shopping, and waiting for them. My vacation days are usually spent getting house or car repairs done or banking."

Another female employee echoed these concerns about too much stress: "As a young, intelligent woman at Honeywell, I often feel pressure from management to move up my career path at a greater pace than I'd care to. With two preschool children, I would like to keep my career growth at a steady rate that keeps me challenged, but not overwhelmed or overworked. I will not move to a job that pushes me to my limits and possibly jeopardizes my healthy family life."

In all, the Honeywell survey showed 57 percent of women employees under 35 with children agreed with this statement: "I am usually too tired or stressed from work to effectively address my family's day-to-day problems."

Men, too, pay the price of stress. "More than half the people now involved in company-sponsored day care are men," says

Dana Friedman, formerly a senior researcher at the Conference Board, a New York think tank, now co-president at the Families and Work Institute. "It is the fathers who are having the most day-to-day exchange" in arranging for care, taking kids to and from the center, and finding time during the day to visit them.

Take, for example, the story of Tom Zilligen told recently in *U.S. News & World Report.* For four years, the divorced, 39-year-old Zilligen was able to compress his work schedule as an advertising sales rep into a 9–3:30 day, allowing him to see his four kids off to school and pick them up before dinner. His commissions were rising and his boss had no complaints—until a new boss, G. Jake Jaquet, arrived on the scene. "We need employees to put in a certain number of selling hours per month. Anything less represents potentially less sales volume," said Jaquet. "If it is impossible for him to work our schedule, maybe he should find an employer who can accommodate his need for part-time work."[14]

Responded Zilligen, "I'm getting an ulcer. I'm almost to the point of telling them, 'Fine, let me go.'"

Recently, 50 "working fathers" at the New York Port Authority attended a seminar on work/family concerns at the Bank Street College of Education. James Levine, seminar leader and director of the college's Fatherhood Project, says, "If you closed your eyes, you would have thought it was the women talking." Stress over work/family problems doesn't follow gender lines.

THE NATIONAL CHALLENGE

In 1990, even the simplest business matters "turn global" for American manufacturers, distributors, and service industries. The attention the nation pays to its work force, including its hidden work force, should take on an urgency born of our competitive spirit and our survival instinct. We cannot hope to compete against equally trained, equally motivated foreign work forces so long as we are

- The only industrialized nation without a maternity or parent leave policy.

- The only industrialized nation providing virtually no kin care for the vast majority of its workers. That care may not come by government program, but come it must.

In sum, who needs kin care? The nation does, if it expects to compete successfully in the 1990s and beyond against countries and blocs of nations that have acted early to build governmental and corporate solutions to the work/family dilemma.

Chapter Two

How Does Your Garden Grow?

Corporate Advantage through Kin Care

P icture this at your office: Your tyke is just a floor or two away, playing happily with other kids and the trained child-care supervisor. You know you can pop in at lunch for a hug or a tear. You know that you're just a phone call away if "something happens."

The question: Are you now, thanks to child and/or elder care in the workplace, a more *productive* employee? Many studies have concluded that the answer is yes (see Tables 2–1 through 2–4).[1] First, you're more likely to *take a job* that comes with satisfactory child care and/or elder care. Second, you're more likely to *show up* at work, especially if your company makes provision for sick-child care or emergency care. Third, you can devote your *attention* wholly to your work, without frequent phone calls home, mad dashes to pick up or drop off kids, or nagging worries about inadequate or haphazard dependent care arrangements.

The 1978 Perry study surveyed 58 on-site child-care centers located predominantly in hospitals. The results: 88 percent of the employers said that their child-care program aided their recruitment efforts; 72 percent noted that the program reduced absenteeism; and 65 percent felt that the program improved the employee's attitude toward the employer.[2] The 1983 Magid study of

TABLE 2-1 Studies of Employer-Supported Child Care

Research Site	Researcher Cited	Sample	Research Design	Major Findings
Federal Office of Employment Opportunity Washington, D.C.	Krug et al. (1972)	50 parents from center 50 in control group	Pre-/posttest of users compared to control group	Center users had greater increase in sick leave. Annual leave taken by users decreased after center opened; it decreased more for nonusers.
Control Data Consortium Minneapolis, Minn.	Milkovich and Gomez (1976)	30 center users 30 parent nonusers 30 nonparents	Posttest of center users compared to two control groups	Lower employee absenteeism and turnover rates were related to enrollment in the center, while no relationship to job performance was found.
North Carolina textile firm	Youngblood et al. (1984)	410 people in company with center and three divisions of another firm with no center	Comparisons of employees in firm with center and those in firm without	Center users higher on job satisfaction, commitment, organizational climate, and lower on turnover. In company with center, 19% drop in absenteeism and 63% drop in turnover rate.
Multiple companies— national	Dawson et al. (1988)	311 employees in 29 companies with various child-care programs	Posttest of employees using various company-sponsored child-care programs	Program users likely to recommend employer, continue with company, work overtime. Child care affected acceptance of promotion. Center yielded greater effects than referrals or financing.
State of New York Children's Place Albany, N.Y.	WRI (1980)	88 users of center one year after opening	Postsurvey of users (66% response)	35% of users said center enabled them to stay working; 73% said absences declined; 47% said productivity increased; 83% said they worried less
Kid's Play—state of Wisconsin pilot day-care center	State (1987)	56 users 35 supervisors of center users	User perceptions surveyed before enrollment, 5 months after opening, and 17 months after. Manager perceptions also surveyed.	89% of users satisfied with center quality; 73% said center helped them be more productive; 82% said center reduced worry and had positive effect on scheduling.
Ina S. Thompson Child Care Center—state of Florida	Department of Administration (1987)	37–62 users 42 supervisors of center users	User perceptions surveyed 9 months after opening, and users interviewed one year later. Interviews with managers.	Users reported positive effects on work. Center helped reduce worry about children. Of center users, 49% said they were absent less, 60% were late less, and 93% would consider child care before changing jobs.
Multiple companies with child care—national	Perry (1978)	58 employers, most with on-site centers	Survey of manager perceptions	Two thirds or more of managers believed that the child-care program helps recruit, lowers absenteeism, and improves attitudes toward company.

Site	Citation	Sample	Method	Findings
Catherine McAuley Health Center Ann Arbor, Mich.	Marquart (1988)	86 parents using hospital-based child-care center or family day-care program; matched to group of other child-care users	Pre-/posttest of hospital center users compared to users of hospital-sponsored family day care and parents using other child care	Users had decreased absences of 1½ days per employee. Recruitment, retention, and recommending employer more likely among users. No differences in job satisfaction, stress, or turnover.
Union Bank Los Angeles	Burud et al. (1988)	87 users one year before center opened and one year later	Pre-/posttest of users compared to control group, parents on waiting list and other bank employees	Center users absent 1.7 days less than other parents; maternity leaves were 1.2 weeks shorter for center users; 61% of job applicants said center was a factor in accepting a job at banks. Turnover and public relations also positively affected.
Dominion Bank Roanoke, Va.	Burge and Stewart (1988)	400 randomly selected employees	Postsurvey of all employees and users	Users believe that the center helped reduce absenteeism, aided recruitment, and improved productivity
Methodist Hospital Arcadia, CA	Burud et al. (1984)	123 users of center	Postsurvey of user perceptions (71% response)	Center helped keep 41% of users; 51% said center was a factor in accepting job; 61% said productivity improved; 79% said morale improved.
Multiple companies with child care—national	Magid (1983)	204 employers with child-care programs, mostly on-site	Survey of manager perceptions	Asked to rank the five most significant effects of their child-care program, managers listed recruitment, morale, lower absenteeism, and lower turnover.
Multiple companies with child care	Burud et al. (1984)	178 employers, most with on-site centers	Survey of manager perceptions	Managers believe that turnover, productivity, morale, and recruitment were positively affected by center, while absenteeism and tardiness were reduced.
Statewide survey of employers—Minnesota	AAUW (1982)	563 firms with and without child care	Survey of manager perceptions in 200 randomly selected companies and subsequent interviews	More than two thirds of companies believed that child-care support would decrease absenteeism and tardiness and increase productivity, recruitment, retention, and morale
Statewide survey of employers—New York	Governor's Commission on Child Care (1986)	1,041 firms with and without child care	Survey of manager perceptions in 10,558 firms	Belief in child care's ability to improve work performance is related to company size, with larger companies more likely to believe that recruitment, retention, absenteeism, tardiness, stress, and morale are positively affected.

Source: Tables 2–1—2–4 adapted from Dana Friedman, *Linking Work-Family Issues to the Bottom Line: A Summary of Research* (New York: Conference Board, 1991).

TABLE 2-2 Perceptions of Managers Regarding Effects of Employer-Sponsored Child-Care Center

	Managers of Center Users			Managers in Multiple Companies with Child Care			Managers in Multiple Companies with and without Child Care	
	Dominion Bank 1988	Wisconsin 1987	Florida 1987	Perry 1978	Magid 1983	Burud 1984	Minnesota 1982	New York 1986
Improves productivity	**48%**	60%	38%		*	49%	72%	32%
Improves motivation	40	43			67	63		
Improves satisfaction		66			170	83		
Improves attitude toward work				55%				
Improves morale	70	**88**			345	**90**	**85**	**44**
Reduces absenteeism	45	71	**62**	**72**	**214**	53	**89**	**42**
Reduces tardiness	33	54	**43**		88	36	67	36
Reduces stress						50		41
Increases scheduling flexibility								
Reduces turnover		23		57	211	65	71	39
Improves attitude toward employer				65				
Increases loyalty/commitment						73		35
Increases women returning from leave		43			208	79		
Improves recruitment				**88**	**448**	85	73	35
Improves public image/publicity		77		60	137	80		
Increases availability of temporary help					26	42		
Improves quality of work force					205	40		
Increases equal employment opportunity					13			
Improves community relations				36				
Improves quality of products/services	30				154	**85**		
Increases profits					48	37		
Reduces training costs							41	14

Boldface numbers indicate the first and second rankings. * The Magid study findings are not percentages; they are rank orderings.

TABLE 2–3
Perceptions of Employees Using Employer-Sponsored Child-Care Centers

	Dominion Bank	Methodist Hospital	Southeastern Hospital	State of Wisconsin	State of Florida	State of New York
Improves productivity	67%	61%	51%	73%	60%	47%
Increases motivation				72		
Increases job satisfaction						
Improves morale		**79**				
Decreases absenteeism	**84**	75	67	72	60	
Decreases tardiness	60	**79**	60	46	57	**83**
Reduces stress						
Improves scheduling flexibility	40	69		**82**		
Able to work more overtime	63	62				
Able to work odd shifts		43	42			
Reduces turnover	70	41	**72**	25	43	35
Improves attitude toward employer					**84**	
Increases women returning from leave		33				45
Improves recruitment		51			81	
Improves public image					87	
Would recommend employer	**74**					
Improves promotability		17				

Boldface numbers indicate the first and second rankings.

TABLE 2–4
Findings from Experimental Studies

	Krug et al. (1972)	Milkovich et al. (1976)	Youngblood et al. (1984)	Dawson et al. (1984)	Marquart (1988)	Union Bank (1988)
Improves productivity/performance		O		*		+
Increases job satisfaction					O	
Improves morale			*			+
Improves organizational climate			*			
Decreases absenteeism	−	*	O	O	+	+
Decreases tardiness	−					+
Reduces stress				*	O	
Able to work overtime						
Reduces turnover		*	*	*	*	+
Increases loyalty/commitment			*		O	
Increases women returning from leave						+
Improves recruitment	+			*	*	+
Would recommend employer				*	*	+
Improves community/public relations						+
Improves promotability				O		

* Statistically significant differences found between center users and companion group(s).
+ Differences found between center users and others, but no statistical test proved it.
O No differences found, or couldn't measure the outcome in question.
− The opposite effect occurred (e.g., absenteeism increased).

204 companies with child-care programs produced a similar list of productivity advantages.[3] In Burud's 1984 study of 178 companies, 90 percent of the managers felt that the child-care program had improved morale, 85 percent pointed to the program's recruitment advantages, and 85 percent said that the program had had a positive effect on public relations. In addition, 65 percent believed child care reduced turnover, 49 percent reported improved productivity, 53 percent reported decreased absenteeism, and 39 percent said tardiness decreased.[4]

In a review of 16 studies of employer-supported child care, Dana Friedman found that in experimental study designs comparing employees who used child-care centers with employees who did not use child-care centers, the centers benefited employers by reducing turnover and improving recruitment. In surveys of employees and managers on their perceptions regarding the effects of child-care centers, the results indicate that both managers and employees using the centers see the greatest benefit of the centers as improved morale. In most of the research done, manager perceptions seem to indicate that child-care centers can reduce absenteeism and increase productivity.

Elder-care responsibilities, like child-care responsibilities, affect the company significantly. Care-giving employees are more likely to report themselves as experiencing poor health, according to the House Select Committee on Aging.[5] In a study conducted by the University of Bridgeport, care-giving employees experienced more headaches, weight changes, anxiety, and depression than other employees and were more likely than other employees to be seeing a doctor because of a chronic health condition.[6] Executives, polled by *Fortune* magazine, reported overwhelmingly (60 percent) that providing elder care by employees or by the executives themselves resulted in stress, late arrivals, early departures, unscheduled days off, excessive telephone use, and absenteeism.[7] If you assume that approximately 20–40 percent of employees are caregivers, these problems could easily cost a company with 1,000 employees over $500,000 annually.[8]

Sold? If the case were that easy to prove, few companies would resist investing the $20,000 to $500,000 or more per year required to underwite a care program. But we inhabit a time of shrinking employee benefits, of expanding medical "deductibles" (a euphemism for *payables*), of family co-payments to medicaid. For many employees, a wide variety of available benefits are offered by means of the so-called cafeteria approach to benefit selection. Under this approach, choosing what you need from the list of benefits turns into a high-stakes game of Russian roulette. The trick is to choose the benefits you need without going bust.

OPTING FOR KIN CARE

But how do *employers* decide whether to make child- and elder-care programs an option at all? "You make it the same way you make any big decision," answers Larry Taylor, vice president of Taylor Corporation. "Is the problem costing us employees? Is it making it hard to get them? Would it be good business? That's always the bottom line, isn't it?"

Taylor has answered the question in his own mind, after 10 years' experience with his company's on-site child-care center. "We see the benefit," he says, "in positive employee feedback, parental peace of mind, a more dependable work force, improvements in recruitment and retention, and higher numbers of women in management. These are the things that make it worthwhile to us."[9]

Nationwide, however, companies have been suspiciously slow to add kin care options to their benefits list. In 1990, only an estimated 10 percent of America's businesses offered kin care assistance to employees. A majority of those businesses—60 percent—provided for kin care only through flexible work hours, which they counted as their response to employees' kin care needs. Few companies provide real elder-care assistance. That leaves a minuscule percentage of American companies with more traditionally defined kin care programs: on-site or near-site centers, consortium centers, contracted care, ill-child nannies, vouchers, and so forth (see Figure 2–1). Many of these select companies are highlighted in Chapter 9.

These figures give the lie to the headlines and sound bites about the growth of kin care programs: "number of programs tripled since 1985," "enrollments in company child-care up 200 percent," and "total company expenditures for child care rise by 80 percent." Percentage rises are always steep—and widely cited for this reason—at the earliest stages of any new development.

FIGURE 2–1
Employers' Family Benefits and Family Policies

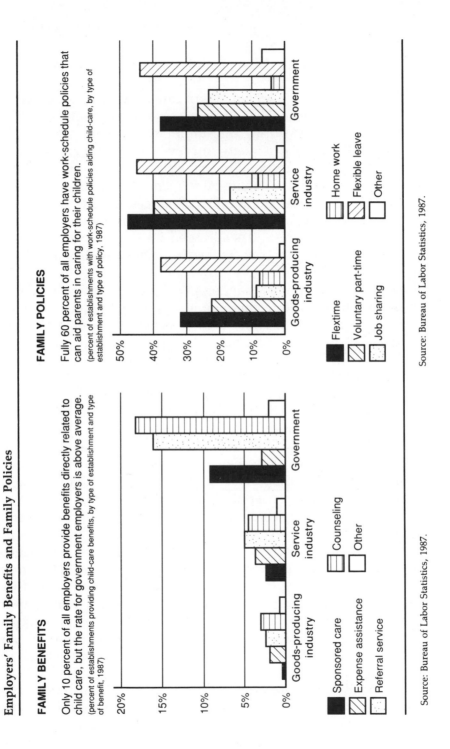

FAMILY BENEFITS

Only 10 percent of all employers provide benefits directly related to child care, but the rate for government employers is above average.

(percent of establishments providing child-care benefits, by type of establishment and type of benefit, 1987)

Sponsored care · Counseling
Expense assistance · Other
Referral service

Source: Bureau of Labor Statistics, 1987.

FAMILY POLICIES

Fully 60 percent of all employers have work-schedule policies that can aid parents in caring for their children.

(percent of establishments with work-schedule policies aiding child-care, by type of establishment and type of policy, 1987)

Flextime · Home work
Voluntary part-time · Flexible leave
Job sharing · Other

Source: Bureau of Labor Statistics, 1987.

25

After all, if two programs expand to four, the increase is 100 percent.

The truth about the growth of kin care in America, however, is revealed in a survey of 10,000 businesses that the Bureau of Labor Statistics conducted during the summer of 1987. As summarized in the *Monthly Labor Review*, the survey "shows that employers as a group have yet to respond in a significant way to the child-care needs of their workers. About 90 percent of establishments with 10 or more employees do not provide direct benefits such as day care or financial assistance."[10] Only 220 corporations, 800 hospitals, and 200 federal and state agencies provide on- or near-site care according to 1990 figures from the Families and Work Institute.[11]

What of the "optimistic reports and comments by experts in the field which indicate that employers are generally becoming more supportive of the child-care needs of their workers"? Those judgments, the researchers note, "are more often than not based on anecdotal evidence rather than surveys with consistent methodologies and definitions."[12] Only 2 *percent* of the 442,000 establishments that reported no child-care benefits or flexible work-schedule policies said that they were "considering" doing something in the future.

Why has American business kept kin care benefits at arm's length? Some corporations may be waiting to see what impact the recent child-care legislation has on managing the child-care shortage. Experts, however, argue that the legislation is unlikely to have a significant impact on the millions of employees who could benefit from an employer response.

The costs of opening a child-care center are still the biggest objection of most employers. The start-up costs can range from $100,000 to $500,000, and most companies subsidize part of the annual operating costs. For example, Little Tikes Company in Hudson, Ohio, subsidizes 35 percent of the operating costs. Campbell Soup Company in Camden, New Jersey, underwrites half the nearly $650,000 annual operating costs of its 106-child on-site facility.

Companies may also worry about liability and insurance premiums for children or elders under corporate care—this in spite of the fact that *INC.* reported in 1988 that "there has not been a successful case against a corporate-sponsored child-care center" and that insurance is affordable (for 30 children, typical insurance costs run between $2,000 and $7,000 a year).[13]

According to JoAnne Brandes, senior counsel for S. C. Johnson & Son (S. C. Johnson Wax), "Liability issues should never be a reason for not getting into child care." Brandes points out that businesses can greatly reduce liability through the legal structure of the program and the establishment of a quality child-care program. "There is nothing you can do that will completely free you of risk in child care, but there are ways to greatly minimize risk." In fact, companies face greater liability problems from daily work practices than from child-care centers. Brandes offered these techniques for minimizing risk:

- Contract the actual operation of the program with a company or agency with child care expertise and require the agency to get insurance with specified limits. Have the center indemnify the company and hold it harmless in case of legal action against the company.

- If the child care program includes transportation, lease the bus driver from a company that carries sufficient liability insurance.

- Contract with a playground company to design and install equipment which operates safely. Be sure to obtain a maintenance contract with the company.

- Contract with a food-service provider and require the provider to indemnify the center.

- Develop and consistently follow written policies regarding discipline, health, transportation, and discharge policies, and make sure parents have a copy.

- Be sure to hire a staff that is equipped to offer first aid and continually provide other training.

- Spend any extra money in the program on establishing lower student/teacher ratios.

- Develop written resource and referral policies, as well as written complaint policies, and require a written disclaimer from parents.[14]

Other experts concur. Liability shouldn't be a reason to say no. Dana Friedman, one of the nation's leading corporate child-care experts and a principal at Families and Work Institute, argues that "the cost of liability insurance is far less than the insurance a corporation needs to cover someone who slips in the lobby and breaks a leg." She continues, "I think the perceived risks concern sex abuse of kids," which, she says, doesn't apply for two reasons. "First of all, it's a felony crime, and no crimes are covered in an insurance policy. Second, it just isn't an issue. No companies with day-care centers are aware of it ever happening."[15]

Corey Gold, director of the Children's Center at Baptist Hospital, points out that clearly written and enforced policies help solve many parent and lawyer concerns. For instance, his center addresses the concern over what happens in the classroom by having classroom doors with glass windows that may not be covered up by posters, artwork, and the like. One can always see what goes on in the rooms. With this concern in mind, when Gold talks with children in his office, his door is always open.

Scott Mies, director of the Fel-Pro Day Care Center, reduced accidents by having the architect build rounded corners into the center.

There's also, inevitably, the problem of organizational inertia. As one human resources director told me, "We don't want to offer another benefit package until we're told we have to."

His statement conveyed an attitude that I confronted again and again in the dozens of extended interviews on kin care that I conducted with corporate decision makers over a two-year period. One message kept coming through loud and clear: "Kin care is a nice idea, but there's just not enough in it for my company."

A survey conducted in 1988 identified other factors that employers saw as obstacles to getting involved in child care. In addition to expense and liability, the respondents regarded the complexity of a child-care system and unfamiliarity with child-care options as major obstacles. Also listed as obstacles were a lack of commitment from top management and a lack of evidence showing that child care provided long-term benefits to the company. Other obstacles mentioned included the following: too few providers of child-care benefits, uncertainty regarding pending legislation, inability to be fair to all employees, lack of knowledge regarding employees' needs, the belief that child care was not a business issue, and objections that might be raised by employees without children.

One chief executive officer, whose business was situated in the "Show Me" state of Missouri, put it this way: "Kin care wouldn't mean more widgets out the door at my company. Now, I grant that some employees might be *happier* if we boarded their kids during the day. But since when is it the goal of a business to make employees happy? This isn't a love-in. As a general rule, employees *don't like work*. They would prefer not to be here. What keeps them working is their need for a paycheck; what keeps them working well is the firm hand of management, with fair rewards and punishments. All the softer things—plush employee lounges, exercise rooms, mountain retreats, and child-care facilities—don't make our electricians connect wires any faster, our painters spray paint any better, or our accountants add numbers any more accurately. American businesses that want to be profitable stay lean and mean, with as few social services as possible."

THE QUESTION OF THE BOTTOM LINE

I couldn't get a word in edgewise at that interview, but I have occasion now to answer this CEO. The attitudes he expressed were the rallying cry of American management 50 years ago, and recall an age when workers labored stolidly in poorly lit and unventilated factories. If an employee quit, good riddance! There was always cheaper help waiting at the employment office. Labor was an unwilling beast that you drove with a stick.

Such management attitudes are summed up well in what Douglas McGregor calls Theory X management principles:

- Work is inherently distasteful to most people.

- Most people are not ambitious, have little desire for responsibility, and prefer to be directed.

- Most people have little capacity for creativity in solving organizational problems.

- People are motivated primarily through monetary rewards and punishments, and through fear of authority.[16]

These assumptions about employees, I believe, continue to delay the arrival of kin care programs in the great majority of American businesses. No matter what their public relations brochures
proclaim, many American businesses are still operated on the
"pay for pain" scheme: employees grudgingly give labor, and
employers grudgingly give pay. Necessary to this scheme are the
"hard drivers," those angry bosses lionized in American corporate life; witness the "Ten Toughest Bosses in America" heralded
by *Fortune* in recent years. In this business mind-set, there is no
place for the concept of kin care.

The management textbooks, of course, say that Theory X principles were passé decades ago—or should have been. New assumptions, new relationships, and new expectations are theoreti-
cally guiding the development of forward-looking companies. As
Apple Computer, IBM, Xerox, and a host of other companies can
testify, the management principles of Theory X just don't apply to
the business realities of the 1990s and beyond. These companies
subscribe, in varying degrees, to McGregor's principles of Theory
Y management:

- Work is as natural as play, if the conditions are
  favorable.

- Self-control is often indispensable to achieving
  organizational goals.

- The capacity for creativity in solving organizational
  problems is widely distributed in the population.

- Motivation occurs for many reasons besides money and
  fear of authority; these reasons include social acceptance,
  self-esteem, and self-fulfillment.

- People can be self-directed and creative at work if they
  are properly motivated.[17]

These principles fit better with the corporate realities of the
1990s. Few companies have the luxury of telling employees to like
it or lump it. Facing a labor shortage and high retraining costs in
the skilled occupations, what company can afford to drive away
good people by managerial anger and verbal abuse? What company can maintain the wrongheaded assumption that employ-

ees—many of whom have spent years in college pursuing their chosen fields—don't *like* what they are doing? What company can seriously cling to the notion, stemming from the milltown days, that "it's the only game in town"?

Finally (and here's the "sell" for kin care), what company would not be well advised to help employees minimize the work/family stresses associated with child and elder care (see Figure 2–2)? Virtually all of the research on the topic demonstrates that a

FIGURE 2–2
Reshaping the Workweek

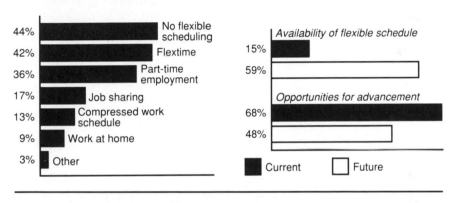

Source: *The Wall Street Journal,* June 18, 1990. Reprinted with permission of Hewitt Associates, 1990.

Source: *The Wall Street Journal,* June 18, 1990. Reprinted with permission of the Conference Board, 1990.

controlled company investment in kin care improves the bottom line. In a survey reported in *INC.* (November 1988), 95 percent of the companies polled said that "the benefits of their child-care programs outweighed the costs."[18] These companies pointed to a familiar litany of advantages: the ability to attract and hold good workers, improved morale, positive public relations, and lower absenteeism.

Moreover, in all of the research I have done and in all of my discussions with the directors of employer-sponsored benefits

and kin care centers, I have yet to find one employer who has
regrets or who has felt that the rewards didn't outweigh the costs.
For example, Karen Leibold, director of work and family at Stride
Rite, has estimated that employees who don't have on-site care
take off a minimum of five days per year for their children. She
has noted that that time off costs more than the cost of providing
child-care benefits.

Kin care, in summary, is not a "good deed" that companies do
for their employees but a *business strategy* for corporate success.
Who needs kin care? America's companies do.

Chapter Three
Birds of a Feather

MEETING THE NEEDS OF EMPLOYEES

W ho needs kin care? Employees do.

In this chapter, you will meet seven faces behind the statistics and surveys already cited: Frances Fields, a single working mother recently off welfare; John and Jennifer Hirsch, a working couple with two preschoolers; Virginia Collins, a divorced attorney with an infant; Eva Richfield, a childless widow with her 82-year-old mother to care for; and Ted and Anita Foster, both employed, who care for their infant, their preschooler, and Ted's 79-year-old father. (Names have been disguised to protect privacy.)

My purpose in telling the personal stories of these people is not to prove a large point through limited examples. The large point, that employees feel they need company-sponsored kin care, needs little support beyond the overwhelming results of the surveys cited in Chapters 1 and 2. My point is simply that kin care has a human face.

THE QUESTION OF BUSINESS MORALITY

The impetus for kin care programs may not lie entirely, or even primarily, in productivity studies and bottom-line analyses. We may individually work for better kin care programs because, in the words one chief executive officer said he couldn't tell his board of directors, "it's just the right thing to do." Companies did not wait for a majority of employees to express a felt need for counseling on alcohol and drugs before instituting programs in those areas. Companies rarely launched longitudinal studies to show that employee drunkenness and drug addiction were linked to bottom-line profits. Instead, companies recognized that these problems threatened the welfare of their employees and went about solving them.

Company kin care programs are instituted for the same reason. As companies learn more about the social responsibility that comes with social power, they are learning, in effect, what good they can and should do, within their means. The "moral maturation of business" is surely too heavy a label to hang on this development, yet in essence the moral relation of employer to employees is at issue here.

There have always been moral limits, and often legal limits as well, to what an employer can do to employees or ask of employees. Obviously, an employer cannot subject employees to cancer-causing asbestos particles without calling down an inevitable and ruinous class-action suit. No more can an employer ask an employee to sacrifice a finger or an ear for the sake of a company project.

But what of the equally dear human extensions of an employee's self—an employee's son, daughter, elderly mother or father? Do employers have a moral obligation to help employees minimize the damage to the employees' relationships with such people (and to the people themselves) brought about by job demands?

A growing number of business leaders say yes, within financial limits. These business leaders defend kin care because of its social and humanitarian merits rather than its effect on productivity. "Meaningful benefits like child care," says Cherie Kester, human resources director for Lucky Stores, Inc., "are really an exchange of value between the employer and the employee. The employee gives value to the employer in the form of labor, and in return the employer gives the employee the tools to manage life circumstances and achieve personal goals. We usually call these tools money, but today true wages include much more."[1]

These large issues animate Leonard Silverman, vice president for human resources at Hoffmann-La Roche, Inc. He is saddened by reports that in some companies "women executives don't have photographs of their children in their offices for fear that absence or lateness will be assumed to be child-care related." For Silverman, the issues go beyond profits to principles: "I believe that employer-sponsored child care, whether it's a thoughtful, well-researched information and referral service or a fully staffed on-site center, demonstrates a corporation's creative commitment to human values and the wisest sort of investment in our nation's future."[2] He quotes Walt Whitman's lines:

> These became part of the child who went forth every day
> And who now goes, and will always go forth every day.

Moral considerations rather than balance sheets lay behind former Labor Secretary Ann McLaughlin's judgment that "child care is *the* challenge to society for the 1990s."

THE FACES OF EMPLOYEES WITH WORK/FAMILY DILEMMAS

Frances Fields

- Age, 28
- Mother of one child, Stephanie, 18 months
- Job: shelf stocker, food store; annual earnings, $12,240

"When I had my child, all my money seemed to just go. The man I had been living with for three years went to California to look for work just before Steph was born, and I haven't heard from him. So I guess he's gone too. My story with welfare was this: I knew, because my mother was on welfare when I was growing up, that I would be eligible for somewhere around $390 a month with a baby, plus food stamps. So I went on welfare and tried to make it for about eight months.

"By this time, Steph was onto a bottle and I could get out if there was someone to watch her. The way welfare works here is that you get a monthly bonus of $125 for two months if you attend a work training class, which is how I got my present job in a grocery store. I paid my next-door neighbor $2 an hour for baby-sitting while I went to the training class from 9 to 12 each day. That was $30 a week, or $120 a month, and just about completely ate up the 'bonus' I thought I was getting. But the training class did get me off welfare.

"What I have now is a full-time job that I don't dislike very much, good health benefits for me and Steph, and, basically, a big cash problem. You see, my neighbor had her own baby and couldn't take care of Steph too. So I have to pay to keep her in a child center called Happy Days. It's just in a lady's home with 10 other kids, nothing fancy. But she charges me $100 a week! When I asked her about it, she told me it worked out to just less than $3 per hour, and I guess that isn't much. But from my job I take home about $800 each month. Take away the $400 I pay to Happy Days, and that leaves me less than $400 to pay rent on and buy food. It's less than I used to have on welfare! So we're basically trying to make it week by week. I don't want to go back on welfare, but it will all depend. I would get a second job, except Happy Days won't keep Steph after 6 P.M., and I do deserve some time with my own child. And, besides, it doesn't make too much sense to go out and get a second job—for what? $6 an hour—when you're paying most of it to the baby-sitter."

The Fate of Single Working Mothers

Frances Fields, who is black, is not atypical of the single working mothers who face crushing child-care costs. As calculated in the *AFL–CIO Newsletter*, women's median income in 1987 was $13,008. Even the most basic child-care costs could be expected to consume at least one fourth of that amount. A minimum-wage worker with two children, the *Newsletter* concluded, "would spend almost all her income on child care—a no-win proposition." In such cases, the only alternative is a return to welfare.[3]

Frances Fields is far from alone in her plight. Almost half of all working mothers are single, divorced, or married to a man earning less than $15,000 a year. Half of all black children live in single-parent homes, and 55 percent of those homes are at or below the poverty level. The poor, concludes a recent *American*

Health article, "are trapped in a kind of child-care Catch-22: The only way off welfare is to work, but working means child care, which most can't afford."[4] The only solution for many working mothers, says Yale psychologist Edward Zigler, is to "put children into environments that may compromise their development."[5] This is a polite reference to frightening realities: preschoolers left home all day with instructions not to unlock the door, infants passed from relative to neighbor to acquaintance in a desperate effort to get to work, latchkey children who rarely see a parent in the daytime, and a four-year-old who is told to play "big sister" during the day as sole caregiver to a two-year-old.

John Hirsch

- Age, 37
- Married to Jennifer, a bookkeeper, who earns $26,500 per year
- Two children: Brad, three; Kim, two
- John's occupation: assistant manager, hardware supply; earnings, $36,200 per year

"Jennifer and I met when we were college seniors. When we graduated, we both thought the tough times and pizza crusts were behind us. We set our sights on kids, a house, a nice car, the big vacation, etc. The American Dream. What we didn't factor in was taking care of the kids while we were earning the money for the American Dream. I won't go into all of it, but the past three years have been one panic after another, all connected somehow with child care.

"First of all, it is damn hard to find a safe place for the kids in our city. The licensed day-care centers all have long waiting lists (which we signed up for anyway). And in the newspaper there are ten 'Sitter Wanted' ads for every caregiver advertising for work. We've probably called 50 numbers out of the paper, and keep coming up with the Big Three responses: (1) 'You're too late'; (2) 'The children would have to be dropped off at my house' (which turns out to be a pit); and (3) 'I may have an opening in about a month.' I guess I thought that in our neighborhood there would just naturally be a teenager in the neighborhood or a woman who didn't work outside the home. It turns out that all the teenagers are in college or at work and all the women are like Jennifer—employed 8 to 5.

"Our situation is this at present: We have both kids in a day-care center, but not our first or second choice. It's the day-care center that had room—4 miles away, in a so-so part of town, not as clean as we'd like. They work on a 40-hour per week contract per child, which means that we pay a total of $280 *per week* to have our two kids looked after during working hours. If we're late, they bill us extra. And there are other interesting rules. If your child is sick, you can't bring the child to school, but you still pay 'to keep the spot open.' If Jennifer has a day off and wants to play with the kids at home or go somewhere, the same rule applies: pay to stay.

"What's amazing about all this to me is that we're both deeply, sincerely *grateful* to the day-care people for what they do for us. We pay out over $1,100 a month to them—virtually all of Jennifer's take-home pay—so that we can work, and that apparently isn't out of line for this city.

"She doesn't want to quit her job for the same reason that I don't want to quit mine: we like being professional people. As much as we love them, neither one of us pictures ourselves home all day with the kids. Besides, they will be in school in a few years, and neither of us wants to put a career on hold until then."

Dual-Career Couples and Kin Care

By income, 'John and Jennifer's combined annual earnings—almost $63,000—place them well up in the middle class. Salaries have become virtually meaningless, however, in light of their expenditures for day care. As Jennifer puts it, "I would be way ahead of the game by taking a $15,000 a year job with a company that provided day care for the children."

Companies have traditionally relied on raises, or possible raises, to motivate employees and assure their loyalty. For more and more dual-career couples, however, the real motivators are such benefits as kin care rather than the lure of higher salaries.

Helen Blank of the Children's Defense Fund in Washington, D.C., says that "the typical cost of full-time care is about $3,000 a year for one child."[6] John and Jennifer would love to find Blank's day-care center, especially in Washington or New York—a center apparently willing to accept about $60 per week to care for a child. In most metropolitan areas, the actual cost is probably double that amount, where openings can be found at all (see Figure 3–1).

Neuville Industries, a North Carolina hosiery manufacturer, has apparently found the key to recruiting and retaining employees who, like Jennifer, literally hand their paychecks to child-care providers each month. Neuville provides a full-service care center to employees at token cost, and thereby achieves an annual turnover rate of 4–8 percent in an industry that averages 50–100 percent. Controller Alan Goodman says that "no one ever leaves."

The two pharmaceutical giants Merck and Hoffmann-La Roche share turf in New Jersey. Hoffman-La Roche was the first to establish a child-care center—with Merck not far behind when it noticed an exodus of female employees to its competitor. For women in Jennifer's financial squeeze, the move to a company with child care—even at a substantial salary reduction—makes good financial sense.

Virginia Collins

- Divorced

- Sole custody of infant, Todd

- Job: attorney; earnings, $79,000 per year

"Before the birth of my son, I led an extremely intense life, with long working hours and many early morning/late night appointments. Problem cases or big opportunities often kept me at the office past midnight for a week or more at a time.

"That lifestyle obviously came to a crashing halt when I gave birth. My parents live 2,200 miles away, I have no siblings, and my husband and I are divorced on less than friendly terms. In other words, there's no one to care for Todd but me. So we manage, with the help of a wonderful woman I hired to spend days with Todd.

"But the interesting aspect to all this is a change I've noticed within myself, and also within the firm for which I work. The senior partners wanted to keep me, and offered to pay half of the expense for my caregiver if I could commit to my usual 60-hour billable week. It took me about five seconds holding my son to

FIGURE 3–1
Paying for Child Care
(Amount Paid by Parents per Year)

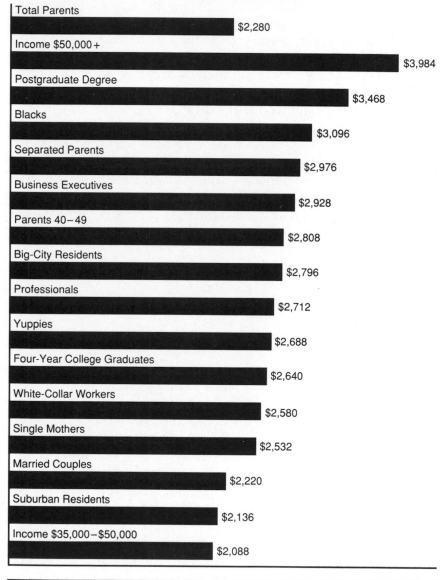

Base: 2,009 parents with children six years old and under

Total Parents	$2,280
Income $50,000+	$3,984
Postgraduate Degree	$3,468
Blacks	$3,096
Separated Parents	$2,976
Business Executives	$2,928
Parents 40–49	$2,808
Big-City Residents	$2,796
Professionals	$2,712
Yuppies	$2,688
Four-Year College Graduates	$2,640
White-Collar Workers	$2,580
Single Mothers	$2,532
Married Couples	$2,220
Suburban Residents	$2,136
Income $35,000–$50,000	$2,088

Source: Philip Morris Companies, Inc., Family Survey II: Childcare (1989). Reprinted from *Personnel*, September 1989.

realize that literally no amount of money could buy away the time I wanted, and needed, to spend with him.

"So I cut my own deal with the firm. I now work a 30-hour week, with considerable flextime based on Todd's changing schedule and my caregiver's availability. I'm earning less, but I don't feel that my career is off track. Day by day, they still see me doing good work at the firm. As Todd grows up, I'll probably add a few more hours to my work schedule.

"But I seriously doubt that you will find me putting in the killer weeks again. Parenting has changed my point of view about who I am and what I really want."

The Possibilities of Part-Time Work

For many professionals like Virginia Collins, the money spent on a caregiver is far less important than the parent's time away from the child. Companies that recognize these priorities can work with employees to make mutually acceptable adjustments.

At the New York law firm Skadden, Arps, Slate, Meagher & Flom, flextime and part-time work are as much the rule as the exception. In several departments of the firm, 25 women work at least 60 percent of a full-time schedule and receive full benefits. Elizabeth Walters, director of professional personnel, explains that "part-time was working so well at our firm with women who wanted to start a family, we decided to expand that program to attract talented women who wished to remain in law but at a reduced schedule."[7]

Corporations may follow this lead. But Lorraine Dusky, consulting editor of *Working Woman,* mulls the question: "If they formalize a two-tier career path, [will corporations] abuse the concept and relegate all women to second-class status? It's one thing to bill fewer hours and be paid accordingly, or for you and your boss to agree that you will not work long hours while the children are young. But it's quite another for a company to force a woman to choose between career growth and stagnation."

Dusky points to NCNB Corporation of Charlotte, North Carolina, as a company that apparently has come up with "the best of both worlds . . . a situation where [an employee] can work part-time but still be in line for promotions, albeit at a slower pace than full-time employees." Of the company's 12,000 employees, 50 are now taking part in the program.[8]

Eva Richfield

- Age, 43
- Widowed, no children
- Job: elementary school secretary; earnings, $22,300 per year
- Sole caregiver for her 82-year-old mother

"In my family, there has always been a tradition of caring for our own. I am my mother's only child. My father died in 1972. So that leaves me to care for her, and I'm not complaining. I do think people should realize, however, what's involved in caring for an elderly parent.

"In total hours, I suppose I spend 40 to 50 hours a week giving care to my mother. And of course this doesn't include time together when we just watch TV or have friends over. Each morning, I help her with her bathroom needs and wash her. I make breakfast and clean up afterward. I drive home 6 miles during my one-hour lunch break to make her lunch, then dash back to school. I make her dinner every night and handle all her medications. She can walk around the house, but I help her when she needs to go outside. This is my life.

"What's a bit harder to talk about, because it sounds petty, is the emotional strain of taking care of an elderly parent. My mother, at 82, has a lot of aches and pains, and a lot of fears and frustrations. Lying in bed or sitting in her chair most of the time, she just doesn't deal with her feelings very well. She gets terribly depressed and takes it out on me in cutting remarks or nagging. Or she puts on the silent treatment for days on end, as if I'd hurt her feelings in some terrible way. That's the part of care-giving that's almost harder than the meal-making, washing, and all the rest. You get so tired of trying to be a friend, a caring person, to someone who seems to have so little left.

"If I weren't around, I suppose my mother would find herself in a rest home. And I really don't know how she or I would pay for it. I've found out the hard way that medicare and medicaid don't cover a lot of her larger medical expenses. I couldn't put my mother in a home even if I could afford it, and, as I've said, I'm not complaining about our life together. A lot of people have it worse. But it has cost me dearly. I think I probably would have remarried if it hadn't been for the fact that I'm an only child and she's my mother."

Women Caring for Women: The Elder-Care Dilemma

As a baby-boomer, Eva Richfield is feeling the force of the Age Wave. Elderly women, such as Eva's mother, tend to have more care-requiring illnesses than men, but also tend to live longer than men. Because these women spent their youth and middle age in periods when women did not commonly work, or worked for low wages, they have contributed relatively little to pension funds or social security. Any assets left by the death of the husband are often spent paying for his nonmedicare medical bills and funeral. Lump-sum payments of insurance benefits often disappear within several years through ordinary living expenses.

The only remaining strategy for many elders is to wipe out their assets altogether, making themselves eligible as indigents for medicaid benefits. But for many families, including Eva's, family mores and traditions may put "going on the dole" out of consideration.

With a growing number of the elderly finding themselves in the position of Eva's mother, states have acted to curtail the spend-all-my-estate route to medicaid access. Indiana was the first state to pass legislation requiring substantial co-payment of a medicaid recipient's expenses by qualifying children. Other states have enacted similar legislation to slow the burgeoning growth of medicaid, particularly for nursing home expenses.

Ted and Anita Foster

- Married for four years, Ted and Anita are both 34
- One infant, Jed, and one four-year-old, Kirsten
- Ted's occupation: carpenter; earnings, $33,000 per year
- Anita's occupation: library assistant; earnings, $19,200 per year
- Sole caregivers to Ted's 79-year-old father

"After Ted's mother died of cancer, his father came to stay with us for a few weeks. It worked out great. He loved Kirsten (the baby hadn't been born yet) and took care of her while Ted and I worked. Everything was going so well that we talked him into staying with us. So he moved out of his rented apartment and moved in. After a couple of years, we had Jed.

"I think the part of this arrangement that we weren't prepared for was Ted's father growing older. Last year, his hearing grew worse to the point that a hearing aid doesn't seem to help much. And no matter how hard he tries, he forgets things—leaving the stove on, not closing the refrigerator door, things like that.

"About the time Jed was born, it was obvious to us that Ted's father couldn't be our main caregiver anymore. We tried to be very gentle in explaining to him that someone else would be coming over to help him with the baby and Kirsten.

"But now we're facing bigger and bigger problems. Ted's father has decided that he doesn't like the woman who takes care of the kids (and, more and more, of him as well). And she told us last week that she really has to charge us more, because Ted's father is almost a third child for her to take care of—and a problem child at that. While he loves the kids dearly, he just doesn't realize that he puts them at risk by forgetting to shut the front door or leaving a medicine cabinet open.

"Ted is extremely defensive about all this. I think it hurts him deeply to see his father becoming . . . well, senile. Ted will hardly talk to me about it. He's either mad at his father or mad at me or mad at the kids or mad at the caregiver. We don't have the option of putting his father in a home. There was no money to speak of, his or ours, and Ted couldn't bear it anyway.

"All in all, I feel like my own life is on hold through all this. I'm just coping as best I can and not really enjoying any of it—not the baby, not Kirsten, not my husband, and certainly not his father. That's probably a terrible thing to say, but I think Ted would have to admit the same thing. About the only time we feel human anymore is when we're at work."

Families in the Middle: Pressure and Breakup

Ted and Anita are members of the "sandwich" generation, responsible not only for at least 18 years of child-rearing but for another, overlapping period of years as caregivers to aging parents. In Anita's words, "I wish I had realized that life was basically over at 25."

The facts and figures regarding both child care and elder care, cited in earlier cases, apply with double fury to the lives of this couple. However painful, it may be worth speculating about what happens when the financial and emotional burdens of care-giving become too much for a marriage to sustain.

Assume for the moment that Ted and Anita divorce. What settlement could possibly provide for the best interests of the many people involved? The court would probably award custody of the two small children to the mother, with visitation rights to Ted. Now saddled with sole responsibility for the children, can Anita continue to work? Even if the court tells Ted to pay Anita reasonable child-care costs and house payments, can Ted—a carpenter—make those payments and also provide basic living arrangements for himself?

And what becomes of Ted's penniless father, now showing marked signs of senile dementia? Does he move in with Ted (if Ted can afford a place to live), and does Ted provide care for him (while working overtime to meet his child-support payments)?

These circumstances are contemplated simply to underline a point: half of all marriages end in divorce due, in part, to the kind of life stresses experienced by Ted and Anita, members of the sandwich generation and caregivers to children as well as elders. The human tragedies precipitated by such breakups prove costly not only to those involved but also to American society as a whole. Ted's father will probably find his way to a bed in a publicly funded facility for his last, sad years. Ted, we surmise, will try to start a new life elsewhere—and, as a nonpayer of child support, will end up as one more target for the justice system, with all the expenses that entails for society.

Anita, finally, may have the hardest row to hoe. She must maintain some life for herself and her children, no doubt without the help of her former husband. Judging from the statistics on remarriage for divorced women with two children, she will probably be the sole supporter of her family for the rest of her life. And one more detail: Anita's own mother wrote to her last week, asking if she could come to stay. She's been very ill, and can't care for herself very well or make ends meet anymore. What's a daughter to say?

LOST WORKERS, LOST LIVES

The circumstances of Frances, John, Jennifer, Virginia, Eva, Ted, and Anita are saddening on a number of levels. All of these people bear burdens that concerted, creative action by companies and government can make light enough to carry. In addition to their work productivity, their human productivity is at grave risk. The "system" relies on their work efforts, yet seems to include pitfalls that undo those efforts. At the same time that we would wish less pain and more joy for these people, we would wish more commitment for ourselves as a society of problem-solving people. Their tragedy is shared, and the blame is not theirs alone, or theirs primarily.

We would also wish that their stories were less *true*. How much more pleasing to contemplate the next-door neighbor who *loves* to care for children for free, or the elderly parent—hale and hearty—who thrives on cooking, cleaning, and care-giving. But the Cleavers aren't even on TV anymore, much less in the neighborhood. The real world of 1990 is, by and large, the world of these five cases: a world of scarce, expensive, and largely untrained care-giving for children; of elders with little money, little strength, and few children to care for them; of hardworking parents sandwiched between heavy responsibilities toward their children and, often at the same time, toward their own aging parents.

Who needs kin care? We all do.

Chapter Four

When the Bough Breaks

CARING FOR CHILDREN

L ast year, near the end of a long meeting on the kin care issues of several companies, a weary voice rose from the back of the room: "We're missing something here. We consider the comfort and happiness of animals in zoos with more fervor and certainly more frequency than we consider the feelings of the children in day care."

Even allowing for rhetorical overstatement, there's a kernel of undeniable truth here. In our eagerness to satisfy company and personal needs for kin care, we spend our fire on facility design, caregiver-child ratios, caregiver certification, employee equity issues, and other admittedly important topics. But in designing kin care to suit our buildings and time schedules, we overlook a primary question: *Is this kin care good for the child or elder?*

Working parents sometimes face this question after the fact. Says Ronald Abalos, director of marketing at the U.S. Postal Service in Phoenix, "I spent more time analyzing the car I bought than the care I got for my child." *Education Week* pointed out in 1990 that "we pay more to those who park our cars and tend our animals than to those who care for our children."[1] Parents feel not a little guilt, it seems. In a 1990 Gallup poll, almost 70 percent of parents gave themselves B or C grades (54 percent and 13 percent) in raising their children.

Working parents want to solve their work/family dilemmas, but not at the expense of their dependents. In this chapter, we will first consider the cautionary advice of many experts regarding kin care alternatives. Then we'll turn to every working parent's question: How can I spot good kin care?

THE QUESTION OF INFANT CARE

It's understandable why half the mothers of children under one year old are back at work full-time (an increase of 100 percent since 1970). First, their firms are not required to offer them maternity leave, paid or unpaid. More than two thirds of working women do not get maternity leave, and many of those who do usually get four months or less—unpaid. So taking several months off for the baby means one of two things for many American working women: resignation or termination. Second, while health insurance may (or may not) pay for most childbirth costs, the ongoing household expenses have to be paid from an ongoing salary. Even a company's "liberal" offer of a few months' *unpaid* maternity leave means little to the single mother or dual-income couple trying to make ends meet.

There may be, in addition, strong peer pressure "not to let the baby slow you down." In several recent surveys, a high percentage of pregnant women across ethnic, economic, and regional boundaries express a common desire to "get back to work after we get into a routine with the baby." Just when American men are learning to discard the Superman uniform, American women seem to be taking it up. The roles are daunting: mother, wife, companion, friend, lover, career woman, civic contributor, and more.

"Being it all," which would stress anyone, is especially stressful for the new working mother recovering from childbirth and adjusting to parenthood. Her first rude awakening (not counting the 2 A.M. feeding) comes in efforts to *find* reliable infant care. Day-care centers of the type listed in the phone directory usually do not take children under 18 months, and often they do not take children who have not been toilet trained. A large California day-care center reports that 40 percent of its requests are for children under two. "My broken record on the phone," says one of the staffers, "is 'No, I'm sorry, we don't take infants.'" Where infant care is available, it will probably be more expensive (up to $150 per week, estimates *American Health*),[2] and often it will not be up to the standards of the parents. Only eight states require care-givers of infants to have any training. Yale psychologist Edward Zigler reports that many states—Florida, North Carolina, and Idaho among them—allow an *8-to-1* ratio between infants and caregiver, and some states even allow a *12-to-1* ratio. Many states have no limits at all.

What Infant Care Means

Consider, for example, what it means for a caregiver to meet the minimal needs of even *four* infants (the 4-to-1 ratio for infant care is better than the 6-to-1 average among the states that regulate infant care). Dorothy Conniff, head of municipal day-care assis-tance in Madison, Wisconsin, has had the opportunity to observe infant care in many facilities over the years. She asks us to "con-sider the amount of physical care and attention a baby needs—say 20 minutes for feeding every three hours or so, and 10 min-utes for diapering every two hours or so, and time for the caregiver to wash her hands thoroughly and sanitize the area after changing each baby. In an 8½-hour day, then, a caregiver working under the most stringent regulation—the 4-to-1 ratio—will have 16 diapers to change and 12 feedings to give. Four diaper changes and three feedings apiece is not an inordinate amount of care over a long day from a baby's point of view.

"But think about the caregiver's day: four hours to feed the babies, two hours and 40 minutes to change them. If you allow an extra 2½ minutes at each changing to put them down, clean up the area, and thoroughly wash your hands, you can get by with 40 minutes for sanitizing. (And if you think about thoroughly washing your hands 16 times a day, you may begin to understand why epidemics of diarrhea and related diseases regularly sweep through infant-care centers.)

"That makes seven hours and 20 minutes of the day spent just on physical care—if you're lucky and the infants stay conven-iently on schedule.

"Since feeding and diaper changing are necessarily one-on-one activities, each infant is bound to be largely unattended during the five-plus hours that the other three babies are being attended to. So, if there is to be any stimulation at all for the child, the caregiver had better chat and play up a storm while she's feeding and changing."

The reality, Conniff concludes, is that "on even this 4-to-1 ratio, babies will not be changed every two hours and they will probably not be held while they're fed. They also will not get the kind of attention and talking-to that is the foundation of language development."[3]

The message here shouldn't be misunderstood. Conniff is not arguing that a working mother should quit, and simply endure poverty at home with the baby. A good day-care facility, she says, can be "a wonderful place, bubbling with energy, joy, and high seriousness." But parents should be the ones who insist on quality care for their babies. What Conniff observes instead is a generation of let's-shut-our-eyes-and-hope-for-the-best parents, willing to "shuffle children off to day-care settings duplicating the sort of deprivation that used to be suffered only by the poorest and most disadvantaged."

The Influence of Infant Care

Even when care and scheduling problems can be resolved satisfactorily, parents may still want to weigh the influence of infant day care on the development of their child. Throughout the 1970s, Penn State child psychologist Jay Belsky was viewed as one of the nation's leading proponents of full-time day care for children. Then he dropped a bomb—his 1986 article in the bulletin of the National Center for Clinical Infant Programs—that is still reverberating in the child-care literature.[4]

Belsky pointed out two things that worried him. First, research was beginning to show that when babies less than one year old are placed in day care, many of them develop weak and insecure parental bonds. This phenomenon seemed to cut across economic and ethnic levels, types of day care, and the location of day care (in-home or out-of-home). "Whether it's a day-care center or a baby-sitter doesn't seem to matter," Belsky noted.

Second, Belsky was worried about the effect that such weak bonding with parents would have on the child's later years. Several follow-up studies showed that weakly bonded children up to

10 years old evidenced behavior patterns that were more disruptive, aggressive, and frustrated than those of strongly bonded children.

Belsky then published his own study, which showed that almost half of the children placed in substitute care for 20 hours or more per week when they were less than one year old developed insecure attachments to their mothers, as measured by the Strange Situation Test. In this test, a 12- to 18-month-old baby experiences seven three-minute episodes, as follows:

- The mother carries the baby into a playroom (new environment) and puts him or her down.
- An unfamiliar adult enters the room and attempts to play with the baby.
- The mother leaves the room.
- The mother returns, and the unfamiliar adult leaves the room.
- The mother leaves the baby alone in the room.
- The same unfamiliar adult returns to the room.
- The mother returns to the room, greets the baby, and picks him or her up.

All of these episodes are videotaped. Based largely on the baby's reaction when the mother reenters the room for the second time, the baby's attachment to the mother is rated as "secure" (the baby is calmed/happy at the mother's return and resumes play easily), "insecure/avoidant" (the baby avoids contact with the mother and seems uninterested in her efforts to initiate play), or "insecure/resistant" (the baby actively resists contact with the mother and won't be calmed by her presence).

Belsky's results are supported by the work of psychiatrist Peter Barglow of Michael Reese Hospital in Chicago, who led a study that examined 110 infants of affluent two-parent families. Half of the infants were cared for full-time by a parent; the other half, whose parents worked, had high-quality day care in the home. In Barglow's study, 50 percent of the infants with nonparental caregivers developed insecure attachments to their working mothers.

Barglow asks this key question: "Is the mother by far the best caretaker for the child in the first year?" His answer: "We think probably yes."[5]

Such studies are often cited in connection with more general judgments by famous child-care experts. Dr. Benjamin Spock, for example, warns that "even at six months babies will become seriously depressed, losing their smile, their appetite, their interest in things and people, if the parent who has cared for them disappears."[6] Burton White, Harvard psychologist and director of the Harvard Preschool Project, states his position unequivocally: "After more than 20 years of research on how children develop well, I would not think of putting a child of my own into any substitute care program on a full-time basis, especially a center-based program."[7] New York child psychiatrist Eleanor Galenson agrees: "Putting infants into full-time day care is a dangerous practice. Psychiatrists have been afraid to come out and tell the public this, but many of us certainly know it to be true."[8]

Day Care and Illness

Add to this bleak picture the statistical fact that children of all ages in day care get sick more often than children who are not in day care. Says Selma Deitch, M.D., editor of the *Health and Day Care Manual for Health Professionals*, "It's the kind of pattern we used to see among kindergartners who were having their first exposure to groups of other children in school."[9] In 1983, the American Medical Association warned that the day-care center was becoming a dangerous source of infections. The Centers for Disease Control charged day-care centers with part of the blame for rising levels of diarrhea, dysentery, epidemic jaundice, hepatitis A, and ear and cytomegalovirus (CMV) infections. The *Journal of the American Medical Association* reported in 1988 that "infants under one year old in day-care centers run a much higher risk of contracting the bacterial disease that is the most common cause of childhood meningitis and epiglottitis."[10]

What's a Working Parent to Do?

Needless to say, the opinions of Belsky, Barglow, Spock, White, Galenson, and others have met with strong rebuttal from advocates of the day-care option for infants. These opinions, say child-care experts Ellen Galinsky and Deborah Phillips, give "parents who were already feeling guilty about leaving their children in someone else's care new reasons to worry."[11]

The counterargument to warnings against nonparental infant care is complex, but it centers on these key points:

1. The Strange Situation Test may be inadequate. A calm baby, undisturbed by a stranger's presence, may go on play-ing with a fascinating toy even when his or her mother ar-rives in the last stage of the test. Why should babies who don't appear to "need" Mommy be judged insecure? Per-haps they are evidencing early signs of independence and security.

2. The number of babies classified as "insecure" is hardly substantial. Most of the babies in parental *and* nonparental care are "secure" as measured by the Strange Situation Test. Ross Thompson, professor of psychology at the University of Nebraska, makes the point that between 26 and 31 percent of infants in full-time child care are classed as insecure.[12] Compare that finding with the findings of Alison Clarke-Stewart, whose compilation of the results of 16 studies on infant-mother attachment showed that 29 percent of infants with part-time or no child care are also classed as insecure. The difference between the two groups, she states, "is not a large enough number to conclude that infants are in danger if their mothers work."[13]

3. A child's later behavior cannot be linked directly to the type of day care that he or she experienced in infancy. A study of five- to six-year-olds who had been cared for as infants at the University of North Carolina's day-care center seemed to show that they were, as a group, more likely to swear, hit, push, kick, and threaten than peers who had been cared for by parents. There is no proven relation, critics of such research claim, between later behavior and forms of infant care. Many other factors could have influenced the children's development, including family stress factors that may have been present when they were placed in day care.

The case is well stated by University of New Hampshire psychologist Kathleen McCartney: "Comparing infants in child care with infants raised exclusively at home may not be very useful. We have no idea whether their differences, if any, are related to their day-care experience, their home experience, or other factors. Is child care a risk factor for infants? Well, it depends. What kind of child care are we talking about? What are the parents' motivations for using child care? What is the infant's personality? We do know that children in high-quality day-care centers do better than those in low-quality centers. We know that young children do better in small groups than in large ones. We know that children do better if their caretakers don't change frequently and are available, empathetic, and sensitive to the child's needs. But beyond that, there's not much that we can say that's backed up by research."

A Consensus View

Parents considering part- or full-time day care for their infants can take heart to some degree from a consensus statement issued by a "summit meeting" of child-care experts, including Jay Belsky, convened by the National Center for Clinical Infant Programs. The statement said: "When parents have choices about the selection and utilization of supplementary care for their infants and toddlers and have access to stable child-care arrangements featuring skilled, sensitive, and motivated caregivers, there is every reason to believe that both children and families can thrive."[14]

As for the issue that day-care kids get sick more often? In a major 1989 article on child care, the *Ladies' Home Journal* sums up the statistics on child illnesses and tells parents to "take heart: the number of colds level off as children get older, and by age three there doesn't seem to be much difference between children at home and those who've been in day care." Many physicians suggest that all children will experience a common array of flus, colds, and other virus diseases as the immune system adjusts to the bugs that cause them; it's a matter of "you can pay me now or pay me later."[15]

DAY CARE FOR PRESCHOOLERS

Much less research has been conducted on the effects of day care on toddlers and preschoolers. Child specialists Samuel J. Meisels and L. Steven Sternberg recommend that parents look for the "three key factors characterizing outstanding programs: The number of children cared for by each staff member is low; the total number of children in a specific classroom or group is moderate; and the qualifications and training of the caregivers meet high standards."[16]

Child-to-Staff Ratio

The National Association for the Education of Young Children (NAEYC) recommends the following *maximum* ratios for nurturing day care:

For infants and toddlers	4 to 1
For age two	6 to 1
For age three	8 to 1
For age four	9 to 1
For age five	10 to 1

Note: Only three states require the 3-to-1 ratio of infants to caregivers recommended by many experts.

These ratios apply to both center-based and family day care. For family settings involving both infants and older children, the NAEYC recommends no more than two infants and three older children per caregiver.

If the recommended ratios sound high to a parent hustling to meet the needs of even two or three children, there's good reason. The economics of child care force most caregivers to despair of achieving the ideal ratios and settle for the just legal and barely tolerable. At the Creative Learning and Child Care Center of Baltimore, owner Donna C. Krause charges a moderate weekly fee of $65 per child; that's $260 a month for each child. Her middle-class clientele simply can't afford more. But even with low overhead, she can afford to hire only 10 people—at low wages—to care for the 80 children in the center. One of Krause's biggest problems is turnover. "The first question a child asks a new person is: 'Are you staying, or are you leaving?' It's devastating."

One quarter of all children below school age receive care in day-care centers. Parents should know that only eight states require caregivers in these centers to have any training in child care. In fact, more than half of the states permit a person with no previous training in child care or development to be the director of a day-care center.[17]

Caregivers for Children

Keeping good caregivers, or any caregivers, is hard. Eileen Nelson reflects on her previous job as director of a child-care center in Minneapolis—a job she quit because she couldn't keep talented teachers. "We just couldn't compete with McDonald's," she says. "They were paying $5.50 an hour, and I was paying $5 to start." At another Minneapolis child-care center, a janitor repeatedly substituted for missing teachers. Working parent Sherry Crowell took her daughter from the center. "It made a joke of all my efforts to find good care," she says.[18] Pay, of course, is the bottom line. In 1990, according to *Education Week*, child-care workers were "the second lowest-paid profession in the nation."[19]

But can parents pay more? The average working parent paid $3,000 per child in full-time care in 1989. The costs of outside-the-home infant care ranged from $3,640 to $7,800. These amounts should be compared with the earnings of the average working mother—less than $13,000 per year.[20]

Of course, other businesses, including fast-food restaurants, also experience high turnover. "It makes no difference to the quality of a hamburger if there's high turnover in McDonald's," says Marcy Whitebook, executive director of the Child Care Employee Project, "but a baby needs to feel secure."[21]

Licensing of Day-Care Facilities

Licensing—a sacred cow for many Americans—is no guarantee of quality child care. There are now 60,000 "licensed" child-care centers in the United States, up dramatically from the number in

1980. However, because no training is required of caregivers or center directors in many states, licensing often amounts to little more than registration, a handy source for municipal fees and taxation. Says Dorothy Conniff, who heads a day-care assistance program in a state with more rigorous standards: "The state license [appears to be] our guarantee to middle-class families that safe and adequate care is being provided. That is a hoax, and a serious one, because few parents have the ability to judge a center's quality for themselves."[22]

Conniff points to the sad spectacle of the "Big Toddler Lineup," a wrongheaded effort by completely untrained staffers to have little ones stand in line long before they are developmentally able to. Why the Big Toddler Lineup in center after center? Because that's what the untrained staffers remember from elementary school.

Just as sad is the repression of natural curiosity and question-asking on the part of three- and four-year-olds by "teachers" intent on forcing preschoolers through boring activities for the sake of "control." Says Conniff, "Whatever children can learn from pasting a picture of a pumpkin on a pumpkin outline is not enhanced the next day by pasting a paper feather on a turkey. This kind of solution to the problem of what to do with children is a terrible waste of their time. The kind of repressive control that keeps them sitting down to meaningless tasks day after day is destructive to their self-esteem and their relationship with learning."

The Franchising of Child Care

America's typical solution to variations in quality is to standardize and franchise. The application of that approach to child care has had mixed reviews. In 1990, five companies dominated the proprietary child-care industry: Kinder-Care Learning Centers, La Petite Academy, Children's World Learning Centers, Gerber Children's Centers, and Children's Discovery Centers. Together, they operate more than 2,600 centers nationwide (see Table 4–1).[23]

In addition to running centers in the general community, these firms also approach companies (or are approached) to provide for their kin care needs. If a company wants its own contracted center, the proprietary chain can deliver site planning, building design, marketing, training of staff, and curriculum plans. Or the

TABLE 4–1
Largest Providers of Child Care

	Year	Number of Centers	Revenues
La Petite Academy	1985	460	$ 82,725,000
	1986	537	104,625,000
	1987	614	130,114,000
	1988	674	152,144,000
	1989	727	173,123,000
Kinder-Care Learning Centers	1985	890	183,810,000
	1986	1,066	220,046,000
	1987	1,122	261,283,000
	1988	1,201	300,139,000
	1989	1,260	343,868,000
Gerber Children's Centers	1985	101	NA
	1986	111	
	1987	117	
	1988	116	
	1989	114	
Children's Discovery Centers	1985	60	3,348,979
	1986	NA	10,127,197
	1987	62	11,035,216
	1988	72	10,611,000
	1989	95	15,720,000

NA = Not available.

company can contract for "slots" in one or more of the chain's area centers.

Some observers have expressed concern, as reported in *Education Week* in 1990, that these area centers may attempt to achieve profitability "by placing children in large groups with poor staff-child ratios and inadequately trained caregivers."[24] In 1988, Kinder-Care's average salary for caregivers and teachers in Detroit, as reported in *Education Week*, was $3.87 per hour. Across the day-care industry, full-time staff members were paid on average only $187 a week. In marketing presentations to potential clients, two of the proprietary chains described the qualifications of their care-giving staff as "18 and warm." A working parent should be wary of turning an infant over to an untrained 18-year-old, working at or below the minimum wage, who is also responsible for at least three other infants.

Even providers with active training programs have difficulty retaining caregivers. For example, staff turnover is publicly reported at 30 percent per year by Kinder-Care, and independent surveys of day-care centers in general put the turnover rate at 41 percent and rising. Staff members in day-care centers have been quitting at a rate three times higher than the rate a decade ago. In the course of a two- or three-year stay in a day-care center, a child on average has to get to know *six* new caregivers—although, as psychologist Karen McCartney points out, the consensus of child experts is that "children do better if their caregivers don't change frequently." To better understand how this high turnover affects the child, a working parent might imagine having six new bosses within 36 months.

Barbara Reisman, executive director of the Child Care Action Committee, sums up: "More than 40 percent of day-care workers leave the field every year because they can't afford to stay in it. Children are suffering, families are suffering, because teachers are leaving in droves."[25]

Where Children Are Cared For

Based on figures from the Institute for Parent/Child Services, we now have approximately 15 million preshool children of working parents. About two thirds of this number, or 10 million children, must be cared for during the day because of a working parent or parents (see Table 4–2).

Who's taking care of the kids? About half are cared for by relatives, including grandparents, or by Mom and Dad as "tag team" caregivers. Of the other half, 24 percent are in family day care, 22 percent are in day-care centers, and the remaining 6 percent are at home with a hired baby-sitter.

With regard to the children in the care of relatives, a few generalizations can be made and a few myths disspelled. Fathers are becoming more involved in child care, looking after 14 percent of preschoolers. Another 7 percent are cared for by working mothers operating out of the home or office. As for the myth, born of lurid headlines, that children are safer in the care of relatives than in other forms of child care, just the opposite is true. The incidence of child abuse is almost twice as high in parental care situations as in nonparental care situations.

TABLE 4–2

Primary Child-Care Arrangements Used by Employed Mothers
for Children Under 5: Fall 1987 (numbers in thousands)

	Total	Percent
Children under 5	9,124	100
Care in Child's Home	2,726	29.9
By father	1,395	15.3
By grandparent	463	5.1
By other relative	298	3.3
By nonrelative	570	6.2
Care in Another Home	3,249	35.6
By grandparent	792	8.7
By other relative	414	4.5
By nonrelative	2,043	22.4
Organized Child-Care Facilities	2,220	24.3
Day/Group Care Center	1,465	16.1
Nursery/Preschool	755	8.3
Kindergarten/Grade School	90	1
Child Cares for Self	24	0.3
Mother Cares for Child at Work	814	8.9

Source: Martin O'Connell and Amara Bachu, *Who's Minding the Kids?* Child Care Arrangements: Winter 1986–87, Survey of Income and Program Participation, Bureau of the Census.

Family Day Care

To some extent, family day care still basks in the warm glow of kids-at-play-with-Aunt Kate. Care situations of this kind tend to be less expensive than day-care centers, with a somewhat lower child-to-caregiver average. (One reason for the difference is simple economics: a woman operating out of her home bears less overhead expense for the business, and can therefore still meet per hour wage goals while taking fewer children.)

But family day care, as working parents know well, can vary widely both in cleanliness and in awareness of what children should, or could, be doing during the day. Family caregivers who "raised" their own children in front of the TV have little motivation to provide developmental or nurturing activities for the children of others. Mother and writer Linda Burton tells in *Reader's*

Digest of her unannounced visit to a family day-care location. "I found that the 'highly recommended' licensed day-care provider confined seven preschoolers to her tiny dining room. They were huddled together, leaning over a barricade, watching a TV in the next room."[26]

I have visited many family day-care facilities. With notable, wonderful exceptions, I found too many of them to be well-intentioned exercises in misunderstanding, frustration, and mismanagement. At one family care center, two five-year-olds were sent "down the block" pushing an infant in a stroller. At most of the care-giving homes, children made the TV area the center of their play, all day, every day. "Breaks" for outdoor exercises were occasionally taken, but just as often skipped if the children were watching TV and were reasonably quiet. Few caregivers made professional pretenses. Some looked the way they felt: overstressed, unkempt, untrained, and underpaid.

Day-Care Centers

Day-care centers not based in homes usually make an effort, at least on paper, to assemble an age-appropriate program for children. The document is usually reviewed by parents who are considering enrolling their children. In many centers, however, the day-to-day activities bear little resemblance to the curricular prose.

In preparing to write *A Mother's Work*, Deborah Fallows visited dozens of day-care centers in several regions. Her observations are summed up in a recent article, "Hard Truths about Day Care."[27] In general, while Fallows "discovered no abuse, little dirt, and adequate physical conditions in most centers, [she] found the average child's experience to be frighteningly empty. A day-care center has a continual 'on' atmosphere, which leaves little time for children to muse, and where the pressure of numbers pushes even gentle and reserved children to react constantly. Grace saying, coat donning, one-at-a-time hand washing—these become exhausting trials in depersonalization. . . . There is much tedium, much bewilderment, many unconsoled tears. Children wandering about, constantly clamoring to go 'to Mommy's house,' are quieted with fibs ('Mommy will be here soon')."

LET THE PARENT BEWARE

In this chapter, we've glimpsed the underside of the rush toward child care in America. The message is clear for parents who love their children: Get to know the caregiver and the care-giving environment well before kissing your children good-bye for the day.

But how can busy working parents spot a good day-care situation as quickly as possible?

We have to know what we're looking for. The best way to use the following checklist is to read it over several times *before* visiting a home-based or center-based day-care facility or talking to staff. Develop, in other words, your own mental list of what you want to *observe* on your first visit, sans clipboard or paper checklist.

Upon visiting the day-care facility, let yourself respond naturally to the environment, without a rigorous attempt to remember each and every evaluative item. After getting to know the facility and its staff, apply the first and most important standard of evaluation:

The Parent's Intuition Test

"Do I feel comfortable and happy with these people, in this environment?"

If the answer is no, don't proceed. Your child probably won't like this care situation either.

Only when the day-care facility has passed the Parent's Intuition Test should you sit down with the director and staff members to discuss specific items on the following checklist.

How to Spot Nurturing Day Care

NAME OF THE CENTER OR FAMILY DAY-CARE FACILITY
DIRECTOR:
ADDRESS:
PHONE:
HOURS:

History

How long has the center been in operation? Where?

What do parents say about it? Are written testimonials available? Can you call a few parents yourself?

Staff

What are the background and training of the center director, or family day-care provider?

How many staff members are employed? What is the child-to-staff ratio?

Maximum Ratios
Recommended by the NAEYC

Infants and toddlers	4 to 1
Age two	6 to 1
Age three	8 to 1
Age four	9 to 1
Age five	10 to 1

What are the qualifications of staff members? What training have they received? Do they receive ongoing training? What kinds of background checks have been done?

What medical emergency training (CPR and first aid) is available at the center?

How many children are in a group? (Group size should not exceed twice the child-to-staff ratios given above.)

What is the pay range of the staff? What turnover does the center experience?

How often are substitutes used? How do the questions in this category apply to substitutes?

Attitudes toward Children

In general, who are the other children? What are they like?

Is the center under contract with any local, county, or state agencies to provide a certain number of its spaces to any particular community group?

Is the center involved in the care of children with special medical or emotional needs?

How do staff members handle discipline?

Are staff members warm, affectionate, playful, and energetic with children?

Can staff members communicate well with parents?

Do staff members have input into the policies and procedures of the center? (Avoid centers whose staff members can't "change the system" to accommodate children.)

Facilities and Equipment

Is there space for active play by preschoolers? Space for safe crawling and toddling by infants?

Is there a safe, fenced outdoor play area free from the hazards of electric wires, nearby heavy equipment, noxious gases, or poisonous plants?

Is the play area appropriately shaded or partially covered for hot-weather or rainy-weather play?

Where do the children rest? Typically, for how long?

Are age-appropriate toys available in abundance? Are the toys in good shape?

Are age-appropriate books available?

Are music and art supplies available?

The Program

What do children do on a typical day? What special activities are planned from time to time?

How do the activities of the various age groups differ?

How did the center settle on its program?

How is the program evaluated to make sure it's working?

Do staff members read to the children? Sing with them? Dance?

Health and Safety

What has the center's accident record been so far?

How are accidents and illnesses handled? Is the parent notified? Are staff members trained to spot medical problems?

What are the hygiene practices of the staff regarding diaper changing, toilet assistance, and food serving? How are the toilet needs of the children handled?

Are the children safe from electric outlets, household chemicals, tools, and other hazards?

Does the center have approved fire detectors? What is the plan for emergency evacuation? Is the plan practiced with the children?

Management of the Center

Who is in charge of the center? How are decisions about the center made?

When parents have questions or concerns about the center, with whom should they speak? When?

Are parents welcome to drop by?

Does the center provide regular reports to parents on the child's experience and progress?

Are the policies and procedures of the center set down in a fact sheet or handbook for parents?

Is the center inspected regularly by local, county, or state authorities? Can you see the results of the most recent inspections?

Does the center carry liability insurance? Is the center owned by a parent company?

What kind of contract or agreement will be signed?

Fees

How much does care cost? When must payment be made?

Can your child be guaranteed a continuing slot in the future?

How are vacations and periods of illness handled with regard to fees?

The following portfolio of useful forms includes questions provided by Lincoln National Corporation, the National Employer-Supported Child Care Project, and the NAEYC for parents who want to screen care providers by phone. It also includes a mail-out questionnaire that can be used to check on center references.

A PORTFOLIO OF USEFUL FORMS AND GUIDELINES FOR PARENTS AND COMPANIES SEEKING CAREGIVERS*

Selection Process

An interview with each possible in-home caregiver gives you a chance to exchange information. It lets you see how that caregiver and your child react to each other. It also lets you see if you feel comfortable with that caregiver.

If a relative or a friend will be caring for your child, you may feel that no interview is needed. But it's still a good idea to share ideas about child care—even if you do it over a cup of coffee at the kitchen table. You may also feel that you do not have as much control over the care of your child as you want. What's important is for both you and your relative or friend to be flexible. You may

---

* Furnished courtesy of Lincoln National Corporation, Fort Wayne, Indiana; Dominion Bankshares, Roanoke, Virginia; the NAEYC and the National Employer-Supported Child Care Project. Many of these forms can be adapted for use in selecting and evaluating caregivers for elders.

find that you can accept a different way of doing things if your child is still well cared for.

If you are interviewing someone you don't know, begin by finding out about the caregiver, rather than by describing the kind of person you are looking for. Some good questions to ask are:

- What kinds of TV programs do you think children should watch?
- What activities do you do with children?
- What do you do when a child disobeys?
- How do you feel about combining homework with child care?

If you are interviewing teenagers for after-school care, pay attention to their attitudes. Ask them if they ever baby-sit or care for brothers and sisters. Find out what activities they participate in. You want to find someone who is responsible and level-headed.

Trust your instincts. If you are not comfortable with a person, do not feel that you have to continue the interview. Once you do begin to feel comfortable, you can talk about some things you want the caregiver to do.

If you are interested in a caregiver, have her spend some time with your child. Be sure to notice your child's reactions. How does the caregiver respond to your child?

Once you've decided on a caregiver, go over with her exactly what the job requires. Some people prefer to write down the arrangements they have agreed to. Writing them down can save misunderstandings later on. Both of you can refer to the list of arrangements if there is a question. Of course, the agreement can be changed as your needs change.

If both parties agree to written arrangements, make sure both parties' signatures are on the agreement paper.

Screening by Phone

Once you have received the names of several prospective care providers, you should contact them on the telephone to narrow your final selection. Arrange interview appointments with those care providers who are best qualified to meet your child's needs as well as your own.

Below are suggested questions to ask during phone screening:

- Why did you choose to do child care?
- Have you worked with children before?
- How long have you worked with children? What ages?
- What kinds of things do you like to do with children?
- How do you handle discipline?
- How frequently do you have openings?
- For what reason have children left your care?
- What role do you think you play in the children's lives?
- Do you smoke?
- Do you have any pets?
- How does your family feel about your day care?
- What other kinds of work experience have you had?
- What do you charge?
- Do you have references available?

Reference Questionnaire

- How long and in what capacity have you known this care provider?
- What is your relationship to this care provider?
- Have you used this care provider's services in the past? Were you satisfied? Will you use his/her services again?
- Would you place your child in her care?
- Explain how you feel this care provider would handle the additional responsibility of caring for other children.
- Do you feel that this care provider is of responsible character and is suitable to provide care and guidance for the children placed in her care?
- Who are the other persons living in this care provider's home that you know? Do you feel that their character would assure the well-being of children?

Sample Form: Agreement with Caregiver

This is an agreement between _____
Name of Nanny/Caregiver
and

Parent's Name
to engage in a "partnership" to provide care for

Name of Child/ren

The details of the arrangement follow:

Caregiver/Nanny: _____ Phone: _____

Address: _____ Zip code: _____

Hours and fees

Hours: _____ Days: _____

Fee: _____ Overtime rate: _____

Weekend rate: _____ Holiday rate: _____

Payment will be given by: Check? Y/N   Cash? Y/N

Child care is needed for these holidays/vactions: _____

Social security number: ___-___-___ Income tax withheld? Y/N

Social security is to be paid by (1) Employer only or
(2) Both employer and employee.

Housework and duties

Housework: _____

Meal preparation: _____

Other: _____

Caregiver is/is not allowed to have guests.

Caregiver is/is not allowed to watch TV other than children's programs.

Caregiver is/is not allowed to smoke while caring for child/ren.

Termination of agreement

(1) Caregiver will give _____ week(s) notice before quitting in order to give sufficient time to find another caregiver.

(2) Parent will give _____ week(s) notice and $_____ when necessary to end this agreement.

_____	_____
Caregiver	Date
_____	_____
Parent	Date

Sample Form: Child-Care Responsibilities and Information

Child's usual schedule (fill in times)

Breakfast: _____ Lunch: _____ Supper: _____ Snacks: _____

Naps: Morning: _____ Afternoon: _____ Evening bedtime: _____

Eating

(List foods)   Breakfast: _____

                    Lunch: _____

                    Supper: _____

                    Snacks: _____

Special foods: _____

Foods *not to be given* at any time (candy, cookies, cake, pop, popcorn, peanuts, other): _____

Child has food allergies to: _____

Toilet Training

Child tells adult he/she has to go to the bathroom? Y/N Needs to be reminded? Y/N

Child uses the word _____ when he/she has to urinate.

Child uses the word _____ for a bowel movement.

Child uses: Potty chair? Y/N Special toilet seat? Y/N Regular toilet? Y/N

Dirty diapers are placed: _____

Sleeping and "Fussy Time"

Child sleeps with _____ for _____ hour(s); has a "fussy time" at _____

Child falls asleep easily? Y/N Takes a while to wake up? Y/N

Play Activities

Indoors: _____

Off limits for play: Stairs? Y/N Upstairs rooms? Y/N Garage? Y/N

Special rooms/special items: _____

_____

Child's Social and Emotional Behavior

Child is afraid of stairs? Y/N Other animals? Y/N _____

Child comforts him/herself by: _____

Child likes to be held? Y/N Rocked? Y/N Sung to? Y/N Read to? Y/N

Child gets frustrated at _____; expresses frustration by _____

Sample Form: Child-Care Responsibilities and Information (*continued*)

Child gets angered at _____; expresses anger by _____
Child gains self-control by: _____
Acceptable discipline: (1) To be sent to his/her room for _____ minutes
                         (2) Loss of privileges: _____
                         (3) Other: _____
Special needs: _____

Regular Medication (if any)
Medication's name: _____ Amount (dosage) _____
Times medication is to be given: _____
Child should be awakened for medication?   Y/N
Storage of medication: Room temperature?   Y/N   Refrigerator?   Y/N

Sample Form: Emergency Information (Place Next to Telephone)

Mother   Name: _____ Work phone: _____
           Place of work: _____ Work hours: _____
Father   Name: _____ Work phone: _____
           Place of work: _____ Work hours: _____
Neighbor Name: _____ Phone: _____
Relative Name: _____ Phone: _____
Doctor   Name: _____ Phone: _____
           Office address: _____

Emergency Instructions
Illness—call: _____
Accident: _____
_____
Fire: _____
_____
Bad weather: _____

Sample Form: Emergency Information (*continued*)

Emergency Medical Care

I hereby give permission to _____
                                        Child-care provider/Nanny

to secure emergency medical and/or emergency surgical treatment for the below-named child/ren while in care. (Make sure you provide signed medical consent form to the provider.)

_____	_____
(1) Child's name	Signature of parent or guardian
_____	_____
(2) Child's name	Date
_____	
(3) Child's name	

Hospital preferred for emergency treatment: _____

Health insurance identification information: _____

General Tax Requirements for Parents with In-Home (Nanny) Child Care

"Generally, household work includes services performed in or about your private home by cooks, butlers, housekeepers, governesses, maids, cleaning people, child-care providers, janitors, caretakers, handy persons, gardeners, and drivers of cars for family use."

1. Household workers are *exempt* from income tax withholding. (They are taxable if both the employer and the employee voluntarily agree.)

2. Household workers are *taxable* for social security tax if they are paid $50 or more in cash in a quarter. Then the employer is also taxable.

3. Employers of household workers are *taxable* for federal unemployment tax if they paid cash wages of $1,000 or more in any calendar quarter in the current or preceding year.

"An employee who wants you to withhold federal income tax from wages must give you a completed Form W-4 (Employee's

Withholding Allowance Certification). If an employee asks you to withhold income tax and you agree, you must withhold an amount from each payment based on the Form W-4 the employee gives you."

Any income tax withholding you pay for an employee without deducting it from the employee's wage is added income subject to income and social security taxes.

Contact your local IRS office for detailed instructions.

Latchkey (Self-Care) Children

A *latchkey (self-care) child* is any child who is regularly left alone during some periods of the day to supervise him/herself.

Parents who consider self-care as a child-care option for their children might review these questions:

- Do you consider your child old enough and mature enough to assume self-care responsibilities?
- Has your child indicated some concerns about trying self-care?
- Is your child able to solve problems?
- Is your child able to communicate with adults?
- Is your child generally unafraid to be alone?
- Can your child unlock and lock the doors to your home unassisted?
- Is there an adult living nearby (neighbor) whom your child knows and can rely on in case of an emergency?
- Do you maintain adequate household security?
- Do you consider your neighborhood safe?
- Has your child exhibited behaviors in the past that concerned you (e.g., playing with matches or dangerous equipment or engaging in violent/aggressive activities)?
- While away from home, are you accessible by telephone?
- Is your child afraid of the dark?
- Does your child have a handicap that requires special attention?

If you are uncomfortable with your answers to any of these questions, it is highly recommended that you delay or abandon plans to leave your child in self-care until you can give comfortable responses to all of the questions.

Self-Care Quiz

Take the following quiz and rate yourself:

Age of your child: 10 or older _____ (1 pt.)   9–10 _____ (2 pts.)   8–9 _____ (3 pts.)   7–8 _____ (4 pts.)   7 or under _____ (5 pts.)

How much time each day will your child be in self-care?

1 hr. or less _____ (1 pt.)   1–2 hrs. _____ (2 pts.)   2–3 hrs. _____ (3 pts.)   3–4 hrs. _____ (4 pts.)   4 or more hrs. _____ (5 pts.)

How much does your child spontaneously tell you about the events occurring in his/her life?

Everything _____ (1 pt.)   Most things _____ (2 pts.)   Some things _____ (3 pts.)   Few things _____ (4 pts.)   Nothing _____ (5 pts.)

How close is the relationship between you and your child?

Very close _____ (1 pt.)   Close _____ (2 pts.)   Neither close nor distant _____ (3 pts.)   Distant _____ (4 pts.)   Very distant _____ (5 pts.)

Will your child be home with younger siblings?

1 other _____ (1 pt.)   2 others _____ (2 pts.)   3 others _____ (3 pts.)

Add the number of points corresponding to your answers. The lower your score, the better your child's chance and yours of managing self-care.

Basic Guidelines for Self-Caring Children

The traditional one-breadwinner family has given way to more dual-career and single-parent families. Many of today's parents are choosing self-care as a child-care option. It is very important that parents prepare their children for this experience.

Guidelines for behavior must be established, and routine as well as emergency procedures must be taught and periodically reviewed.

Below are some guidelines for self-caring children.

Using the Phone

- **Never** tell the caller your name, address, or phone number or say that you are alone, even if the caller asks.

- Say that your mother or father is busy, and get the caller's name and message.
- Keep emergency numbers by the phone.

When Someone's at the Door

- Answer through the door; **never** open it.
- Unless you have permission to let the person in, **don't,** even if it is someone you know.
- Say, "My mother (or father) is busy. Can I take your message?"
- Doors should be locked at all times.

When Playing Outside

- **Never** talk to strangers. Parents should "define" who strangers are.
- If a stranger approaches you, move away to a safe place and tell an adult.
- Stay within the boundaries that you and your parents have established.
- Discuss with parents whether you can accept an invitation to a neighbor's or friend's house.
- Never give your name to a stranger.

Household Emergency

- Be familiar with first aid, and review the contents of the first aid kit periodically.
- The first aid kit should contain:
    Bandages/sterile pads in assorted sizes
    A small scissors
    Calamine lotion to treat insect bites/poison ivy
    Iodine to clean cuts
    A thermometer/aspirin
    An icepack to limit swelling
    A bottle of ipecac to induce vomiting

- Discuss and practice emergency procedures in case of fire, accidents, or severe weather. **Do not attempt to put out a fire!**

- The severe weather kit should contain:
  A portable radio
  A flashlight
  Extra batteries
  Food that needs no cooking or refrigeration
  Candles and matches

Arriving Home Alone

- Be alert. Have your key ready.

- If you must carry a house key, keep it out of sight so that no one will know you are going home alone.

- If you lose your key, go to a safe place and call your parents.

- Go straight home after school. Wandering around the neighborhood is an invitation to trouble.

- Have your parents ask a friendly neighbor if you can come to his/her place *in case of an emergency*.

- If bigger kids threaten to take your belongings or bully you, just let them have their way and leave quickly. Tell your parents when they return home.

- Call your mother or father to report your safe arrival home.

Questionnaire for Parents

This questionnaire has been designed by the staff of the National Employer-Supported Child Care Project to assess parents' feelings about the child-care program used by their children. Since we are interested in obtaining an overall view of how parents feel, you need not identify yourself on the questionnaire. Please complete all questions to the best of your ability. Thank you for taking the time to give us feedback on the program in this way.

1. Overall, how satisfied are you with this child-care program? Would you say that you are (check one choice):

   __1. Extremely satisfied

   __2. Very satisfied

Questionnaire for Parents (*continued*)

___3. Satisfied

___4. Dissatisfied

___5. Very dissatisfied

___6. Extremely dissatisfied

___7. Don't know

2. On a scale from 0% (totally dissatisfied) to 100% (perfectly satisfied), what percent best shows how satisfied you are? _____%

3. Was this program your first choice of care?

___ Yes

___ No

If no, what type of arrangement would you have preferred? _____

4. In terms of convenience for you, would you say that this program is (check one choice):

___1. Extremely convenient

___2. Very convenient

___3. Convenient

___4. Not very convenient

___5. Not at all convenient

___6. Don't know

5. In terms of dependability, being able to count on it every day, would you say that this program is:

___1. Extremely dependable

___2. Very dependable

___3. Dependable

___4. Not very dependable

___5. Not at all dependable

___6. Don't know

6. In terms of how good the price is for you, how satisfied would you say that you are with the price of this program?

___1. Extremely satisfied

___2. Very satisfied

___3. Satisfied

___4. Not very satisfied

Questionnaire for Parents (*continued*)

___5. Not satisfied at all

___6. Don't know

7. In terms of how competent the staff is, would you say that the staff of this program is:

___1. Extremely competent

___2. Very competent

___3. Competent

___4. Not very competent

___5. Not at all competent

___6. Don't know

8. Would you say that the physical aspects of the facility (the building, grounds, and equipment) are:

___1. Excellent

___2. Good

___3. Adequate

___4. Fair

___5. Poor

___6. Don't know

9. In terms of teaching your child new things, would you say that this program does:

___1. An excellent job

___2. A very good job

___3. An average job

___4. Not a very good job

___5. Not a good job at all

___6. Don't know

10. In terms of loving and understanding your child, would you say that the staff is:

___1. Extremely loving and understanding

___2. Very loving and understanding

___3. Loving and understanding

___4. Not very loving and understanding

Questionnaire for Parents (*continued*)

___5. Not at all loving and understanding

___6. Don't know

11. In terms of giving your child opportunities to get along with and get to know other children, would you say that the program does:

___1. An excellent job

___2. A very good job

___3. A good job

___4. Not a very good job

___5. A bad job

___6. Don't know

12. Which of these statements describes your feelings about leaving your child at the program?

___1. I'm always worried

___2. I worry often

___3. I worry sometimes

___4. I rarely worry

___5. I never worry

___6. Don't know

13. How would you say your child feels about the program overall?

___1. Likes it very much

___2. Likes it

___3. Does not like it

___4. Does not like it at all

___5. Don't know

14. How would you say your spouse feels about your child-care service?

___1. Likes it very much

___2. Likes it

___3. Doesn't have strong feelings one way or the other

___4. Does not like it

___5. Does not like it at all

___6. Don't know

___7. Not applicable (single parent, separated, divorced)

Questionnaire for Parents (*continued*)

15. Have you experienced any of the following benefits as a result of the child-care program (check all that apply)?

    ___1. The child-care program was a factor in your decision to take your current job.

    ___2. The child-care program is a factor in your continuing to work here.

    ___3. Your job performance has been affected positively by the child-care program.

    ___4. You have a more positive attitude toward the company because of the child-care program.

    ___5. The child-care program has allowed you to miss less time from work.

    ___6. The child-care program has made it possible for you to work overtime or odd work shifts.

    ___7. The child-care program has made it possible for you to accept a promotion or a change in jobs.

    ___8. You have recommended your employer to others because of the child-care program.

    ___9. Other benefit (describe): _____

16. Are you a single parent?

    ___ Yes

    ___ No

17. Are you:

    ___ Male

    ___ Female

18. How many children do you have in the program, and what are their ages?

    Number of children ___

    Ages _____

19. What are the major advantages of this program? _____

    _____

    _____

20. What are the major disadvantages of this program? _____

    _____

    _____

Questionnaire for Parents (*continued*)

21. Do you have any suggestions for change? ————————————————

————————————————————————————————

————————————————————————————————

Date completed ——————————

Thank you for completing the questionnaire.

Chapter Five

To Grandmother's House We Go

CARING FOR ELDERS

E lder-care programs require the same careful scrutiny by adult children and other caregivers that is required for child-care programs. It's well beyond the scope of this book to describe and account for the conditions of elder care in the homes of elders, the homes of elders' children, rest homes, convalescent hospitals, and other elder living/care-giving arrangements. But "fact sheets" on the elderly and their circumstances will help paint the cloudy picture of care for elders in the 1990s and the foreseeable storms beyond. After presenting the facts on the elderly, we will consider guidelines and suggestions for adult children caring for elders. Taken together, these facts, guidelines, and suggestions go far to explain why so many companies, listed in Chapter 9, are acting now to provide long-term care insurance, medical co-payment insurance, and/or other support systems for their aging work forces.

How Many of Us Are Elderly?

- Americans now 65 or older number 29 million, and there are now more than 10,000 Americans who are over 100 years old.

- By 2030, the number of Americans 65 or older is expected to swell to 65 million, or almost one quarter of the entire population, at which point there will be as many elderly citizens as children.

How Many of the Elderly Need Daily Assistance?

- Of the elderly between the ages of 65 and 74, 17 percent need assistance with the activities of daily living; 6 percent get that assistance.
- Of the elderly between the ages of 75 and 84, 28 percent need assistance with the activities of daily living; 12 percent get that assistance.
- Of the elderly 85 years of age or older, 49 percent need assistance with the activities of daily living; 31 percent get that assistance.

Table 5–1 identifies the many challenges the elderly may face.

Who Cares for the Elderly?

- Family and friends perform 80 percent of the services for the frail elderly, usually without pay.
- Of the caregivers for the elderly, 33 percent are themselves 65 or older.
- Of the caregivers for the elderly, 50 percent are employed either full- or part-time.
- Two thirds of all the caregivers for the elderly are women. Daughters are 11 times more likely than sons to be such caregivers.
- One third of all the caregivers for the elderly are near or below the poverty line. In 1986, the Older Women's League reported that care-giving for the elderly often impoverishes caregivers who started with substantial savings.
- About 25 percent of all workers have elder-care responsibilities.

TABLE 5–1
Performance Limitations Often Associated with Selected Conditions

Limitation	Alzheimer's disease	Cerebral palsy	Heart disease	Multiple sclerosis	Normal aging	Parkinson's disease	Rheumatoid arthritis	Spinal cord injury	Stroke, cerebral trauma	Visual impairment	Hearing impairment	Pregnancy	Short stature	Obesity
Inability to Use Lower Extremities		×	×	×		×	×	×	×					
Reliance on Walking Aids		×	×	×	×	×	×	×	×					
Difficulty in Bending and Kneeling		×		×	×	×	×	×	×					
Difficulty in Handling or Fingering		×				×	×	×	×					
Loss of Coordination		×		×		×	×	×	×					
Loss of Upper Extremity Skills		×				×	×	×	×					
Difficulty in Reaching		×		×	×	×	×	×	×			×	×	
Limitations of Stamina or Strength		×	×	×	×	×	×	×	×			×		×
Speech or Communication Problems	×	×		×		×		×	×		×			
Poor Balance		×	×	×	×	×	×	×	×					×
Severe or Complete Loss of Sight or Hearing				×	×				×	×	×			
Difficulty in Interpreting or Processing Information	×			×	×	×		×	×					

Source: Zola: ''Aging and Disability: Toward a Unifying Agenda,'' *Educational Gerontology*, 14 (1988), pp. 302–303.

- A survey conducted by the American Association of Retired Persons (AARP) found that 31 percent of the caregivers for the elderly were management staff, that 12 percent of care-giving daughters and 14 percent of care-giving wives had to resign their jobs, and that 38 percent of the caregivers for the elderly reduced their work participation.[2]*

- Caregivers for the elderly are more likely to be addicted to antidepressant drugs than the persons they care for, according to a Duke University study.

Who Will Go to Nursing Homes?

- About 25 percent of working adults can expect to be in a nursing home during their elder years.

- The probability of spending time in a nursing home is 40 percent for persons 65 and older.

- If a husband and wife both live to age 65, there is a 70 percent chance that at least one of them will spend time in a nursing home.

- If a husband and wife have four parents who live to age 65, there is a 90 percent chance that at least one of those parents will be cared for in a nursing home.

Figure 5–1 presents a graph depicting the projections for nursing home admissions.

---

* An AARP and Travelers Foundation 1988 national survey found that approximately 8 percent of the sampled households were currently providing assistance to one or more disabled persons aged 50 or older or had done so within the previous 12 months.[3] According to Andrew E. Scharlach and his associates at the University of Southern California Andrus School of Gerontology, this means that approximately 7 million American households were involved in elder care.[4] The AARP-Travelers study also found that 42 percent of the caregivers were currently employed full-time and that 13 percent were employed part-time. Other studies have indicated the extent to which employees take care of their elderly relatives. A *Fortune* magazine study has reported that 13 percent of employees provide such care, and other estimates have been as high as 20–40 percent.[5]

FIGURE 5–1

Nursing Home Population Projections: Persons 65 Years and Older by Age Group, 1980–2040

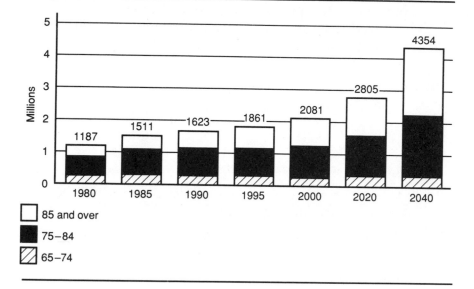

Source: K. Manton and K. Liu, *The Future Growth of Long-Term Care Population:* Projections Based on the 1977 National Nursing Home Survey and the 1982 Long-Term Care Survey, March, 1984.

Who Finances Health Care for the Elderly?

- In 1990, the cost of elderly care in a nursing home ranged from $20,000 to $50,000 a year and the cost of elderly care at home or at an adult day-care center was about $15,000 a year. As a general rule, medicare does not cover these expenses.

- During the 1980s, medicare paid for approximately 50 percent of the medical expenses of the elderly.

- Elderly Americans now use more of their own income for medical care (16 percent) than they did before medicare (15 percent).

- Elderly Americans who don't have social security due to long-term unemployment or undocumented work must pay for medicare insurance.

- Married women who care for their elderly spouses often
  end up in poverty. Medicare and private health
  insurance rarely cover most nursing home expenses.
  Medicaid eligibility comes only after the couple's income
  and assets have been almost totally depleted and the
  husband has been put in a nursing home. Medicaid
  takes a portion of his social security and pension
  income, leaving the wife with almost nothing. If she
  sells their house to make ends meet, medicaid will stop
  all payments until the funds she acquires have been
  spent on health care.

By the 1987 U.S. Census Bureau definition of "poverty line" for
the elderly ($99 per week for a single elderly person, $125 per
week for a couple), one in seven of the elderly were below that
poverty line. The elderly continue to have a higher poverty rate
than any other population group.

If federal programs for the elderly did not exist, 52 percent of
the elderly would fall below the poverty line. The annual cost of
such programs in 1989 exceeded $350 billion. (The annual cost of
all forms of federal child-care assistance is $6.9 billion.)

What Are the Facts about Widowhood?

- There are five widows to every widower.

- Ninety percent of all widows are over the age of 55.

- The average age of widowhood is 56.

- A married woman can expect to live, on average, 10
  years as a widow.

Do Families Take Care of Their Own?

- The percentage of the elderly who lived alone or with a
  spouse was approximately the same in 1890 as in 1990.
  Older adults were not "taken in" by care-giving children
  any more frequently in the "good old days" than they
  are today.

- Although families are more mobile now than they were a century ago, three fourths of the elderly have at least one child who lives close to them. (More than half of the elderly live within 10 minutes of at least one child. This statistic has remained relatively constant for 20 years.)

Are the Elderly Retiring or Working?

- The participation of older adults in the labor force has declined rapidly over the past 30 years.

- In 1950, 50 percent of men over 65 were employed; by 1984, only 16.3 percent of men over 65 were employed.

What Are the Facts about the Physical Decline of Elderly Males?

Table 5–2 tells the story of what physical ailments the elderly may face.

TABLE 5–2
Average Decline in Human Male, Ages 30–75

Factor	Percent Decline
Brain weight	44
Velocity of nerve impulse	10
Number of taste buds	64
Blood supply to brain	20
Output of heart at rest	30
Kidney filtration	44
Vital capacity of lungs	44
Maximum oxygen uptake	60

What Are the Top 10 Chronic Conditions of the Elderly?

Tables 5–3 and 5–4 identify chronic conditions and leading causes of death for the elderly.

TABLE 5–3
Top 10 Chronic Conditions of the Elderly
(in Order of Frequency)

1. Arthritis
2. Hypertension
3. Hearing
4. Heart conditions
5. Orthopedic impairment
6. Sinusitis
7. Visual impairment
8. Diabetes
9. Varicose veins
10. Arteriosclerosis

TABLE 5–4
The 10 Leading Causes of Death in Older People
(in Rank Order)

1. Diseases of the heart
2. Malignancies
3. Cardiovascular diseases
4. Accidents
5. Chronic obstructive pulmonary disease
6. Pneumonia and influenza
7. Diabetes
8. Suicide
9. Chronic liver disease and cirrhosis
10. Atherosclerosis

What Do We Know about Life Expectancy?

The Social Security Administration does actuarial studies, making projections on life expectancy. Table 5–5 depicts these projects. Or, take a life expectancy quiz (see Table 5–6) to make your own projections.

TABLE 5–5
Life Expectancy at Birth and Age 65 by Sex and Calendar Year, 1900–2050

	Male		Female	
Year	At Birth	At Age 65	At Birth	At Age 65
1900	46.4	11.3	49.0	12.0
1910	50.1	11.4	53.6	12.1
1920	54.5	11.8	56.3	12.3
1930	58.0	11.8	61.3	12.9
1940	61.4	11.9	65.7	13.4
1950	65.6	12.8	71.1	15.1
1960	66.7	12.9	73.2	15.9
1970	67.1	13.1	74.9	17.1
1980	69.9	14.0	77.5	18.4
1990	71.8	15.1	78.9	19.0
2000	72.7	15.6	80.1	19.6
2010	74.1	16.0	80.8	20.1
2020	74.6	16.4	81.4	20.5
2030	75.2	16.8	82.0	20.9
2040	75.7	17.1	82.6	21.4
2050	76.3	17.5	83.1	21.8

Source: Social Security Administration, *Social Security Area Population Projections*, 1989; Actuarial Study no. 105, by Alice Wade, A.S.A.

TABLE 5–6
How Long Will You Live? A Quiz

Personal Facts

Starting score:	<u>72</u>
If you are male, *subtract 3*.	_____
If female, *add 4*.	_____
If you live in an urban area with a population over 2 million, *subtract 2*.	_____
If you live in a town under 10,000 or on a farm, *add 2*.	_____
If any grandparent lived to 85, *add 2*.	_____
If all four grandparents lived to 80, *add 6*.	_____
If either parent died of a stroke or heart attack before the age of 50, *subtract 4*.	_____

TABLE 5-6 (*concluded*)

If any parent, brother, or sister under 50 has (or had) cancer or a
heart condition, or has had diabetes since childhood, *subtract 3*.   _____

Do you earn over $50,000 a year? *Subtract 2*.   _____

If you finished college, *add 1*.   _____

If you have a graduate or professional degree, *add 2 more*.   _____

If you are 65 or over and still working, *add 3*.   _____

If you live with a spouse or friend, *add 5*. If not, *subtract 1* for every
10 years alone since age 25.   _____

Lifestyle Status

If you work behind a desk, *subtract 3*.   _____

If your work requires regular, heavy physical labor, *add 3*.   _____

If you exercise strenuously (tennis, running, swimming, etc.) five
times a week for at least a half hour, *add 4*. Two or three times a
week, *add 2*.   __ ____

Do you sleep more than 10 hours each night? *Subtract 4*.   __ ____

Are you intense, aggressive, easily angered? *Subtract 3*.   _____

Are you easygoing and relaxed? *Add 3*.   _____

Are you happy? *Add 1*. Unhappy? *Subtract 2*.   _____

Have you had a speeding ticket in the last year? *Subtract 1*.   _____

Do you smoke more than two packs a day? *Subtract 8*. One or two
packs? *Subtract 6*. One-half pack to one pack? *Subtract 3*.   _____

Do you drink the equivalent of 1½ ounces of liquor a day?
Subtract 1.   _____

Are you overweight by 50 pounds or more? *Subtract 8*. By 30 to 50
pounds? *Subtract 4*. By 10 to 30 pounds? *Subtract 2*.   _____

If you are a man over 40 and have annual checkups, *add 2*.   _____

If you are a woman and see a gynecologist once a year, *add 2*.   _____

Age Adjustment

If you are between 30 and 40, *add 2*.   _____

If you are between 40 and 50, *add 3*.   _____

If you are between 50 and 70, *add 4*.   _____

If you are over 70, *add 5*.   _____

Add up your score.
This is your life expectancy.   _____

Source: Robert F. Allen, Ph.D., and Shirley Linde, *Lifegain* (Burlington, Vermont: Human Resources Institute, Inc.).

Where Do the Elderly Live?

According to the House Select Committee on Aging, one quarter of the elderly are physically impaired and require the assistance of another person. Of this group, 20 percent (1.4 million) receive such care in nursing homes. The rest (4.6 million) live in the community and function as best they can.

Some areas will experience the Age Wave more dramatically than other areas. The New York State Data Center projects that the number of the elderly on Long Island will increase by more than 100 percent between 1980 and 2000. Locales in Florida, Arizona, California, and other "sunshine states" will see even more rapid increases in their elderly populations.[6]

Almost half of the elderly now live in eight states—California, New York, Florida, Pennsylvania, Texas, Illinois, Ohio, and Michigan. By the year 2020, the entire country will have the same concentration of the elderly in its population that Florida has now.

GUIDELINES AND SUGGESTIONS FOR ADULT CHILDREN GIVING ELDER CARE

When thinking about elder care, most of us may be overwhelmed by the difficulty of identifying alternatives, evaluating the many options, and finally making the right choice for our loved ones. This section offers a beginning in thinking about the many issues involved in providing elder care.

Assistance from the Community

Communities throughout the country provide a plethora of services that help caregivers provide assistance to the elderly. Caregivers should assess the availability and quality of services related to equipment needs, mental health services, social services, education and advocacy services, medical services, and other sources of home care-giving assistance.

> **1.** *Equipment.* Look for vendors or organizations that provide adaptive equipment (beds, walkers, special telephones, etc.) for purchase or loan. Knowing what a medical supply

house offers in terms of equipment, information, and assistance is one of the first steps in finding how "elder friendly" a community might be.

2. *Mental Health Services.* How available are support groups, bereavement counseling, family counseling, or individual therapy? These services provide the caregiver with much of the support needed to manage the emotional challenges of elder care.

3. *Social Services.* Many communities provide case management and assessment services in addition to a family service agency and other social work support agencies. Case management would include assessing the factors that affect an elderly person's physical, social, and psychological well-being; consulting with family members and/or other caregivers; developing a comprehensive care plan; and coordinating services and community resources.

4. *Education and Advocacy Services.* Look for IRS aid for the elderly, insurance information regarding the unique needs of the senior citizen, medicare/medicaid information, organizations involved with aging and/or care-giving such as the AARP, legal services, general elder-care information and referral services, and disease-specific information.

5. *Medical Services.* Managing the medical needs of elder care is challenging enough even when basic medical services are available. Assess the community for emergency aid, convalescent homes, nursing homes, home nursing care, home health aides, hospices, gerontologists, pharmacy consultation, and rehabilitative services (such as physical and occupational therapy).

6. *Other Home Care-Giving Assistance.* Sometimes the most supportive help comes from a community that provides a wealth of home care-giving assistance, such as adult day-care centers, crime prevention programs, escort services, friendly visitors, handyman services, homemaker services, nutrition information and assistance (e.g., "Meals on Wheels"), respite care both in and outside the home, shopping services, and transportation assistance.

The community services identified here are just some of the areas that caregivers of the elderly must be concerned with. Evaluating the quality of the services and how well they meet your elder-care needs is similar to the evaluation process used to assess child care. Many of the forms and questionnaires provided in Chapter 4 can be easily adapted for assessing elder-care options. Other questions and advice that caregivers of the elderly should consider include the following:

- When looking at a facility, evaluate its physical layout and note whether the necessary adaptive measures have been taken. For example, does the facility work, or can it be adjusted for walkers, wheelchairs, etc.?

- Speak privately with those who provide care. What are the concerns of these caregivers? What approaches do they take? Compare these approaches with the approaches that are taken in a home setting.

- Evaluate how consultants and/or professionals help the caregivers handle such things as incontinence, multiple medications, mobility, confusion, and the caregivers' own needs.

- Determine the availability of services in the community. Contact services and ask questions regarding cost (both payment and billing procedures), eligibility, the contact person, hours of operation, accreditation or licensing, employee/volunteer training, and possible barriers (such as transportation difficulties, eligibility restrictions, and unsuitable office layouts). Obtain brochures and sample application forms.

- Ask for references regarding the use of services. Check the references out. Were people satisfied? Did the primary caregivers get the assistance and support they needed? How was the elderly person treated? What were his/her thoughts while receiving care?

Companies and Elder Care

As of mid-1988, according to a *Personnel Journal* survey involving 101 companies and over 1 million employees, corporations weren't doing much to assist workers who were also caregivers for elderly parents and relatives. Two thirds of the companies surveyed agreed that "elder care is something personnel executives should be concerned with," but only 1 in 10 of the companies had studied the problem. The other companies had "no plans to address the elder-care issue" or didn't "know of any plans to start any type of elder-care assistance program or employee benefit." Of the 101 companies surveyed, only 3 had an elder-care benefit for their employees.[7]

There are bright spots here and there in the corporate response to the need for elder care. IBM in 1988 instituted a three-year personal leave policy that employees can use to care for children or elders. A company hot line helps employees deal with elder-care emergencies. In addition to IBM, a number of companies— Johnson & Johnson, John Hancock Mutual Life Insurance Company, Warner-Lambert Company, and other companies identified in Chapter 9—offer extensive resource and referral programs for elder care. These programs are very similar to the resources and referral programs for child care. Usually, the services used are referred to as consultation and referral services. As with the child-care program, the service contracts out with community-based organizations throughout the country. Employees work with specialists who furnish them with detailed information on and referrals to providers of elder-care services. In addition, the service offers other kinds of help to employees who are caregivers of the elderly—giving information, suggesting caregiver support groups, and discussing elder-care issues.

The services provided include information and referrals on medical services, home health workers, housing alternatives such as retirement communities, home meal delivery, nursing homes with different levels of care, senior citizen centers and other community programs, special transportation services, and case management services that can contact your older relative or help evaluate his/her needs. Information regarding nutrition, financial matters, and legal matters is also typically provided. Employees can ask about themselves as well as about relatives. Anytime the employee has an elder-care question or concern, the consultation and referral service provides the desired information and a "listening ear."

The Travelers is one of about 35 companies providing long-term health care insurance that employees can purchase. The monthly premiums run from $10 a month for a 32-year-old employee to $97 a month for a 62-year-old. The benefits include $50 a day for in-home elder care and up to $100 a day for elder care in nursing homes. In 1988, Stride Rite Corporation expanded their on-site child care center to 79 children and 24 elders and plans to expand further. With a high staff-to-participant ratio, the center hopes to involve both ends of the generational spectrum in mutually satisfying activities. "The goal," said a company spokesperson, "is that they will give a lot to each other."

These forward-looking programs can awaken the efforts of other corporations to the growing need for elder-care action.

And they had better. The National Association of Area Agencies on Aging polled employees responsible for elder care and found that 77 percent of them reported that their elder-care responsibilities interfered with their jobs.[8] Another survey, by the New York Business Group on Health, found significant reductions in productivity among such employees.[9] What's the bottom line here?

One study estimated the average annual cost of employee elder care at $2,500 per care-giving employee. This figure represents money lost through absenteeism, time off during business hours, missed overtime, reductions in productivity because of added stress and fatigue, and the expenses associated with unnecessary job turnover, rehiring, and training.[10] This number is significant, say Andrew E. Scharlach, Beverly F. Lowe, and Edward Schneider, authors of *Elder Care and the Workforce,* if you consider that it can translate to $500,000 per year (assuming that 20 percent of the employees have care-giving responsibilities) in lost wages for a company with 1,000 employees.[11]

One of the research staffers for the House Select Committee on Aging saw this in his crystal ball: "As far as elder care is concerned, we're heading for a train wreck beginning in the 1990s. Medical costs are skyrocketing, elders are living longer and getting poorer, and the federal and state governments are backing away from their support to full medicare and medicaid benefits. That adds up to a huge burden for the working children of the elderly. One way or another, in lost days or stress or resignation, these working children pass that burden along to their companies."

THE FINAL CONSIDERATION

Well before architectural plans have been analyzed, budgets approved, staff hired, and marketing undertaken for kin care, one question should guide development efforts more than any other: What is best for the children and elders in care?

Chapter Six
If Wishes Were Horses

KIN CARE ALTERNATIVES AND COSTS

What do you picture when you think of company-sponsored kin care? I asked that question of 100 Georgetown University MBA students from many industries and many states. The most common answer—given by some 70 percent of these students—went something like this: "I picture dropping my kid off at a child-care center in my office building, or at least close by."

Unfortunately, the on-site model of kin care, while only one of many approaches, remains the "do-or-die" option in minds of many company leaders. As a salty chief executive officer told me, "Either we do it *right* [i.e., with an on-site center] or we won't do it at all." More than 95 percent of American companies don't do it at all, often to their own disadvantage and that of their employees. But before exploring alternatives to the on-site center, we should give this most popular concept of kin care its due.

THE CONCEPT OF AN ON-SITE OR NEAR-SITE KIN CARE CENTER

By luck or by design, some company buildings already meet the "Big Six" requirements for an on-site kin care center:

(1) Clean air.

(2) Quiet surroundings.

(3) Safe entry and exit paths.

(4) Good natural lighting.

(5) Easy emergency access (fire, ambulance, rescue).

(6) Sufficient space for activities, rest, eating, and hygiene.

These requirements would disqualify a bright, sunny room in the path of oil fumes from a nearby refinery; a large, empty room that can be reached only by walking past lathes and milling machines; a boardroom that is no longer used because of the high noise level from nearby power generators.

On-site kin care centers are typically placed in "corner" locations of corporate buildings, preferably on the ground floor. Such locations are most likely to provide natural lighting, easy access without stairs, and an outdoor patio or play area. Firms also place their kin care centers at a nearby location, on company grounds, or, in the case of a consortium, in a location convenient to the employees using the facility.

Financial arrangements for the on-site center may be trickier to plan than the center itself. Some companies choose to set up their on-site centers as independent divisions within the company, or even as a separate subsidiary or nonprofit agency (with possible tax and liability advantages for the company).

Table 6–1 provides one estimate of the financial considerations in undertaking a center. (See Table 6–2 for examples of costs of different corporate centers.)

Other companies have leased space, at advantageous rates, to commercial providers of kin care services or to government services. In some cases, such arrangements allow noncompany children and/or elders to use the center on a space-permitting basis.

Advantages of On-Site and Near-Site Kin Care Centers

- Employees like the convenience of bringing a child and/or elder to work instead of a separate location.

- A parent or adult child is nearby to handle unusual upsets and assist in emergencies.

- The company can closely monitor the quality of its kin care services, for which it is both liable and responsible.

TABLE 6–1
One On-Site Center's Estimate of Financial Considerations

The start-up costs included approximately $30,000 to buy equipment and materials. The cost of the building will vary, of course, depending on the area of the country and the type of facility. The building cost was around $100,000.

Salaries	65.00%
Rent	14.00
Building maintenance	0.14
Depreciation (furniture and fixtures)	0.33
Telephone expense	0.57
Speakers (parenting seminars)	0.03
Travel	0.26
Conferences and meetings; staff development	0.69
Subscriptions/publications	0.02
NAEYC dues	0.01
Music, creative storytelling teachers	0.16
Tuition assistance for staff	0.07
Taxes and licenses	0.01
Supplies (including diapers, art materials, toy and small equipment repair and replacement)	5.70
Meals and snacks	11.40
Insurance	1.33
Miscellaneous	0.04

- The hours of the center can be adjusted to the needs of the company and the employees.

- The visibility of the center can heighten the morale and loyalty of employees, with distinct public relations advantages.

- Staff can often be recruited on a part-time or full-time basis from among company personnel.

Disadvantages of On-Site and Near-Site Kin Care Centers

- The setup costs may be high.

- The amount of use may vary until the center has been fully subscribed; staff may not be fully utilized.

TABLE 6–2
Annual Company and Parent Costs for an On-Site Child-Care Center

Organization	Product or Service	Annual Cost to Organization	Employee Cost (after Company Subsidy)	Center Opened	No. of Children in Center
Hoffman–La Roche Nutley, N.J.	Pharmaceuticals	$3,000–5,000 per child	$1.50/hour	1980	165
Rex Hospital Raleigh, N.C.	Health care	$66,000 annual budget	$40/week for one child or $9.50/day or $2/hour for part-time	1969	NA
Nyloncraft, Inc. Mishawaka, Ind.	Plastic molding	$20,000 annual loss	$25/week	1981	160
American Savings Bank Stockton, Calif.	Banking	NA	$125/month for one child and $100/month for each additional child	NA	135
Union Bank Los Angeles, Calif.	Banking	NA	$80/week for infants and $60/week for children ages one and older	1987	58
First National Bank of Atlanta Atlanta, Ga.	Banking	NA	$42 or $46/week depending on child's age (no company subsidy)	NA	120
Certified Grocers of Florida Ocala, Fla.	Retail grocers	NA	$30/week for infants and toddlers, $25/week for others	1984	105
Mercy Richards Hospital Bakersfield, Calif.	Health care	NA	$170/month (preschoolers only)	1982	156

Source: *Personnel*, May 1988, p. 69.

- Liability costs may be high, depending on the area and on the number of users.

- Out-of-office workers, including sales and technical representatives, may find an on-site center less convenient than other forms of care-giving.

- Waiting lists for a popular on-site center may engender charges of favoritism and other forms of ill will on the part of employees.

- An on-site center may be impractical for employees who drive long distances to work and therefore can't bring their children. Employees who take public transportation may be similarly disadvantaged.

Table 6–3 describes what many companies provide in their on-site centers.

EXAMPLE OF A SUCCESSFUL NEAR-SITE KIN CARE PROGRAM

The Fel-Pro Day Care Center

Walking through the Fel-Pro Day Care Center in Skokie, Illinois,[1] one is reminded of a childhood lost. Rounded corners, curved Plexiglas windows, skylights, creative and innovative toys, crawl-through equipment, a renovated red caboose in the playground, lots of stimulating educational materials in bright, and cheerful classrooms all made me want to relive my childhood or, at the least, enroll my daughter there. The children, used to the publicity and the visitors this center draws, greeted me warmly and then returned to their activities. As director Scott Mies said to me, "Our architect, Steve Forsyte, had a fresh, innovative approach to design. Although the outside of our building looks like part of the industrial workplace, the interior and the playground represent the wonderful world of childhood."[2]

The center is located in a building just adjacent to the company's premises. The offices were vacant, and the space was just right. Mies had carte blanche to work with the architect in the design of the center and was instrumental in making sure that the center met his goals, philosophy, and standards regarding early

TABLE 6–3
Selected Characteristics of On-Site Child-Care Centers

Organization	Number of Children in Center	Age Range of Children in Center	Hours Open per Day	Days Open per Week	Staff	Facilities	Curriculum
Hoffmann–La Roche Nutley, N.J.	56	NA	NA	NA	3 teachers; 3 teachers' assistants; 2 research interns; 1 cook	NA	Reading, math, science, creative art, music, drama, safety, health nutrition
Rex Hospital Raleigh, N.C.	NA	18 months to 6 years	6 A.M.–6 P.M.	7	1–7 teacher/child ratio	3-bedroom, ranch-style house	NA
Nyloncraft, Inc. Mishawaka, Ind.	160	NA	24 hours per day	NA	27, including 6 certified teachers	6,000 sq. ft.	NA
American Savings Bank Stockton, Calif.	135	2 years to 10 years	7 A.M.–7 P.M.	Mon.–Fri.	18	33-room facility	Sewing, drama, computer, music, math, science
Union Bank Los Angeles, Calif.	58	3 months to 5 years	NA	NA	1–7 teacher/child ratio for four-year-olds; 1–6 for one–three-year-olds; 1–4 for infants	NA	NA
First National Bank of Atlanta Atlanta, Ga.	40	15 months to 6 years	7:30 A.M.–6 P.M.	Mon.–Fri.	Director, 3 preschool teachers, 2 associate teachers	NA	NA
Certified Grocers of Florida Ocala, Fla.	50 max.	3 months to kindergarten	NA	NA	Director, staff of 10	Kitchen, 5 classrooms, multipurpose room	NA
Mercy Richards Hospital Bakersfield, Calif.	156	Infant to 12 years	6 A.M.–midnight	7	NA	NA	NA

Source: *Personnel*, May 1988, p. 61.

103

childhood development. Six separate classrooms (each with its own bathroom), two central playrooms, a teachers' lounge, a kitchen, and an office make up the center. The outside playground is spacious, with age-appropriate equipment, and the ground is a mixture of grass, asphalt, and woodchip surfaces.

The center enrolls 45 children ranging from two to six in age, and it operates 7 A.M.–5 P.M. A full-scale kindergarten program is now also running. The weekly tuition for full-time care is $80 per week, which represents about 40 percent of the actual cost. The company subsidizes the remainder. The teachers are degreed and certified. Staff turnover is practically nonexistent. Mies attributes this to the fact that staff members have full status as Fel-Pro employees, with all of the attending benefits. Enthusiastic, motivated assistants are recruited from college programs in early childhood development and do their teacher training at the center. The director is always getting unsolicited résumés from well-qualified teachers.

A waiting list exists for parents who want to enroll their children. Bob O'Keefe, vice president of human resources, estimates the list at 10–11. Enrollment is based on seniority (years of service with the company), and white-collar and blue-collar workers are evenly represented among the enrollees. "A lot of companies are afraid of this balance issue, but we find there's no problem. . . . As long as you're running a quality program, the parents are really happy to use it," says O'Keefe.[3] O'Keefe should know. His grandchildren are enrolled.

O'Keefe, Mies, and President Paul Lehman had some advice for companies beginning programs. "Get professional help with the start-up—that's what we did, and it's real important." What else should companies consider? Approximately 2–10 percent of the employees generally participate in on-site day care, and the other 90–98 percent might feel threatened because so much is spent on so few. "The rest of the benefits package (for other employees) should be in order and communicate that the company cares."

In addition to providing a strong benefits package to all employees, Fel-Pro has a center that plays a part in the company. The children take field trips into the plant, their artwork is posted in the corridors, and overall, the whole work force views the successful center with pride.

Other companies still find excuses not to consider a center. Lehman, who hears from other corporate executives that they are not ready to pay the kind of price it takes to have a quality kin care program, has this to say: "I agree with a lot of what's being said. Day care is expensive, and there are legitimate arguments against this route, but when all is said and done, I think you just have to take the risk. . . . We get so many questions all the time about insurance, liability, costs, etc., but there is a point where you have to stop hiding behind these questions, answer them, and move on. People are afraid to take the step, to make these kinds of commitments. . . . We think there's a bottom-line result from treating people decently."[4]

(For more information regarding the start-up of other quality programs, see the start-up stories on MCCARE and ABIG in Chapter 7.)

KIN CARE CONSORTIA

Several companies may join together to fund and manage a kin care consortium, located on-site at one of the companies or, more commonly, at an off-site location somewhat equidistant from all of the partners to the joint venture.

Gail Bjorklund, assistant director of the Fairfax County Employer Child Care Council, reports on the popularity of consortia: "Several consortia have developed here in northern Virginia. They are popular because of the large number and percentage of small businesses in this area that are unable to operate a center on their own. With consortia, they can get together . . . [Consortia] are popular because of the flexibility."[5]

Partnership interests in a consortium may be unequal, as would be the case when a small company with limited kin care needs enters into a consortium with larger companies that have substantial kin care needs. Spaces for children and/or elders in the consortium care center are usually apportioned according to the employer's percentage of participation in the consortium. To avoid misunderstandings and miscues, partners should work out agreements regarding management, liability, and withdrawal from the consortium at the outset.

Siting and environmental standards are the same for a kin care consortium as for an on-site center, as are many of the advantages and disadvantages. In addition, employers and employees contemplating a consortium arrangement for kin care should consider the following advantages and disadvantages.

Advantages of the Consortium Approach to Kin Care

- Since the costs are divided among partners, they may be lower than comparable costs per participant in an on-site center. When a developer assumes the cost of creating the space, the costs are reduced even further.

- Liability is shared. Because the consortium is often established as an independent entity, the partners may be legally distanced from claims arising out of damage or injury suits. Companies provide seed money to initiate the kin care venture through charitable contributions or as a necessary business expense. Their decision-making capacity on the incorporating board is limited solely to business-related decisions. These two factors break the line of liability linking employers to the venture.

- Companies with too few participant children and/or elders for an on-site center can gain most of the advantages of an on-site arrangement.

- Community relations and intercompany employee relations are strengthened.

- A decline in use by one company/partner can be offset by the larger participant pool that other partners provide.

- Employers with multiple locations can generally replicate the model anywhere. The first consortium can serve as a pilot and then be used as a basis for other consortia at other locations.

Disadvantages of the Consortium Approach to Kin Care

- The financial stability of the consortium depends in large part on the financial stability of all its partners.

- The demand for spaces in the consortium may quickly (and often unexpectedly) overwhelm the available spaces and resources. The consortium may not have the flexibility to expand to meet that demand.

- The rules for who may use the consortium and how much they pay (or co-pay with their company) may differ widely for various partners in the consortium, especially when different unions are involved. Policy setting, paperwork, and procedural problem solving may become unmanageable for staff.

- As an inevitable meeting place for employees from different companies, the consortium may unwittingly lead to the loss of personnel by some member companies as employees discuss job opportunities and problems.

- Public relations advantages, while still substantial for member companies, are diluted in that no single company gets credit for the consortium.

- The policies and standards of the consortium may become a matter of controversy and bitterness between the employees of different companies. Member companies may find it difficult to resolve these disagreements. Furthermore, arguments over the consortium may spill over into other intercompany relations.

EXAMPLE OF A SUCCESSFUL KIN CARE CONSORTIUM

The Tyson's Corner Play and Learn Children's Center

The Tyson's Corner Play and Learn Children's Center in Tyson's Corner, Virginia, opened in October 1987. It currently enrolls over 70 children, 12 of whom are on scholarships funded by the original contributors to the consortium.

Managed by Play and Learn Services, Inc., a consulting firm specializing in the development and operations of consortium day care, the center grew out of a need for child care among a large number of organizations, many of which were small businesses.

The issue of care was first addressed by TyTran, Inc., which commissioned a study by Play and Learn Services to explore the child-care needs of the area and detail a plan to meet those needs.

The study developed a plan for child care that required a developer to create a child-care facility and a consortium of companies that would collectively contribute $100,000 in exchange for reservations of space in a nonprofit, tax-exempt child-care center.

TyTran endorsed the study, the funding commitment was met, and Play and Learn Services was hired to implement the plan. Corporate contributors formed an incorporating board of directors that performed all the legal and financial functions necessary to establish the center as an independent entity. Once that was done, the board appointed an operating board of directors (made up of parents, staff, and consultants) that made the program and policy decisions for the center. The incorporating board was then

FIGURE 6–1
A Model for Consortia Day Care

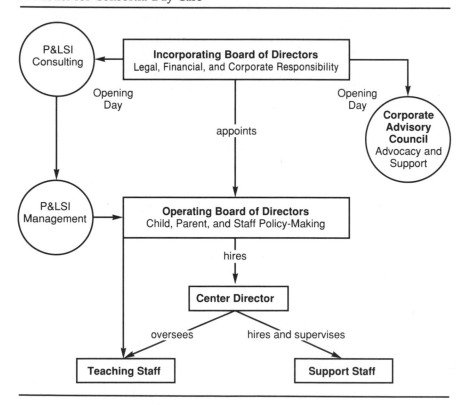

Source: Provided courtesy of Play and Learn Services, Inc., Chantilly, Virginia, 1990

dissolved. The board of directors hired a center director who implements policy and oversees the daily operations of the center. Play and Learn Services provides technical assistance and management support for the program.

Once the initial funding goals were met, the Tyson's Corner center could operate independently of its original corporate support. The center's finances are enhanced through corporate funds generated by an annual renewal of priority enrollment status. These funds help the center provide scholarships and other special services. Companies in the consortium pay a $1-per-person fee for the total number of employees working in proximity to the center. Over 20 companies started up the consortium, and over 30 companies are currently participating in it. The cost to employees varies, depending on how their company chooses to subsidize child care.

In short, the consortium works by combining the commitment of a developer, the resources of employers, the involvement of working parents, and the technical assistance of a child-care consulting firm. A model of how this consortium works is provided in Figure 6–1. Play and Learn Services, Inc. has used this approach in developing and managing six successful consortia centers, two in Maryland and four in Virginia.[6]

EXTENDED SCHOOLDAY KIN CARE

Working parents with school-age children need to provide kin care during the hour or two before school and during the hours from the end of the schoolday to the end of the workday. Companies have difficulty in providing such kin care through on-site centers, which are often too far from the children's schools to be of use. Neighborhood services, therefore, have grown up to replace the unsatisfactory "latchkey" arrangement for kin care. (Under this arrangement, as the term suggests, children simply have a key to the house or apartment and provide for themselves before and after school.)

In many communities, extended schoolday kin care is provided by churches, youth groups, the YMCA/YWCA, private individuals in their homes, and by the schools themselves. Companies can make financial arrangements with these care providers to ensure spaces for their employees' dependents. In some cases, such as care provided by religious institutions, companies will probably prefer to subsidize the employee instead of entering into contracts that presume a particular religious bias or interest.

Advantages of Extended Schoolday Kin Care Programs

- The company makes no capital investment in facilities.
- The cost per participant is usually low.
- The company may have little or no liability exposure.
- Working parents can minimize arriving late and leaving early.
- The quality of care is generally good, with activity-based programs suited to the participant's age and interests.
- The location of the care center is usually convenient for both the parents and the children.
- Use of the care center is easily arranged, terminated, and adjusted for vacations and other schedule changes.
- Parents use company telephones much less than they would under a latchkey arrangement, in which case a number of "checkup" calls have to be made during the workday.

Disadvantages of Extended Schoolday Kin Care Programs

- Companies cannot count on the existence or availability of community-based programs to solve the kin care needs of their employees.
- The existing extended schoolday programs may not be flexible enough to meet wide swings in employee demand for them.
- Companies have little or no control over the location, staffing, or standards of care providers.
- Companies that deal directly with care providers such as religious organizations or private individuals may face awkward liability and public relations problems. For example, a company may not want to be associated too

closely with a particular religious group or to take the risk of having its name tarred by the misdeeds or mismanagement of a private care provider.

- Companies may have little control over the hours of operation of the care provider.

- Companies may pay widely varying amounts for the care available to different employee dependents. These differences in support may be hard to justify.

EXAMPLES OF SUCCESSFUL EXTENDED SCHOOLDAY PROGRAMS

BASE

One successful program, the Braintree After School Enrichment (BASE) program in Braintree, Massachusetts, was founded by Roselyn Karll, the administrative director of the program. BASE started as a result of a proposal Karll wrote six years ago. Karll says, "Partnerships with business are the key to keeping programs like this up and running."

At first, the BASE program was run in two rented rooms in Braintree High School. After two years, BASE moved into a public school facility that housed several offices of the Department of Health and Human Services. No longer being used as a school, the complex had a cafeteria, gym, and other facilities that made it ideal for an after-school program. BASE provides after-school activities for 80 children from 2 P.M. to 6 P.M. The program was recently expanded to start at 7 A.M. to help the kindergarten population. According to Karll, "By opening early, we enable children to attend their home-based schools and the BASE program. We transport the children to and from the individual schools." The program charges $50 per week. BASE is a private, nonprofit organization that has received the support of the school district.

"The staff works directly with BASE, although the schools have supported us by renting us space and making recommendations to parents about the program. Word of mouth is how we get most of the kids." Getting corporate support is the next step. "We are in the planning stages of developing a partnership with companies whereby companies subsidize the program in exchange for priority enrollment of their employees' children," says Karll. "I have also written and had a grant funded through the League of Women Voters for After School Family Day Care. This program will provide after-school care for nine-year-olds and up. Now, we need to get matching funds from companies. In the past, smaller businesses seemed really interested. Dentists, doctors, and lawyers can give nominal funds for the program, say $10 a week, and subsidize the costs for their employees. Both large and small companies can make a difference. The answer lies in approaching companies and asking for small donations for parents who couldn't otherwise afford the program. We plan to offer sliding scale fees to help parents."[7]

These are the kinds of programs already operating in the community that invite company participation and partnership.

Corporate-School Partnerships: ABIG

A creative program being discussed by many was proposed by Edward Zigler, education specialist at Yale University. The schools offer a reasonably priced solution to many child-care and/or elder-care concerns. Zigler refers to this program as "schools of the 21st century" where the school tries to work out the problems faced by working parents. The needs of over 2 million latchkey kids and even senior citizens could be served if schools were resource centers for parents and caregivers. The schools of the 21st century are another possibility in thinking about private-public partnerships. American Bankers Insurance Group (ABIG), in Miami, Florida, has already made this connection by operating a public school on company grounds as a partnership with the Dade County School District. In addition to ABIG's satellite school, extended schoolday programs are offered.

Beulah Richards, principal of Cutler Ridge Elementary School and the satellite school at ABIG (see Chapter 9), recently received a special award for community service in Dade County from the Dade Coalition for Community Education. The award recognized her work as host principal at ABIG's satellite school and her development of a principal-operated before- and after-school care program.

Richards started the before- and after-school program at Cutler Ridge and extended the program to her satellite school at ABIG, 2 miles down the road. Working parents pay $1.50 per day for before-school care from 7:15 A.M. to 8:15 A.M. and $20 per day for after-school care from 2 P.M. to 6:15 P.M. During school vacations, the program includes "campcare" from 7:15 A.M. to 6:15 P.M. During the program, children engage in supervised recreation, arts and crafts work, supervised homework, and see movies/videos. The program also provides campcare during the winter and spring school vacations.

According to Richards, the program is "self-supporting." Usually, an assistant principal, teacher, or aide from the school serves as program manager and the school hires activity directors at the minimum wage to work with the children. The directors are usually high school or college students who are carefully screened, meet Department of Health and Rehabilitative Services (HRS) requirements, and want to work part-time with children. Richards indicates that the program has been a "smash success" with ABIG. Phil Sharkey, vice president at ABIG, concurs.[8]

SICK-CHILD/SICK-ELDER KIN CARE

Sick children and sick elders cause more absenteeism, lack of concentration, personal use of company resources, unauthorized use of sick leave, and general stress than any other care-related problem. The solution, companies find, does not necessarily lie in an on-site or off-site infirmary. Parents have a natural need and desire to be with their sick children during the worst periods of sickness.

Company-provided infirmaries have been useful to employees, however, for the fluish or recovering child or elder. Company-provided nurses (typically LPNs—licensed practical nurses) for in-home care of dependents have also been useful. Some hospitals have worked with area businesses to set up a corridor for sick child care separate from ordinary hospital admitting procedures. More commonly, companies simply extend the rules governing an employee's own sick leave, personal time, or vacation leave to include caring for a sick child. This approach, however, does not solve the problem of the absent worker.

The applicability of the following advantages and disadvantages depends to a large extent on the approach to sick-child sick-elder care taken by the company.

Advantages of Sick-Child/Sick-Elder Kin Care Programs

- Company resources are directed at the most common cause of employee absenteeism, stress, and lack of productivity.

- Knowing that sick-child/sick-elder emergencies can be "covered" enables employees to plan more effectively, increases employee loyalty, and may reduce employee turnover.

- Since the company is in the "care business" only on an occasional, case-by-case basis, considerably less investment may be required for such programs than for other forms of kin care.

- Public praise and improved public relations may result.

Disadvantages of Sick-Child/Sick-Elder Kin Care Programs

- Heavy outbreaks of flu and other illnesses can decimate a work force that is allowed to use sick leave and vacation time for sick-child/sick-elder care.

- Parents of chronically ill children or elders may ask the company for too much scheduling flexibility.

- It may be inadvisable to bring contagious or susceptible dependents to a common-care center.

- Transporting an ill dependent to care sites may be inadvisable.

- The costs of staffing, equipment, and facilities may be prohibitive.

- Liability issues may be posed for companies that assume a care-giving position with regard to sick children or elders.

- Employees may not exercise good judgment in deciding whether to bring sick children or elders to a common-care center. Such centers will probably be unable to provide adequate care for the very sick.

EXAMPLES OF SUCCESSFUL SICK-CHILD/SICK-ELDER KIN CARE PROGRAMS

Baxter Healthcare, Champion International, and Du Pont

Extending Sick Pay for Sick Family is a program being used at Baxter Healthcare Corporation. This new program allows employees to use their own sick pay when needed to care for a sick family member. Generally, sick pay is up to 15 days of pay replacement for illness. More and more companies are letting employees use this approach.

Champion International Corporation has developed *Wee Care*, a program that helps working parents when a sick child is unable to attend school or a day-care facility. Coordinated with the Fort Hamilton–Hughes Memorial Hospital, the program provides safe, comfortable, and affordable care for sick children 24 hours a day, seven days a week. Employees preregister before using the program, so that when the unexpected occurs, they can go right to the hospital's pediatric unit. *Wee Care* provides routine infant formulas; routine meals; hospital pajamas; diapers; entertainment and diversion appropriate to the child's age, clinical condition, and desired activity level; age- and condition-appropriate amounts and types of supervision (including the administration of doctor-prescribed medication provided by the parent); and care. The employee pays $3 per hour for the first eight hours of service and $2 per hour for each additional hour of service. Champion subsidizes the remaining costs.

Du Pont provides a similar program called *Sniffles 'N Sneezes*. Employees receive a 50 percent discount for first-time use of the sick-child care center.

EMERGENCY CHILD CARE

Emergency child care is intended to help employees solve problems arising from the breakdown of their regular child-care arrangements. Such situations as the illness of child-care providers and unexpected school closings present significant problems for many employees. Several organizations are recognizing that unexpected child-care problems often spell major problems for the organization.

Consider the experience of one law firm. A managing partner tells this story: "We were working on a critically important case. One of the attorneys who played an important role in the preparation suddenly called in to tell us that her nanny called in sick and as a consequence she couldn't make it to work until she found alternative arrangements. The deadline for filing [briefs] was approaching, and we were in real trouble." The firm subsequently made arrangements for an emergency care center that employees could use when the unexpected occurred. Satisfaction with the center is high, and several associates have indicated that one of the reasons they came back to work was the responsiveness and understanding of the firm's managing partners with respect to child care.

An emergency care center, like a full-care center, can be licensed by the state to assure adherence to local regulations regarding health, safety, fire, and day-to-day operations. It would then operate similarly to a full-care center, except that parents would use it only when their regular child-care arrangements break down. Sick children are not eligible to use an emergency care center. Emergency care centers are typically licensed for 20–30 children.

EXAMPLES OF EMERGENCY CARE

Fannie Mae, Arnold & Porter

The Fannie Mae emergency care center is a good example of how this type of kin care works. The center is licensed for emergency care only. The program can accommodate 20 children, including no more than 4 under the age of two. Parents preregister for future use of the center so that staff has the necessary health and background information on each child. When parents need to use the center, they call ahead and, space permitting, the child can be accommodated on a first-come, first-served basis. A waiting list is maintained. The daily fees are $15 for children under two and $10 for children over two. Discounts are available for employees with more than one child. If the center is needed for less than four hours, a flat fee of $5 is charged. According to Julie Goldstein, who runs the Fannie Mae center, this method works only when parents understand that the center is to be used for emergency purposes only.[9]

Arnold & Porter, another law firm that has an emergency care center for the children of employees, has reaped many benefits from the center. According to its director, Maria Elwood, the center saved the firm, located in Washington, D.C., $400,000 in its first year of operation.

FAMILY KIN CARE

Within the limits defined by their state, individuals can open their homes to children and elders for day care. Most states allow one adult to care for up to four infants *or* six older children. More children can be taken in if this caregiver/child ratio is maintained (group family care). Guidelines for home safety, hygienic facilities, food provisions, and indoor/outdoor play areas are suggested by many states and enforced by some. In some areas, family care providers have joined into networks to share training, substitute care providers, the participant pool, and the purchase of equipment and supplies.

Having a network of family care centers handy can ease the crunch for companies and their employees during school "snow days" or school vacation days that aren't also company vacation days. Many family care centers are willing to take extra children on such occasions. Companies try to notify these care centers well in advance of the anticipated overload period.

Advantages of Family Kin Care Programs

- Little or no capital investment by the company is required.
- The fees paid to care providers are usually moderate.
- Working parents and their dependents may feel good about the home environment provided by family care.
- The locations of family care centers are usually convenient for employees and their dependents (especially children who go to neighborhood schools).
- Working parents can leave children of varying ages at the same family care center.

- The hours of family care centers are usually more flexible than those of on-site centers or other kin care arrangements.

Disadvantages of Family Kin Care Programs

- The care providers have generally received little formal training in child care or elder care. (On the other hand, the care providers usually have a great deal of experience.)
- Especially in care situations involving children of various ages, there may be little or no attempt to provide age-appropriate activities or playthings.
- Standards of cleanliness, individual attention, and supervisory control are usually out of the hands of both the parents and the company. What you don't see is what you get.
- The company may face liability exposure if it contracts with unlicensed, uninsured care providers.
- The company accrues little public relations value or community visibility.
- Due to low wages, staff turnover in group family care settings is extremely high.

EXAMPLE OF A SUCCESSFUL FAMILY KIN CARE PROGRAM

America West Airlines

In addition to establishing a strong center-based program, America West Airlines was one of the first companies in the country to establish a home-based family care program. Plans for implementing the company's child-care programs were drawn up by Michael Conway, America West's president and chief operating officer.

The coordinated family care program comprises a network of family homes sprinkled throughout the Phoenix and Las Vegas areas—more than 50 in Phoenix and more than 10 in Las Vegas. These homes provide care for children six weeks of age and older. The caregivers are fully trained, and employees have the opportunity to interview and select the family home that best meets their individual needs.

The family caregivers participate in the food program of the U.S. Department of Agriculture (USDA) and are inspected by the local health and fire departments. The company has a toy-lending library that supplements the facilities of the family homes with educational toys and equipment. An America West home care specialist visits the homes biweekly. The company also provides initial and ongoing training programs that enhance the caregivers' child development skills. The in-home caregivers are independent contractors running small businesses. Each caregiver is carefully screened and trained before being accepted as part of the network. The caregivers agree to fingerprinting and FBI background checks, substance abuse screening, ongoing child development training, licensing, completion of a pediatric first aid course, and CPR training. According to Daphne Dicino, senior director for corporate communications, "The small ratios of children in the home foster a feeling of 'extended family,' while enabling the caregiver to provide flexible, loving, quality care to each child."[10]

ELDER DAY CARE

As the Age Wave puts more and more employees into the role of caregivers to elderly parents and other relatives, companies are beginning to consider ways to assist. Few companies have established on-site elder-care centers. Many more have worked with community agencies, private care providers, and church organizations to establish "drop-in centers." These homelike settings (which, in fact, are often located in private homes) welcome the elderly, including the frail elderly, for an hour or the entire business day.

Elder drop-in centers differ from nursing homes primarily in that they provide no overnight accommodations. The supervisory personnel tend to have less medical training than the supervisory personnel of nursing homes, though most of them have had extensive experience in working with the elderly. Social and recreational activities help seniors fill their days enjoyably.

The fees vary widely, according to program and region. Some elder centers don't consider themselves "care" centers at all, and consequently charge only the minimum dues necessary to pay for food and activities. These centers often receive considerable subsidies from public and private agencies. Elder centers that provide higher levels of physical care, however, may charge rates that, hour for hour, are comparable to those of a nursing home.

In some areas, nursing and convalescent homes have lounge and recreation space during the day for "visitors." A few companies have negotiated with these homes to provide space for elder dependents of employees.

A variant of the elder-care center is the intergenerational center, which serves both the elderly and young children. This does not imply that the elderly take care of the young children. Under supervised conditions, however, many elders do enjoy giving care and attention to children, and vice versa. But working parents should be wary of any arrangement based on the premise that the elderly and the young can take care of each other.

Advantages of Elder Day-Care Programs

- Neither families nor the company incur the expense of 24-hour nursing home or hospital care for the frail elderly, who can often delay or avoid institutionalization by spending days at an elder-care center.

- Liability for the company is limited, especially considering the precarious health of some elderly dependents.

- Employees are unexpectedly absent less often and are less likely to tie up company phones with personal calls.

- The company reaps public relations benefits if the elder day-care center is identified by the community as a company project.

- The elderly person's satisfying social life during the day lessens the stress of elder care.

Disadvantages of Elder Day-Care Programs

- The charges of some elder-care centers are high.

- Equitable balancing of company subsidies for elder care may be difficult since employees in one area may have access to elder care that is less expensive than comparable care in another area.

- Since use of elder-care centers by employees may vary week to week as the health and interests of the elder dependent change, the company may find it impractical to reserve slots in elder-care programs on a steady basis.

- The company and its employees have little control over the standards, procedures, and personnel at elder-care centers independent of the company.

- The truly frail elderly, including those who are bedridden, may not be served by most elder-care centers.

EXAMPLES OF SUCCESSFUL ELDER DAY-CARE PROGRAMS

The Stride Rite Intergenerational Day-Care Center

The Stride Rite Intergenerational Center is a prime example of a high-quality day-care program for both children and elders. The design of the center encourages informal interaction between children and elders while also enabling the two groups to be separate from each other. The center is divided into two wings that are both linked and separated by a large central area. The elders' wing has three rooms, which have been designed to accommodate a variety of activities. The elder-care part of the program serves 24 elders 60 years of age or older. A carefully planned and supervised curriculum fosters regular daily contact between the elders and children along with separate activities for the two groups.

The center also serves as a teacher-training site for students and as a research site for faculty from Wheelock College. The company works closely with the college and Somerville-Cambridge Elder Services, Inc. (SCES) to best serve elder needs.

SCES, an experienced human services agency, screens elder clients and develops the adult day-care curriculum and training models. It also offers ElderLink, a resource and referral service that employers and employees use. Stride Rite provides workshops, seminars, and support groups that are designed to foster greater awareness of elder-care issues.

Wang Laboratories

The U.S. Administration on Aging, along with Wang Laboratories in Merrimack Valley, Massachusetts, and Elder Care Services of the Merrimack Valley, is conducting an experimental program for adult dependent care. The program makes adult day-care services available to those Wang employees who have primary care responsibilities for an impaired elderly person. Under this program, employees discuss their needs with a counselor of the Wang Employee Assistance Program (EAP). The counselor then makes referrals to Elder Care Services of the Merrimack Valley. Elder Care Services informs employees of the availability of day care and arranges for an appropriate day-care setting and for transportation as needed. The U.S. Administration on Aging subsidizes a portion of the cost of the day care. This program is an excellent example of a private-public partnership.

Upjohn In-Home Care

The Upjohn Company in Kalamazoo, Michigan, provides care at a reduced rate for dependent children, adults, and elderly family members through a home health care agency. The agency's program includes Companion Care, which provides care for up to three dependents at a time, giving emotional and physical support, preparing meals, and maintaining a safe, clean home. Employees pay $3.25 an hour, and Upjohn pays the balance. Home Health Aide Care, available for mildly ill children, adults, or elders, provides monitoring but not professional nursing. Aides give basic personal care, administer medication, and provide emotional and supportive care. Employees pay $3.50 per hour, and the company pays the rest. Employees may use the In-Home Care programs for planned or unplanned needs. Each employee is limited to 20 days a year and normally up to 10 consecutive days at a time.

LONG-TERM CARE INSURANCE

Long-term care insurance, a relatively new benefit for the 1990s, is another kin care alternative addressing the unique problem of a "graying America." In Chapter 5, we discussed the fact that about half of all senior citizens will eventually require some type of long-term care. The cost of such care can deplete assets and place a heavy burden on the elder's extended family. Several companies are responding to this need by offering long-term care insurance. The insurance is a choice that flexible benefits programs often give employees. The insurance benefits cover a variety of nursing and custodial expenses for people who cannot perform the activities of daily living. The types of care include nursing home care, adult day care, home health care, and the services of professional care advisers. Several companies offer the plan to retirees and their spouses and to surviving spouses. Other companies let the employees' parents and parents-in-law also enroll.

EXAMPLES OF SUCCESSFUL LONG-TERM CARE INSURANCE PROGRAMS

Chevron Corporation, Johnson & Johnson, and Sovran Financial Corporation

Chevron, J & J, and Sovran Financial Corp. are among the few companies that offer long-term care plans. Johnson & Johnson's plan allows employees and their spouses, parents, parents-in-law, and grandparents to enroll. The Johnson & Johnson plan is underwritten by Continental Casualty Company, one of the CNA companies. CNA—(800) 621-0839—will answer questions that employers or employees have about long-term care. Chevron's plan covers retirees, their spouses, and surviving spouses and is underwritten by Metropolitan Life. Sovran offers long-term care insurance to the employee for the employee's spouse, parents, and in-laws.

RESOURCE AND REFERRAL SERVICES

Some companies have expressed a bit of chagrin at offering "only" resource and referral (R & R) help for employees with child- or elder-care responsibilities. If resource and referral services are thought of as nothing more than a list of phone numbers and a few brochures, then the chagrin is justified. But done right, such services can forge a vital link between the employee who needs kin care assistance and the many agencies and individuals willing to provide that assistance.

Well-conceived resource and referral services are usually sited in a high-traffic, high-visibility area within the company. The staffers of such services are good listeners as well as good information sharers. Employees seeking referral help want someone in the company to "really listen" to their problems and concerns.

Keeping resource information current and growing can be a full-time job, though many companies ask a personnel employee to handle that task along with other duties. Employees must be assured, by the way the resource and referral services are advertised within the company, that their personal concerns and circumstances will be held in complete confidence. (Many employees fear that family burdens of any kind, once known in the company, may disqualify them from advancement.)

In some companies, the resource and referral specialist has a background in social work or clinical evaluation. If trained to do so, such a specialist can, at the invitation of employees, go out "into the field" to visit homes and assess what's needed in the way of kin care assistance. Resource and referral programs that do not have an individual so trained on their staff can contract with area professionals to provide in-home evaluations. Many companies, particularly those whose employees are located all over the country, contract with national resource and referral providers such as Work/Family Directions, Inc. and The Partnership Group, Inc. to administer R & Rs. These firms subcontract out with local community-based organizations that help employees in a particular geographic location. In addition to working with referral agencies, these and similar firms also offer specialists who work on-site with the company, and provide extensive workshops, seminars, and a wide variety of other helpful resources.

Advantages of Resource and Referral Kin Care Programs

- There is little liability for the company so long as specific medical or rehabilitative therapies or courses of action come about by referral, not by recommendation on behalf of the company.

- The cost is relatively low, depending on the range of the services offered and the degree of their use by employees.

- Since the services are available to all employees on an as-needed basis, company expenditures for the program are equitable to all employees.

- Employees can work out individualized solutions to fit their particular kin care needs.

- The company establishes good relations with a wide number of local health and human services providers.

- Employee needs can be tracked as a basis for developing necessary on-site services, focus seminars, and other programs.

Disadvantages of Resource and Referral Kin Care Programs

- Employees may view the program as "too little, too late" to meet their pressing needs.

- As a result, the resource and referral services may be underutilized. In some companies, these services quickly gain an unfair reputation as a "white elephant" that no one uses.

- Employees may be upset if the recommendations of the resource and referral services prove to be unsatisfactory or too expensive.

- The success of the program depends almost entirely on the level of services provided by agencies and individuals outside the company.

EXAMPLES OF SUCCESSFUL RESOURCE AND REFERRAL KIN CARE PROGRAMS

Chevy Chase Bank (Chevy Chase, Maryland) and Branch Electric Company (Washington, D.C.)

To meet their resource and referral needs, Chevy Chase Bank and Branch Electric Company have contracted out with Child Care Management Resources (CCMR), a child-care counseling firm headquartered in Bethesda, Maryland. Carol Ann Rudolph, former director at the National Institutes of Health (NIH) day care center and president of CCMR, says that the resource and referral program is a "unique child-care service that is particularly helpful and cost effective for smaller employers. . . . Every employee receives kid-gloved treatment from a specialist who comes to the worksite and meets with employees on an individual basis. . . . In many ways, it is like an Employee Assistance Program for child care."[11]

Branch Electric Company, with only 200 employees, feels that the program really helps meet its employees' family needs. The employees of Chevy Chase Bank are located in many branches. Typical of employee response to the program are such comments as these: "It's helpful to speak with a consultant who has thorough and complete knowledge of child care and the problems we parents face"; "The personal contact and counseling are superb"; and "The counselor does the research, and that helps."

Phillips Petroleum Company (Bartlesville, Oklahoma)

Phillips Petroleum Company contracted with The Partnership Group, Inc. to provide both child-care and elder-care services to its employees. Employees' families are provided with immediate, practical information about child care and elder care in addition to receiving referrals for programs and services that will better meet their individual needs. Specialists work with each family, and referral specialists provide information on child care and elder care options over the phone. The ChildCare Solution and The ElderCare Connection, two services of the R & R, provide counseling, referrals, educational materials, on-site workshops, and a videotape library. The ChildCare Solution also offers a resource development service that involves special programs to recruit and train additional caregivers in the community. Robert Nash, manager of compensation and benefits at Phillips Petroleum, indicates that "the service has been well received by employees. The vast majority of those who have used the service have found it helpful in addressing immediate needs and would use it again in the future."[12]

IBM (Purchase, New York)

Most of the companies whose kin care programs are showcased in Chapter 9 use a resource and referral program; in general, the feedback regarding these programs has been very positive. IBM, a pioneering company in this area, has compiled statistics on the use of its R & R. Says IBM: "The single most important benefit for those using the service is the in-depth personalized counseling about elder-care issues." It reports that "16,000 employees, retirees, and spouses have used the elder-care service to find care for 15,000 people" and that "43,000 IBM families received referrals for child care." "Through our new $25 million fund for dependent care initiatives, IBM expects to increase the supply and improve the quality of child care in the country," says Ted Childs, program director of work/life program, IBM United States.[13]

VOUCHERS AND COMPANY-NEGOTIATED DISCOUNTS

Companies that resist the notion of having children and/or elders on-site or in company-sponsored off-site centers may nevertheless be enthusiastic providers of vouchers and negotiated discounts. A voucher is the company's scrip, convertible to cash payment by the care provider, for care services rendered to the children or elders of a company employee. (In many cases, the company simply requires employees to turn in their kin care receipts for full or partial reimbursement.)

Company-negotiated discounts work as follows: The company offers an independent care provider a certain amount of kin care business for a specified discount (usually 10–20 percent). In addition, the company usually pays a portion of the remaining charges; this payment, too, is usually 10–20 percent. In the best of discount situations, an employee may be paying only 50–60 percent of the going rate for care services (after both the discount and the company payment have been subtracted). Employees can pay their portion with pretax dollars through a Dependent Care Assistance Plan (DCAP), reducing their actual costs even more.

Advantages of Voucher and Company-Negotiated Discount Programs

- The payments involve little liability exposure for the company.

- The company's expense is usually limited to accounting, check disbursement, and use verification. Usually, the company does not incur any capital investment costs or any additional staff costs.

- The services are selected by the employee, not the company.

- The company does not become involved in facility inspection, staff training, program review, policy-making, or administration of kin care sites.

- Employees view the voucher and discount system as minimally intrusive into the details of their personal lives.

Disadvantages of Voucher and Company-Negotiated Discount Programs

- The company has little control over money misspent on kin care services that do not resolve employee problems.

- If adequate services are unavailable in the community, vouchers and discounts are meaningless.

- The costs can mount quickly as more and more employees find ways to qualify for company payments.

- In the case of discounted services, employees must use specific care vendors. This may prove inconvenient or objectionable.

EXAMPLES OF SUCCESSFUL VOUCHER AND COMPANY-NEGOTIATED DISCOUNT PROGRAMS

Hasbro, Inc. (Pawtucket, Rhode Island)

Hasbro, Inc. has developed a program called Kid Care, a network of over 35 licensed child-care centers and many in-home care providers enrolling children from infancy through age 13. Hasbro employees are given priority enrollment throughout the network. To use the voucher program, parents can research the listings of child-care locations at the Human Resources Department. Parents are encouraged to visit the child-care centers in order to select the one that best meets their individual needs. Once a child has been accepted by a center, Human Resources issues the parent a voucher that allows Hasbro's portion of the payment to be paid directly to the care provider. Hasbro subsidizes the parents' costs based on family size and income. The voucher also enables parents to receive a reduced rate for child-care services within the Kid Care network. The company has negotiated additional discounts for families enrolling more than one child.

National Discounts

Such child-care chains as Children's Discovery Centers, Children's World Learning Centers, Gerber Children's Centers, Kinder-Care Learning Centers, La Petite Academy, and Rocking Horse Child Care Centers offer companies corporate discounts for enrollment. Parents at a company without a child-care program can often band together to negotiate group discounts through the company or even on their own. Companies that have secured national discounts are listed in Chapter 9.

KIN CARE THROUGH FLEXIBLE WORK ARRANGEMENTS

By far the most common response of American companies to the kin care needs of employees is one or more of these flexible working arrangements:

- *Flextime.* Employees can schedule work hours around kin care commitments.

- *Flexible place/telecommuting.* Employees can occasionally work at home or at another location.

- *Half-day vacations.* Employees can use vacation time or personal days for half-day breaks to handle kin care situations such as doctor appointments and teacher conferences.

- *Job sharing.* Employees can perform a certain percentage (usually half) of a particular job. They receive prorated salary and prorated or full benefits.

- *Permanent part-time.* Employees can limit the time they spend on the job by doing part-time work. Their benefits and salary are usually prorated. Their advancement is typically slowed.

- *Schedule compression.* Employees can complete their week's work in a few long days—four 10-hour days, for example—instead of the usual workweek.

Advantages of Flexible Work Arrangements for Kin Care

- The company's out-of-pocket costs for resolving kin care problems are very limited (though the spin-off expenses of some of the arrangements may be costly).

- The company has virtually no liability for the kin care decisions made by employees.

- Company morale rises as employees enjoy the freedom to shape the use of their time. Recruitment and public relations also benefit.

- In some industries, productivity tends to rise as time-conscious workers try to accomplish tasks more efficiently.

- Turnover may tend to drop if employees cannot find comparable programs in other companies.

Disadvantages of Flexible Work Arrangements for Kin Care

- The scheduling of groups, such as work teams, and of group activities, such as meetings, may be difficult.

- Monitoring the work schedules of individual employees may be problematic. Some employees may abuse flexible scheduling to work less than the company pays them to.

- Employees may be unwilling or unable to give up their flexible schedules during times of heavy production, rush orders, or seasonal surges.

- The most talented employees may be tempted to work on a part-time or job-sharing basis while using most of their energy and talent in other enterprises, including consulting.

EXAMPLES OF SUCCESSFUL FLEXIBLE WORK ARRANGEMENTS FOR KIN CARE

Marriott Corporation (Bethesda, Maryland)

When Sherri Cline, lodging marketing services accounting assistant, decided to leave Marriott Corporation in the summer of 1989, this seemed to be her only option. The conflicts between her personal and professional roles seemed insurmountable. Frank Camacho, vice president of lodging marketing services, had an innovative response. Sensitive to Cline's parenting and commuting concerns, but also concerned about losing a valued employee, Camacho suggested an alternative work schedule. Now Cline divides her full-time schedule into three days at home and two days at headquarters. Her responsibilities are the same: she coordinates all accounting, payroll, benefits and computer-related functions, and supports 22 people. Most of her work is completed in a home office outfitted with a desk, a file cabinet, an on-line computer, and a facsimile machine. During her two days at headquarters, she meets with coworkers, obtains signatures, copies materials, and divides her in-box into tasks for home and headquarters. "I have an ideal situation," says Cline. She leaves her son with a neighborhood family care provider two days a week, and she likes giving him this opportunity to spend time with other children. Camacho is pleased to report that his only expense has been the purchase of a fax machine, which, he says, is "much less expensive than replacing an employee." "If you can understand the criteria for getting the job done, the volume, and

have an employee you are comfortable can work well independently," argues Camacho, "I'd certainly recommend you
consider flexible job arrangements that make life easier for the
employee."[14]

Hallmark Corporation (Kansas City, Missouri)

Hallmark Corporation has established a Job Share Clearinghouse
so that an employee can research the possibility of sharing a
single full-time position with another employee on a part-time
basis. To get started, an interested employee completes a Job
Share Candidate form and submits it along with an internal ré-
sumé. The candidate forms are circulated to all personnel managers and to other job share candidates with similar skills and
experience. The clearinghouse provides employees with information about other interested Hallmarkers, markets employees
who are interested in a job share, and provides employees and
managers with assistance and support in creating job share
arrangements.

UNUM Life Insurance Company (Portland, Maine)

At UNUM Life Insurance Company, flexible working hours are
designed to encourage maximum productivity and to assist employees in balancing work and family obligations. The company
has established "core hour" guidelines for the hours 9:30 A.M.–
3 P.M., Monday through Friday. A non–core hour schedule is
worked out with an employee's supervisor to best meet both the
employee's family needs and the needs of the company.

FLEXIBLE BENEFITS FOR KIN CARE

Beginning in 1981 with the Economic Recovery Act, the federal
government clearly indicated its path with regard to kin care
programs. Direct payments to care providers would give way to
tax incentives motivating employers to offer or provide access to
kin care services. As a result, employees now confront a "menu"
of benefit choices—the so-called cafeteria approach—instead of a
fixed benefits package. Here are some of the most popular kin
care choices:

1. *Medical Co-Payment Insurance.* Also known as medigap, this insurance option protects employees against deductibles, co-payments, and other charges not covered by medicare and medicaid.

2. *Dependent Care Assistance Plans (DCAPs).* Under the IRS provision for such plans, employers can provide certain kin care services (for example, vouchers and direct payments to vendors) without including the amounts paid for these services in the employee's taxable income. Employers receive tax incentives for programs developed under this provision. Employees may be required to participate in paying for DCAP's through salary reduction.

The DCAP provision also describes the Flexible Spending Accounts, Reimbursement Accounts, and other programs that companies use so that employees can benefit from IRS regulations. The IRS now allows employers to hold up to $5,000 of employee pretax contributions for use in paying insurance premiums, medical bills, care expenses, and so on for qualifying health services. Any funds not used during the year are forfeited. Thus, employees can pay for dependent care with pretax dollars.

3. *Tax Planning.* Under the terms of the Child and Dependent Care Tax Credit for Workers, employees may claim credits on qualifying expenses of up to $2,400 for one dependent and up to $4,800 for two or more dependents. (These expenses must be for services not covered under any Dependent Care Assistance Plan provided by the company.)

Advantages of Flexible Benefits for Kin Care

- Employees meet their dependent care needs primarily from their own resources, through careful selection of available programs.

- The company makes little capital investment that is not compensated by tax credits for providing flexible benefit options.

- The company has virtually no liability for the health and care services selected by employees.

- The company cannot be charged with inequitably distributing benefits.

Disadvantages of Flexible Benefits for Kin Care

- Under the cafeteria approach to benefits, employees must often choose one benefit to the exclusion of other needed benefits.

- If quality kin care services are unavailable in the area, the employee's ability to pay for them is meaningless.

- For complex cafeteria plans, the company's administrative and processing costs may be high.

- Employees may be unskilled, or unlucky, in choosing the benefits that they or their dependents need most. Company education programs may prove difficult and costly to develop and deliver.

- Flexible benefits may do relatively little to address emergency kin care situations, such as the sudden illness of a child or the unexpected arrival of an elderly parent in need of care.

EXAMPLE OF SUCCESSFUL FLEXIBLE BENEFITS FOR KIN CARE

Most of the companies listed in Chapter 9 provide some type of flexible benefit plan, primarily DCAPs. DCAPs are a company's least expensive way to provide some form of kin care assistance.

Johnson & Johnson (New Brunswick, New Jersey)

Johnson & Johnson in New Brunswick, New Jersey, calls its DCAP the Dependent CareAccount. Under this plan, employees estimate the amount they think they will spend on dependent care per year. They can deposit up to $5,000 of that amount into their CareAccount. The deposit comes out of their paychecks in equal, tax-free amounts. It goes into a special account in the employee's name. An employee who has a dependent care expense pays it and then files a claim. The employee is reimbursed from the money that has been put aside in the CareAccount. Employees do not pay federal income or social security taxes on this money.

Employees are encouraged to compare the CareAccount with the Child and Dependent Care Tax Credit to determine which of these plans saves them more on taxes. The CareAccount reduces taxable income and thus reduces taxes; the tax credit directly reduces federal income tax by a percentage of dependent care expense. Employees are provided with work sheets so that they can make this comparison.

Eligible expenses reimbursed by the CareAccount include expenses for child or adult day care, expenses for baby-sitting inside or outside the home, and expenses for a housekeeper, a relative, or other caregiver who cares for dependents.

Chapter Seven

This Is the House That Jack Built

STARTING KIN CARE PROGRAMS

T he real business of this chapter is a step-by-step approach by which working parents or company decision makers can get a kin care program up and running.

But first we should glance back at the origins of kin care in our country. Like its modern-day manifestation in company-sponsored kin care programs, child care in America began as a response to a business problem. With the growth of factories and large urban centers in the 1800s, many children of working parents were left to wander the streets or, in worst cases, locked up for the day in basements or leashed to bedposts. Social reformers and philanthropists stepped in to establish "day nurseries," a few of them underwritten by companies, for the care of these children.

Care meant physical protection from weather, hunger, and street abuse. A modicum of medical attention was available to children, as were elementary lessons in personal hygiene. The day nurseries were located in church basements, settlement houses, or private residences. The children came primarily from the families of poor shopkeepers and factory workers, many of them immigrants. The typical hours of care were the same as the typical working hours of the parents: dawn to dusk.

136

Distinct from the day nursery, though similar in name, was the "nursery school." It was primarily intended for the children of the upwardly mobile middle class, those merchants, professionals, and others who couldn't afford the governesses and nannies of the rich but nevertheless wanted their children to have developmental enrichment. The nursery school employed child specialists to nurture the children's intellectual, emotional, and social growth.

In time, the curricula and techniques of the middle-class nursery school became a model for day nurseries and other programs serving the lower classes. The warehousing of children, where it still occurred, was brought under governmental regulation and remediation.

With the call-up of women for war-related jobs in the 1940s, the day nursery and the nursery school merged quickly into the concept of the child-care center, and child-care centers exploded in numbers. After the war, however, the thousands of child-care centers shut down as women returned to the roles of homemaker, wife, and mother. Where the need for child-care facilities still existed, it was largely filled by women willing to look after an additional child or two at home.

This pattern of child care continued through the 1950s up to the first sallies of the War on Poverty in the 1960s. Programs such as Head Start were begun to provide early intervention for economically disadvantaged children. At the same time, other forces such as the women's movement and household economics drew women out of the home again and into the workplace. Child-care centers were again needed—and the need was met in large part by church and government "preschools" and kindergartens.

The economic recessions of the 1970s added impetus to the creation of child-care facilities. The median income of young working couples fell by 16 percent between 1973 and 1983. The mom-at-home pattern of the 1950s was no longer an option for couples intent on purchasing a house, living in a safe neighborhood within a major metropolitan area, or saving for family goals, including their children's education.

Federal and state governments, also affected by the recessions of the 1970s, opted to provide less and less support for child care. Most memorable was Richard Nixon's 1971 veto of child development funds on the ground that they augured a "communal" approach to child-rearing. In the past two decades, reported *Time* in 1989, "funding for direct day-care subsidies for low- and middle-income families has dropped by 28 percent."[1]

And so back to the future. We have come full circle, from the church-basement day nurseries of the 1800s to the church-basement child-care centers of the 1990s. "What was once a problem only of poor families," writes Sheila Kamerman, Columbia University professor of social policy and planning, "has now become a part of daily life and a basic concern of typical American families."[2]

DOING IT RIGHT

Whether spawned in the musings of the chief executive officer or in the grumblings of the rank and file, the idea of starting a kin care program can grow to maturity in six steps. Your company can follow these steps alone or together with another company, a union, or a government organization. It can choose whether to involve professional consultants who specialize in developing kin care programs.

Step 1: Discover What Employees Need

It's tempting to skip this laborious step and simply look at other area businesses, saying, in effect, "XYZ Corporation, with the same number of employees as our company, built an on-site care center. That's what we need."

Skipping the needs assessment step is a recipe for day-care disaster. A somewhat embarrassed Virginia company, for example, spent $105,000 as an up-front fee for a partnership in an attractive child-care consortium facility 4 miles from its office. When the center opened, two children of its employees showed up for its 26 reserved spaces. "We simply didn't figure that employees would prefer to use child care closer to home," a company representative said.

In 1989, the International Foundation of Employee Benefit Plans surveyed 243 employers across industries in the United States. Of these employers, 40 percent said that they offered some form of employer-sponsored child-care benefits. But fully half of the employers who offered child-care benefits said that these benefits were hardly ever used—on average, they said, less than 5 percent of their employees used child-care benefits. Here's the explanation: Only 26 percent of the employers said that they had designed their child-care benefits based on specific needs identified by employees.

The needs assessment process doesn't have to begin by vote of the board of directors. A group of interested employees in the company can distribute their own needs assessment, then take the results to the human resources department. Because it is usually the function of this department to *generate* programs, it may be wise to work with the department from the beginning in the needs assessment process. Otherwise, company politics may sabotage a good idea.

At Columbia Hospital for Women, an employee anonymously dropped a brochure from Child Care Management Resources, a consulting firm in Bethesda, Maryland, onto the desk of the human resources director. Curious, the director phoned Carol Ann Rudolph, the contact person named in the brochure. The ball kept rolling to produce the hospital's present counseling, resource, and referral program for kin care.

A "grass roots" approach—the kin care program initiated by interested employees—is not uncommon and can be successful. Margery Sher, of Fried & Sher, Inc., a child care development consulting firm located in Herndon, Virginia, says that "employees with a personal interest in beginning a child-care center have successfully banded together, worked diligently, and seen their dream come to fruition." Although the task may often be difficult, Sher contends that it is doable.

In consulting with firms developing child-care centers, Sher tells how employees on their own time have compiled information and statistics to enlighten their employers about demographic trends. "Some daring employees met with success when they presented management with a petition in favor of a child-care center with thousands of signatures." She emphasizes that management must be convinced that the employee group is serious and capable of undertaking such a major project.[3]

The American Airlines child-care program is one example of a grass roots start-up. According to Veronica Zollo, a senior analyst with American, First Class Academy, a near-site child-care center, came into being as a direct result of an idea suggested by a reservations sales representative.[4]

Whether assessing needs from the bottom up or the top down, be careful not to rely on employee anecdotes alone ("I'll bet lots of my friends with elderly parents would use a center!") as evidence of need. The vocal few may not represent a company-wide trend. Surveys of employees are critical. A sample elder-care survey instrument is obtainable from the American Association of Retired Persons (AARP) as part of its *Caregivers in the Workplace Program Kit*. The kit includes the basic materials needed to develop an employer-sponsored elder-care program (surveys, information on caregiver fairs, seminars, problem solving, and other resources). To arrive at substantive data regarding employee needs with respect to child care, one can use the accompanying types of needs surveys. These surveys can be adapted fairly easily for use in assessing the need for elder-care alternatives as well.

Corporate Day-Care Center Questionnaire

1. Personal data:
   a. Male ☐   Female ☐
   b. Age: Under 25 ☐   25–30 ☐   31–35 ☐   36–40 ☐   41 or over ☐
   c. Exempt ☐   Nonexempt ☐
2. What is your current work location?
   Downtown   ☐
   Branch   ☐
   Operations Center ☐
3. Do you have dependent children under the age of 13 living at home?
   Yes ☐   No ☐
   If yes, how are they cared for while you work?

   _____

   _____

   _____

   _____

   _____

4. If you are currently paying for child-care services, please complete the following for each child:

Corporate Day-Care Center Questionnaire (*continued*)

Age of Child	Weekly Cost for Child Care	No. of Days per Week	No. of Hours per Day
_____	_____	_____	_____
_____	_____	_____	_____
_____	_____	_____	_____
_____	_____	_____	_____

5. What hours of the day and days of the week do you need child-care services?

   Monday _____   Thursday _____

   Tuesday _____   Friday _____

   Wednesday _____

6. If a day-care center were established at the Operations Center, would you be interested in enrolling your preschool-age children?

   Yes ☐   No ☐

   If yes, please list the age of each child:

   _____   _____   _____   _____

   If no, why not?

   _____

   _____

   _____

   _____

7. Because of transportation problems, it would be difficult to provide an after-school program. However, if there were a summer program for school-age children (5 through 12 years old), would you be interested in enrolling your children?

   Yes ☐   No ☐

   If yes, please list the age of each child:

   _____   _____   _____   _____

   If no, why not?

Corporate Day-Care Center Questionnaire (*continued*)

_____

_____

_____

_____

8. Are you currently expecting a child?

   Yes ☐   No ☐

   If yes, would you be interested in enrolling this child in the day-care center?

   Yes ☐   No ☐

   If yes, at what age? _____

   If no, why not?

   _____

   _____

   _____

   _____

9. Fee schedules cannot be determined until the costs of operating the day-care center have been determined. However, if your answer to Question 6, 7, or 8 was yes and if a sliding scale fee schedule similar to the one outlined below were in place, would you enroll your child (children)?

   Infants to two years old: $30/week minimum or 12½% of an employee's weekly salary up to a maximum of $50/week.

   Two years old and up: $25/week minimum or 10% of an employee's weekly salary up to a maximum of $40/week.

   Yes ☐   No ☐

   If yes, what is your annual salary? _____

   If no, why not?

   _____

   _____

   _____

   _____

10. Comments:

   _____

   _____

Corporate Day-Care Center Questionnaire (*concluded*)

Source: Provided courtesy of Lincoln National Corporation, Fort Wayne, IN.

Child-Care Survey

If you have any children aged 12 or under living at home *and* you use child-care arrangements regularly . . .

Please check this box ☐ -1   Then answer all of the questions (Questions 1–24) on this form.

If you have any children aged 12 or under living at home *and* you do *not* use child-care arrangements regularly . . .

Please check this box ☐ -2   Then *just* answer Question 1a and Questions 10–24 in Sections 2, 3, and 4. (Do *not* answer questions 1b–9b.)

Child-Care Survey (*continued*)

If you do *not* have any children aged 12 or under living at home . . .

Please check this box   ☐ -3   Then answer only the questions in Section 4
(Questions 22–24).

Section 1: Present Child-Care Arrangements

1a. Please list the number of children you have in each of the following age
groups who are living in your home. (Record the actual number in the
spaces below.)

1b. Please list the number of children you have in *each* of the age groups
shown who regularly use child-care arrangements while you work.
(Record actual number(s) below.)

Age	Question 1a Live in Home	Question 1b Regularly Use Child Care
18 months or younger	————	————
1½ years (18 months) to 2½ years	————	————
2½ years to 5 years	————	————
5 to 6 years (kindergarten age)	————	————
6 to 12 years	————	————

Now please answer the remaining questions in this section by recording
the requested information in the specific age group column(s) that apply
to your children 12 or younger who regularly use child care.

Note: If you have two or more children in the *same* age group using
child-care arrangements, record the information for the *youngest*
child only.

2. Which of the statements listed below best describes the child-care
arrangements you now use while you are working? (Check as many as
apply.)

Child-Care Survey (*continued*)

Arrangement	18 Months or Less	1½ Years to 2½ Years	2½ Years to 5 Years	5–6 Years— Kinder-garten Age	6–12 Years
Spouse	☐ 1	☐ 1	☐ 1	☐ 1	☐ 1
Paid friend/neighbor/ relative in my home	☐ 2	☐ 2	☐ 2	☐ 2	☐ 2
Unpaid friend/ neighbor/relative in my home	☐ 3	☐ 3	☐ 3	☐ 3	☐ 3
Paid friend/neighbor/ relative in his/her home	☐ 4	☐ 4	☐ 4	☐ 4	☐ 4
Unpaid friend/ neighbor/relative in his/her home	☐ 5	☐ 5	☐ 5	☐ 5	☐ 5
Nursery school	☐ 6	☐ 6	☐ 6	☐ 6	☐ 6
Child-care center	☐ 7	☐ 7	☐ 7	☐ 7	☐ 7
Paid sitter in his/her home	☐ 8	☐ 8	☐ 8	☐ 8	☐ 8
Paid sitter in my home	☐ 9	☐ 9	☐ 9	☐ 9	☐ 9
Child cares for self and/or siblings	☐ 0	☐ 0	☐ 0	☐ 0	☐ 0
Other (please specify)					

3. Which of the statements listed below best describes where your current child-care facility is located? (Check as many as apply.)

Child-Care Survey (*continued*)

Location	18 Months or Less	1½ Years to 2½ Years	2½ Years to 5 Years	5–6 Years— Kinder- garten Age	6–12 Years
In my own home	☐ 1	☐ 1	☐ 1	☐ 1	☐ 1
Close to my home	☐ 2	☐ 2	☐ 2	☐ 2	☐ 2
Close to my child's school	☐ 3	☐ 3	☐ 3	☐ 3	☐ 3
Close to my work	☐ 4	☐ 4	☐ 4	☐ 4	☐ 4
On my way to work	☐ 5	☐ 5	☐ 5	☐ 5	☐ 5
Inconvenient—not close to home, school, or my work	☐ 6	☐ 6	☐ 6	☐ 6	☐ 6
Other (please specify)					

4. How far away, in minutes, is your child-care facility? (Estimate number of minutes in spaces below.)

	18 Months or Less	1½ Years to 2½ Years	2½ Years to 5 Years	5–6 Years— Kinder- garten Age	6–12 Years
Minutes from your home (record zero *if at home*)	____	____	____	____	____
Minutes from your work	____	____	____	____	____

Child-Care Survey (*continued*)

5. Which *months* during [this year] did you use child-care arrangements?

Months	18 Months or Less	1½ Years to 2½ Years	2½ Years to 5 Years	5–6 Years— Kinder- garten Age	6–12 Years
January	☐ 1	☐ 1	☐ 1	☐ 1	☐ 1
February	☐ 2	☐ 2	☐ 2	☐ 2	☐ 2
March	☐ 3	☐ 3	☐ 3	☐ 3	☐ 3
April	☐ 4	☐ 4	☐ 4	☐ 4	☐ 4
May	☐ 5	☐ 5	☐ 5	☐ 5	☐ 5
June	☐ 6	☐ 6	☐ 6	☐ 6	☐ 6
July	☐ 7	☐ 7	☐ 7	☐ 7	☐ 7
August	☐ 8	☐ 8	☐ 8	☐ 8	☐ 8
September	☐ 9	☐ 9	☐ 9	☐ 9	☐ 9
October	☐ 0	☐ 0	☐ 0	☐ 0	☐ 0
November	☐ X	☐ X	☐ X	☐ X	☐ X
December	☐ R	☐ R	☐ R	☐ R	☐ R

6. Which days of the week do you now use child-care arrangements on a regular basis?

Days of Week	18 Months or Less	1½ Years to 2½ Years	2½ Years to 5 Years	5–6 Years— Kinder- garten Age	6–12 Years
Monday	☐ 1	☐ 1	☐ 1	☐ 1	☐ 1
Tuesday	☐ 2	☐ 2	☐ 2	☐ 2	☐ 2
Wednesday	☐ 3	☐ 3	☐ 3	☐ 3	☐ 3

Child-Care Survey (*continued*)

Days of Week	18 Months or Less	1½ Years to 2½ Years	2½ Years to 5 Years	5–6 Years— Kinder- garten Age	6–12 Years
Thursday	☐ 4	☐ 4	☐ 4	☐ 4	☐ 4
Friday	☐ 5	☐ 5	☐ 5	☐ 5	☐ 5
Saturday/Sunday	☐ 6	☐ 6	☐ 6	☐ 6	☐ 6

7a. On an average day, at about what time do you *start* using your child-care arrangements? (Record in spaces below.)

7b. On an average day, at about what time do you *stop* using your child-care arrangements? (Record in spaces below.)

Question 7a Time Start Using	18 Months or Less	1½ Years to 2½ Years	2½ Years to 5 Years	5–6 Years— Kinder- garten Age	6–12 Years
Before 6 A.M.	☐ 1	☐ 1	☐ 1	☐ 1	☐ 1
6 A.M.–6:59 A.M.	☐ 2	☐ 2	☐ 2	☐ 2	☐ 2
7 A.M.–7:59 A.M.	☐ 3	☐ 3	☐ 3	☐ 3	☐ 3
8 A.M.–8:59 A.M.	☐ 4	☐ 4	☐ 4	☐ 4	☐ 4
9 A.M.–9:59 A.M.	☐ 5	☐ 5	☐ 5	☐ 5	☐ 5
After 10 A.M. (please specify time)	_____	_____	_____	_____	_____

Child-Care Survey (*continued*)

Question 7b
Time Stop Using

Before 3 P.M. (please specify time					
3 P.M.–3:59 P.M.	☐ 1	☐ 1	☐ 1	☐ 1	☐ 1
4 P.M.–4:59 P.M.	☐ 2	☐ 2	☐ 2	☐ 2	☐ 2
5 P.M.–5:59 P.M.	☐ 3	☐ 3	☐ 3	☐ 3	☐ 3
6 P.M.–6:59 P.M.	☐ 4	☐ 4	☐ 4	☐ 4	☐ 4
7 P.M.–7:59 P.M.	☐ 5	☐ 5	☐ 5	☐ 5	☐ 5
After 8 P.M.	☐ 6	☐ 6	☐ 6	☐ 6	☐ 6

---

8. How much per week do you currently pay for child-care arrangements for each child?

Amount per Week	18 Months or Less	1½ Years to 2½ Years	2½ Years to 5 Years	5–6 Years— Kinder-garten Age	6–12 Years
Nothing	☐ 1	☐ 1	☐ 1	☐ 1	☐ 1
$25 or less	☐ 2	☐ 2	☐ 2	☐ 2	☐ 2
$26–$35	☐ 3	☐ 3	☐ 3	☐ 3	☐ 3
$36–$45	☐ 4	☐ 4	☐ 4	☐ 4	☐ 4
$46–$55	☐ 5	☐ 5	☐ 5	☐ 5	☐ 5
$56–$65	☐ 6	☐ 6	☐ 6	☐ 6	☐ 6
$66–75	☐ 7	☐ 7	☐ 7	☐ 7	☐ 7
$75 or over	☐ 8	☐ 8	☐ 8	☐ 8	☐ 8

9a. Overall, how satisfied are you with your current child-care arrangements?

Child-Care Survey (*continued*)

	18 Months or Less	1½ Years to 2½ Years	2½ Years to 5 Years	5–6 Years— Kinder- garten Age	6–12 Years
Very satisfied	☐ 4	☐ 4	☐ 4	☐ 4	☐ 4
Somewhat satisfied	☐ 3	☐ 3	☐ 3	☐ 3	☐ 3
Not very satisfied	☐ 2	☐ 2	☐ 2	☐ 2	☐ 2
Not at all satisfied	☐ 1	☐ 1	☐ 1	☐ 1	☐ 1

9b. What is there about your current child-care arrangements that made you give them the rating in Question 9a above? (Please answer as completely as possible.)

_____

_____

_____

_____

_____

_____

Section 2: Opinions about Child-Care Arrangements (to be answered by all persons with children 12 years of age or younger)

10. Now, we would like to obtain your opinions about the importance or lack of importance of specific elements or features of child-care arrangements that might be available.

Listed below are a series of statements about child-care arrangements. For each of them, please check the rating phrase that best describes how important or necessary you feel that item is for your child or children 12 or younger. (Check only *one* box for *each* statement.)

Child-Care Survey (*continued*)

Statements	Absolutely Necessary	Very Desirable	Nice but Not Necessary	Not Needed
Available for child care before school opens	☐ 4	☐ 3	☐ 2	☐ 1
Available for child care after school closes	☐ 4	☐ 3	☐ 2	☐ 1
Provides sick care	☐ 4	☐ 3	☐ 2	☐ 1
Similar cost to current care method	☐ 4	☐ 3	☐ 2	☐ 1
Lower cost than current care method	☐ 4	☐ 3	☐ 2	☐ 1
A cheerful environment	☐ 4	☐ 3	☐ 2	☐ 1
Available only to Johnson Wax employees	☐ 4	☐ 3	☐ 2	☐ 1
Individual attention	☐ 4	☐ 3	☐ 2	☐ 1
A learning environment	☐ 4	☐ 3	☐ 2	☐ 1
Special outings/field trips	☐ 4	☐ 3	☐ 2	☐ 1
Written disciplinary policy	☐ 4	☐ 3	☐ 2	☐ 1
Staff has more training than minimum licensing	☐ 4	☐ 3	☐ 2	☐ 1
A warm social environment	☐ 4	☐ 3	☐ 2	☐ 1
Available to non-Johnson employees	☐ 4	☐ 3	☐ 2	☐ 1

Child-Care Survey (*continued*)

11. If Johnson Wax were to offer some type of child-care assistance program(s), which of the types of programs listed below would you be most interested in? (Check as many as apply.)

Types of Programs

Booklets/pamphlets on child care	☐ 1
Information and referral service on licensed care facilities	☐ 2
Sick-child care program	☐ 3
Local child-care service for overnight business trips	☐ 4
Newsletters	☐ 5
Parent seminars	☐ 6
Support groups	☐ 7
Summer camp	☐ 8
Child care for school holidays	☐ 9
Company-established center in the Racine community funded by users	☐ 0
Company-established center at Waxdale funded by users	☐ 1
Company-established center at Racine administrative complex funded by users	☐ 2
None	☐ 3

Other (specify) _____

_____

_____

_____

12. If Johnson Wax provided its employees with a child-care center at a cost similar to that of other centers in the area, how likely would you be to enroll one or more of your children in this center rather than in their current care facility?

Definitely would enroll one or more of my children	☐ 5
Probably would enroll one or more of my children	☐ 4
Might or might not enroll one or more of my children	☐ 3
Probably would not enroll one or more of my children	☐ 2
Definitely would not enroll one or more of my children	☐ 1

Child-Care Survey (*continued*)

13. What are the three most important things you would look for if you were considering enrolling one or more of your children in a child-care center provided by Johnson Wax for its employees? (Please answer as completely as possible.)

   1. _____

   _____

   2. _____

   _____

   3. _____

   _____

14. Why would you not be interested in enrolling one or more of your children in a child-care center provided by Johnson Wax? (Please answer as completely as possible.)

   _____

   _____

   _____

   _____

   _____

   _____

15. If Johnson Wax had provided its employees with a child-care center for the entire year of 1984, with a cost and services similar to those of other centers in the area, how many of your children do you think you would have enrolled? (Please specify number of children by each age group.) [Note: The 1984 date reflects the time frame initiated by Johnson Wax in developing their child care center.]

18 months or younger	_____
1½ years to 2½ years	_____
2½ years to 5 years	_____
5–6 years (kindergarten age)	_____
6–12 years	_____
Total	======
None—would not enroll any of my children	☐ 1

16. Listed below are a number of possible locations for a child-care center. For each location, please check the one phrase that best describes how

Child-Care Survey (*continued*)

desirable or convenient *each* location would be for you? (Record only one rating per location.)

Locations	Very Desirable	Desirable	Undesirable	Very Undesirable
On Waxdale premises	☐ 4	☐ 3	☐ 2	☐ 1
Within one-half mile of Waxdale premises	☐ 4	☐ 3	☐ 2	☐ 1
On Racine administrative premises	☐ 4	☐ 3	☐ 2	☐ 1
Within a few blocks of Racine administrative premises	☐ 4	☐ 3	☐ 2	☐ 1
Between Waxdale and Racine administrative premises	☐ 4	☐ 3	☐ 2	☐ 1
At Armstrong Park	☐ 4	☐ 3	☐ 2	☐ 1

17. How far away from your work location, in minutes, would you be willing to go to take advantage of a child-care center provided by Johnson Wax at a cost similar to that of other centers in the area?

Less than 5 minutes	☐ 1
5–10 minutes	☐ 2
11–15 minutes	☐ 3
16–20 minutes	☐ 4
21–25 minutes	☐ 5
26–30 minutes	☐ 6
31 minutes or more	☐ 7

Child-Care Survey (*continued*)

18. If Johnson Wax provided its employees with a child-care center, what is the *maximum* amount of money you would consider paying for the care of one child for five full days per week?

$25–29	☐ 1
$30–34	☐ 2
$35–39	☐ 3
$40–44	☐ 4
$45–49	☐ 5
$50–54	☐ 6
$55–59	☐ 7
$60–64	☐ 8
$65–69	☐ 9
$70–79	☐ 0
$80–89	☐ 1
$90–99	☐ 2
$100 or more	☐ 3

Section 3: Classification Data Section (to be answered by all persons with children 12 years of age or younger)

19. For each working adult living in your household, please check the one statement that best describes that person's work location.

	Self	Spouse	Other Adult	Other Adult
Waxdale	☐ 1	☐ 1	☐ 1	☐ 1
Main administrative complex in Racine	☐ 2	☐ 2	☐ 2	☐ 2
Other Johnson Wax location in community	☐ 3	☐ 3	☐ 3	☐ 3
Non–Johnson Wax location in community	☐ 4	☐ 4	☐ 4	☐ 4
Outside Racine area	☐ 5	☐ 5	☐ 5	☐ 5

20. Are you: Male   ☐ 1   Female   ☐ 2

Child-Care Survey (*continued*)

21. Which of the following statements best describes your household (parental status)? (Check one.)

One-parent family (single parent)   ☐ 1

Two-parent family   ☐ 2

Two parents sharing custody/care of children in separate
households   ☐ 3

Noncustodial parent (no custody of children)   ☐ 4

Other (specify) _____

Section 4: Comments Section (to be answered by all employees)

22. What advantages, if any, would there be for you if Johnson Wax provided a child-care center for employees that would be funded by its participants? What other advantages or benefits would there be? (Please answer as completely as possible.)

_____

_____

_____

_____

_____

_____

23. What concerns, if any, do you have about Johnson Wax providing a child-care center for its employees that would be funded by its participants at a cost similar to that of other centers in the area? What other concerns do you have? (Please answer as completely as possible.)

_____

_____

_____

_____

_____

_____

Child-Care Survey (*concluded*)

24. What other thoughts or comments would you like to share with us regarding the possibility of Johnson Wax offering *any* type of child-care assistance (i.e., referrals, supporting current programs, etc.)?

_____

_____

_____

_____

_____

_____

Thank you very much for your time and help! Please return this completed questionnaire *promptly* in the enclosed postage-paid envelope.

Source: Provided courtesy of S. C. Johnson & Son, Inc., Racine, Wisconsin.

Child-Care Survey

We would appreciate hearing from everyone, even if you do not have children or do not have a need for child care. The information you provide will be very helpful.

☐ If you *don't* have children under six years living with you, check this box; then answer questions 1–3, attach any comments, and return the survey to Human Resources.

☐ If you *do* have children under six living with you, check this box; then answer all of the questions below, attach any comments, and return the survey to Human Resources.

1. *a.* 1 ☐ Male   2 ☐ Female

   b. Age: 1 ☐ 25 or under   2 ☐ 26–30   3 ☐ 31–35

   　　　　　4 ☐ 36–40   　　　　5 ☐ 41 or older

   c. 1 ☐ Exempt   2 ☐ Nonexempt

   d. 1 ☐ Part-time   2 ☐ Full-time

   e. Regular work hours: _____

   f. Regular workdays: ☐ Monday–Friday   ☐ Other _____

   g. Location: 1 ☐ Operations Center   2 ☐ Downtown

   　　　　　　　3 ☐ Branch

   h. Length of service: 1 ☐ Less than 1 year   2 ☐ 1–5 years

   　　　　　　　　　　　3 ☐ 5–10 years   4 ☐ 10 or more years

Child-Care Survey (*continued*)

2. Do you plan to have children within the next five years?

   1 ☐ Yes   2 ☐ No   3 ☐ Have not decided

3. During the past 12 months, has your work been more difficult or inconvenient when other employees had child-care problems? For example, has your work been delayed when they had to stay home with their children? (Circle appropriate number.)

| | Minor | Moderate | Major |
No Effect	Difficulty	Difficulty	Difficulty
1	2	3	4

If you *don't have children under six,* stop here. Thank you for your help. Please feel free to add comments, and then return the survey. If you *do* have children five or under, please continue.

4. Please indicate the ages of your children under six living with you:

Child #1	Child #2	Child #3	Child #4
1 ☐ 0–6 mos.	1 ☐ 0–6 mos.	1 ☐ 0–6 mos.	1 ☐ 0–6 mos.
2 ☐ 6–12 mos.	2 ☐ 6–12 mos.	2 ☐ 6–12 mos.	2 ☐ 6–12 mos.
3 ☐ 1–1½ yrs.	3 ☐ 1–1½ yrs.	3 ☐ 1–1½ yrs.	3 ☐ 1–1½ yrs.
4 ☐ 1½–2 yrs.	4 ☐ 1½–2 yrs.	4 ☐ 1½–2 yrs.	4 ☐ 1½–2 yrs.
5 ☐ 2–2½ yrs.	5 ☐ 2–2½ yrs.	5 ☐ 2–2½ yrs.	5 ☐ 2–2½ yrs.
6 ☐ 2½–3 yrs.	6 ☐ 2½–3 yrs.	6 ☐ 2½–3 yrs.	6 ☐ 2½–3 yrs.
7 ☐ 3–3½ yrs.	7 ☐ 3–3½ yrs.	7 ☐ 3–3½ yrs.	7 ☐ 3–3½ yrs.
8 ☐ 3½–4 yrs.	8 ☐ 3½–4 yrs.	8 ☐ 3½–4 yrs.	8 ☐ 3½–4 yrs.
9 ☐ 4–4½ yrs.	9 ☐ 4–4½ yrs.	9 ☐ 4–4½ yrs.	9 ☐ 4–4½ yrs.
0 ☐ 4½–5 yrs.	0 ☐ 4½–5 yrs.	0 ☐ 4½–5 yrs.	0 ☐ 4½–5 yrs.

5. Sometimes child-care arrangements affect parents at work. During the past 12 months, have you had difficulties related to child care in any of these areas? (Circle the number.)

Child-Care Survey (*continued*)

	No Problem	Minor Problem	Moderate Problem	Major Problem
Traveling on the job	1	2	3	4
Attending training for job	1	2	3	4
Scheduling vacation time	1	2	3	4
Working desired schedule or overtime	1	2	3	4
Returning to work after birth of child	1	2	3	4
Ability to do job well; concentration	1	2	3	4
Level of stress	1	2	3	4
Other (describe)_____	1	2	3	4

6. Approximately how many days have you been absent in the past 12 months because of child-care difficulties? _____

7. Approximately how many days have you been absent in the past 12 months because your child was ill? _____

8. Approximately how many days in the past 12 months have you missed part of a day (e.g., arrived late, left early, had significant interruption) due to child-care difficulties? _____

9. Have you ever considered quitting your job at this company because of child-care difficulties? 1 ☐ Yes   2 ☐ No

10. How many times have you had to change your child-care arrangements over the past two years?

    1 ☐ None   2 ☐ Once   3 ☐ Twice   4 ☐ Three times

    5 ☐ More than three times

11. Here are some common problem areas for working parents who need or use child care. Have you had problems in any of these areas in the past 12 months? (Circle the number.)

Child-Care Survey (*continued*)

	No Problem	Minor Problem	Moderate Problem	Major Problem
Cost of care	1	2	3	4
Convenience of location	1	2	3	4
Transportation	1	2	3	4
Schedule to match work and child care	1	2	3	4
Quality of care	1	2	3	4
Dependability of care	1	2	3	4
Finding care for sick child	1	2	3	4
Finding temporary/ emergency care	1	2	3	4
Finding care for child under two	1	2	3	4
Finding care for child two– five years old	1	2	3	4
Other (describe) _____	1	2	3	4

For Questions 12–15, your answers for Child #1 should refer to the same child whose age you gave for Child #1 in Question 4. Follow the same procedure for Child #2, and so forth.

12. What is the average amount you pay per week for child care for each child while you work? (Include care during school vacations and summer, overtime, emergencies, etc.)

Child #1	Child #2	Child #3	Child #4	
1 ☐	1 ☐	1 ☐	1 ☐	Under $20
2 ☐	2 ☐	2 ☐	2 ☐	$20–24
3 ☐	3 ☐	3 ☐	3 ☐	$25–29
4 ☐	4 ☐	4 ☐	4 ☐	$30–34
5 ☐	5 ☐	5 ☐	5 ☐	$35–39
6 ☐	6 ☐	6 ☐	6 ☐	$40–44

Child-Care Survey (*continued*)

Child #1	Child #2	Child #3	Child #4	
7 ☐	7 ☐	7 ☐	7 ☐	$45–49
8 ☐	8 ☐	8 ☐	8 ☐	$50–54
9 ☐	9 ☐	9 ☐	9 ☐	$55 or more

13. What type of care do you currently use for your children? If any child is cared for in more than one arrangement, mark the one used for the most hours.

Child #1	Child #2	Child #3	Child #4	
1 ☐	1 ☐	1 ☐	1 ☐	Relative in your home or the relative's home
2 ☐	2 ☐	2 ☐	2 ☐	Unrelated person in your home
3 ☐	3 ☐	3 ☐	3 ☐	Unrelated person in his or her home
4 ☐	4 ☐	4 ☐	4 ☐	Day-care center
5 ☐	5 ☐	5 ☐	5 ☐	Other (describe) _____

14. If Dominion were to establish a child-care center at the Operations Center on Plantation Road, indicate for each of your children the likelihood that you would utilize the facility for that child.

Child #1	Child #2	Child #3	Child #4
1 ☐ Definitely	1 ☐ Definitely	1 ☐ Definitely	1 ☐ Definitely
2 ☐ Probably	2 ☐ Probably	2 ☐ Probably	2 ☐ Probably
3 ☐ Probably not	3 ☐ Probably not	3 ☐ Probably not	3 ☐ Probably not
4 ☐ Definitely not	4 ☐ Definitely not	4 ☐ Definitely not	4 ☐ Definitely not

Child-Care Survey (*concluded*)

15. When do you usually need child care? (Check all that apply.)

Child #1	Child #2	Child #3	Child #4	WEEKDAYS:
1 ☐	1 ☐	1 ☐	1 ☐	Before 7 A.M.
2 ☐	2 ☐	2 ☐	2 ☐	All or part of 7 A.M.–6 P.M.
3 ☐	3 ☐	3 ☐	3 ☐	All or part of 6 P.M.–11 P.M.
4 ☐	4 ☐	4 ☐	4 ☐	Other (describe) _____

16. Would you use an in-house child-care referral service to help you find the care you want?

1 ☐ Very likely

2 ☐ Somewhat likely

3 ☐ Somewhat unlikely

4 ☐ Very unlikely

Thank you very much for taking the time to answer these questions. Please feel free to add comments. Then return your survey to human resources.

Source: Provided courtesy of Dominion Bankshares Corporation.

Involving a Consultant.   At the stage of needs assessment, you may already choose to involve one of the many consulting firms that provide kin care advice and services. "All it takes is a phone call," says a spokesperson for one such firm, The Partnership Group, Inc. (TPG).[5]

TPG provides resource and referral (R & R) services to over 92 corporate clients nationwide under its *ChildCare Solution* and *ElderCare Connection* trademarks. It subcontracts to community-based, nonprofit agencies that can help employees find quality care for their dependents.

If you hire TPG to conduct your needs assessment, a representative from the firm might begin by asking such questions as these: How many employees do you have? Where are they located? What dependent care benefits do you offer? What is the demographic mix at the company? How many of your employees have taken maternity leave?

Once the needs assessment has led to the development of a suitable program for your company, a project manager from TPG works closely with your company to design a communications program for employees at all levels. The goal is to "get the word out" on kin care developments through brochures, paycheck inserts, posters, displays, and other communication channels. On-site workshops and seminars are also available.

To provide employer-sponsored child care for clients, Marriott Corporation works in partnership with a specialist in the field: Corporate Child Care, Inc. in Nashville, Tennessee. Marriott benefits from working with a team that has extensive experience in professional, worksite child care. In fact, Marriott has recently gone into the business of setting up child-care centers for its corporate clients. Working with Corporate Child Care, Inc., it offers these clients employer-sponsored child care as a service additional to hospitality and contract service.

Dave Gleason, executive vice president and chief operating officer of Corporate Child Care, Inc., and Diane Huggins, director of corporate communications, both indicate that a partnership of the kind CCC has with Marriott offers distinct advantages. "We give great attention to recruiting, screening, hiring, and training staff; tailoring the curriculum we offer; and designing a safe, sound facility and playground. We place a significant emphasis on risk management and ongoing quality assurance. . . . Programs are tailored for the clients and their employees."[6]

The costs for such consultant services vary; they are based on an in-depth analysis of the company and its needs. TPG notes that consultant services regarding Dependent Care Assistance Plans (DCAPs) are the least expensive, while consultant services regarding on-site care centers are the most expensive. The costs of consultant services regarding R & Rs falls somewhere in between.

The National Association for Child Care Resource and Referral Agencies, located in Rochester, Minnesota, lists among its members many reputable consulting firms that help employers set up kin care benefits.

The Consultant's Role. Margery Sher, a principal in Fried & Sher, Inc., describes the role of the consultant for firms starting up kin care programs:

> The consultant must first discover how the client perceives his problem—where is the client coming from? Each corporation or government agency has its own culture and its own goals. The consultant cannot assume that what is true for one employer is true for another—even employers in the same field. No two hospitals are exactly alike, and no two government agencies are the same. The consultant must not try to force the ugly stepsister's foot into Cinderella's shoe.
>
> Sometimes the client may come to the consultant with a preconceived idea of what is needed. In that case, the consultant must verify that the suggested solution is indeed a good one. A child-care benefit should solve a problem—either existing or foreseen—and the price of the care should not be greater than the price of the illness.
>
> Sometimes the client has only a global understanding of solutions. When a client asks, "Should we consider child care?" the consultant must help the client restate the question to, "Should we consider a child-care benefit (or work-family benefit), and if so, which one will work best for us?"
>
> From an employee's point of view, problems can be categorized into problems of availability, affordability, accessibility, and quality. From the employer's point of view, the problems may appear as absenteeism, tardiness, turnover, low morale, and decreased productivity. A solution must:
>
> - Eliminate the most glaring child-care problems of the employees.
> - Reduce the specific problems of the company.
>
> A careful study must be performed by the consultant in order to determine correctly the problem and the appropriate solution. First, a corporate needs assessment must be undertaken. What are the corporate problems? Are they tardiness or absenteeism? Are children at work on school holidays or snow days? Are problems company-wide, or do they appear only in certain departments or on certain shifts? What are competitors doing? What do demographic projections show relevant to future employee recruitment? What are the attitudes of managers toward child-care issues?

Next, the consultant must conduct an employee needs assessment. Two types of information should be gathered: qualitative and quantitative. Qualitative information can be gathered by leading focus groups. Focus groups are a vehicle for illustrating problems on a human level, and for understanding how personal problems become translated into corporate problems. Quantitative information is gathered through the use of a written survey instrument.

Third, the consultant must assess the child-care marketplace. What is happening in the geographic area? What problems are there with existing services? Can the company work with an existing provider to improve quality, expand services, or extend hours?

When all of this information has been gathered, the consultant must summarize the need and evaluate the numerous child-care benefits possible in order to recommend the best match for the client. Child-care benefit options are numerous, and a creative consultant can suggest new ones which might work perfectly in a particular situation. The basic options are: on-site or near-site child-care centers, child-care centers sponsored by a consortium of companies, school-age child-care programs, emergency child-care programs, sick-child care programs, resource and referral programs, voucher programs, vendor programs, Dependent Care Assistance Plans, provision of capital for expansion of existing programs, and parenting seminars.

This lengthy process of assessment is essential to avoid a corporate cure more costly in human and financial terms than the illness. Consultants must also abide by the Hippocratic oath!

Once the consultant and the client agree on the proper child-care program to implement, if any, the consultant begins the next phase: program development and implementation. This phase must also be customized for the client. Even if the option selected is a child-care center, and the consultant has developed many child-care centers, the process must begin at the first step with the client having input into every design and operating decision in order to be certain that the end product will meet the unique needs of that specific client.

In every circumstance, the consultant must customize solutions so that they reflect the culture and goals of the client. The path to a finished product is slow and winding, but if the consultant pushes through a straight and quick path to a child-care benefit, most likely the result will not meet the client's needs. The consultant is not a salesman pushing a product; the consultant is a diagnostician and creator of customized solutions. The resultant shoe must fit the client's foot exactly.[7]

Step 2: Consider All Your Options

Once you hold before you a clear picture of your company's needs, it's time to ponder the pros and cons of *many* kin care systems before choosing your company's cup of tea. In Chapter 6, you will find a dozen tried-and-true approaches to kin care spelled out, with accompanying corporate examples as well as suggested advantages and disadvantages.

Let's say, for example, that your survey data show a strong disposition on the part of your employees to choose their own child care, in their own neighborhoods. Obviously, an on-site center isn't a prudent choice. In that case, you will probably investigate vouchers or Flexible Spending Account plans for your people. Or your survey data may reveal a hidden problem with elder care. Perhaps many of your senior managers are trying to give their all to the company while caring many hours per week for elderly parents. In that case, you may opt to reserve spaces for these dependents in a daytime drop-in center for elders.

The key is to let your kin care design be driven by documented company needs, not by fads or hearsay.

Step 3: Match Your Tentative Program with Available Resources

Some companies may question the desirability of developing a tentative plan *before* seeking resources to fund it. "Don't you have to know your budget before shopping for kin care programs?" a human resources director asked me. Yes and no. Yes, you have to be generally aware of the company's financial capabilities and level of commitment. But no, the choice of a kin care option should not be based entirely on prior assumptions about the size of the budget. Many companies have discovered that really good ideas have a way of earning their budgets as they develop. If a kin care plan can be devised that saves money in the form of reduced recruitment, training, and turnover costs; the powers that be in the company may be disposed to fund it beyond anyone's initial dreams (as happened in the ABIG case discussed later in this chapter).

What does kin care cost? That depends, of course, on the programs selected. Resource and referral programs often cost no more than a secretary's salary, and sometimes far less. Integrated Genetics pays $3,500 a year for access to 1,300 care providers in their area and four on-site seminars for employees. More typical costs for the resource and referral programs of midsize companies are $1 per month per employee, assuming heavy use of 6–8 percent. Programs involving other flexible benefits (flextime, job sharing, Flexible Spending Accounts, and so forth) require some initial expense for changing accounting and management procedures and for continuing administrative expenses.

The high-cost spread, of course, is the on-site care center. Companies usually forge partnerships of sorts with their employees to fund such centers. A 50–50 split is not uncommon. Taylor Corporation, for example, puts up $1,000 a year per child, thus funding about 40 percent of the required operating costs of its on-site center. Employees pay the balance through tuition. The on-site centers of larger companies typically have operating budgets in the $100,000–500,000 range. To minimize past-due accounts, employee co-payments are usually handled by payroll deduction.

It is possible, of course, for a company to pass along virtually all the operating expenses of the care center to the employees using it. But the economics of child and elder care are harsh. For a caregiver to earn $8 an hour (only $320 per week) caring for four infants, each set of parents would have to pay about $4 an hour to the care center to cover the caregiver's salary plus benefits and the company's administrative costs. If an infant is in care for 40 hours a week, that's a payment of $160 per week, or $640 per month, for care!

Another alternative, taken much too often, is to pay the caregiver too little, which leads to undesirable turnover, which leads in turn to a poor care experience for children, which leads to the gradual death of the care center. Or a company may be fortunate enough to obtain a steady supply of capable volunteers to assist the regular care staff.

Most forward-thinking companies often bite the bullet of expense as a necessary investment in their employees. Group 243 Incorporated, an Ann Arbor, Michigan, advertising company, runs a highly successful on-site center. "I think I could run ours at break-even," says Carey Ferchland, senior vice president of corporate administration, "but it would mean lower salaries, greater staff turnover, worse staff-child ratios, and, in general, a lower-quality program. And that's not what we want."[8]

Step 4: Sell the Program Internally and Externally

This is a delicate stage for the growing project. You have a tentative plan and a budget line for development. But in a few weeks your program will begin to step on some company toes. Perhaps you'll be taking away some cherished office space, moving some walls, rearranging accounting ledgers, and even walking some children and elders through company halls. At this point, the project will need support from top to bottom in the company.

The goal in Step 4, then, is to *communicate* your plans, hopes, and dreams to all the stakeholders, from top brass to maintenance staff. Sell the merits of the coming program to potential users of the facility or service as well; studies show that as few as 15–20 percent of the parents who indicated *interest* in the care center actually use it in its first year.

The message you communicate will probably have these basic components:

- Here's what we're going to be doing in the next few months (or weeks). Specify where, when, and how.
- Here's why (the benefits of the program for the company and its employees).
- Here's how it will affect you.
- Here's what to do or whom to contact if you have questions or concerns.

Organizations of all types resist change, especially when that change seems to benefit only a select few in the organization. It's not uncommon for a company with 1,000 employees to have only 25 children in its on-site center. The many must understand that their interests are being served by this benefit to the few.

This is also the time to make sure you've successfully "sold" the program to external regulators and community organizations. In setting up its on-site child-care center, Official Airline Guides, Inc. (OAG) kept close contact with the Oak Brook, Illinois, Zoning, Health, and Fire departments and with the Illinois Department of Child and Family Services. Any one of those agencies, given cause, could have delayed the scheduled opening of the OAG center. Liability insurance was easily arranged through an outside carrier.

Step 5: Actualize the Kin Care Program

This is the day of the grand opening. Whether cutting the tape to a new on-site center or simply sending out the first of the company's child-care vouchers, publicize the moment as widely as possible to enhance the company's image and to encourage participation by employees. Figure 7–1 is a sampler of the press coverage garnered by firms providing outstanding kin care benefits.

Step 6: Monitor and Improve the Program

In a sense, this step brings us back full circle to a needs assessment. But now we're interested in monitoring the needs of the fledgling program. You'll no doubt want to monitor the program's vital signs (probably with the aid of a computer spreadsheet): daily numbers of children or elders served, staff time, operating costs, utilities, and so forth. But just as important are the qualitative measures of the program's success. These can be based on interviews or questionnaires directed toward parents, staff, children, elders, employees not using the care center, senior management, community members who have heard of the care center, and other sources.

One company used the following questionnaire to gather after-opening information from parents about a near-site child-care center:

FIGURE 7–1

2 Part IV / Wednesday, September 20, 1989 ★   **Los Angeles Times**   The Wall Street Journal Wednesday, September 20, 1989

Survey Rates Apple No. 1 in Perks for Mothers

Firm Cited for Superior Pay, Benefits Package and On-Site Child-Care Center

By NANCY RIVERA BROOKS,
Times Staff Writer

IBM grants new mothers leaves of up to three years with benefits. Media giant Gannett offers $2,500 in adoption aid. SAS Institute, a computer software developer in Cary, N.C., runs a free on-site child-care center, according to a survey of the best companies for working mothers released Tuesday.

But the clean diaper award—if there were such a thing—would go to Apple Computer, the Cupertino-based computer manufacturer. The fourth annual survey by Working Mother magazine put Apple Computer at the top of a list of 60 pace-setting companies based on pay, advancement opportunity, benefits and child-care support.

Although the roster includes some extraordinary policies, mom-my-friendly companies are still unusual in the American workplace, the magazine's editor said.

"We see these 80 companies as role models," said Judsen Culbreth, editor of Working Mother, a New York-based publication with a circulation of 460,000. "They have caught on to the idea that to be good to working parents is to be competitive edge."

THE BEST COMPANIES FOR WORKING MOTHERS

Company rankings are based on the following criteria: pay scales (compared to the competition); opportunities for advancement; support for child care; financial, referrals and/or actual care) and benefits (maternity leave, parental leave, adoption aid, flextime, part time work, job sharing and support for care of the elderly)

The National Top 10

Company	City	Business
Apple Computer	Cupertino	A leading maker of personal computers
Beth Israel Hospital	Boston	Teaching hospital of Harvard Medical School
Du Pont	Wilmington, Del.	Largest U.S. chemical company
Fel Pro	Skokie, Ill.	Makes gaskets, sealing products and specialized lubricants
Hoffmann-La Roche	Nutley, N.J.	Maker of prescription drugs, vitamins and diagnostic products
IBM	Armonk, N.Y.	World's largest computer manufacturer
Merck	Rahway, N.J.	Largest U.S. maker of prescription drugs
Morrison & Foerster	San Francisco	Nation's 12th largest law firm
SAS Institute	Cary, N.C.	Produces computer software products
Syntex	Palo Alto	Makes prescription drugs, diagnostic systems and veterinary products

California companies that made the list

Company	City	Business
Apple	Cupertino	

REST OF THE BEST

Here are the rest of the 1989 roster of the 60 best companies for working mothers published in the October issue of Working Mother magazine. The companies are listed alphabetically.

Aetna Life & Casualty, Hartford, Conn.
America West Airlines, Phoenix
Amer. Bankers Ins. Grp., Miami
American Express, New York
AT&T, New York
Arthur Andersen, Chicago
Baptist Hospital, Miami
Barrios Technology, Houston
Campbell Soup, Camden, N.J.
Champion Intl., Stamford, Conn.
Corning, Corning N.Y.
Digital Equipment, Maynard, Mass.
Dominion Bankshares, Roanoke, Va.
Dow Chemical, Midland, Mich.
Eastman Kodak, Rochester, N.Y.
First Atlanta, Atlanta
Gannett, Washington
General Mills, Minneapolis
Grieco Bros., Lawrence, Mass.
Group 243, Ann Arbor, Mich.
Hallmark Cards, Kansas City, Mo.
Hechinger, Landover, Md.
Herman Miller, Zeeland, Mich.
Hewitt Associates, Lincolnshire, Ill.
Hill, Holliday, Connors, Cosmopulos, Boston
Johnson & Johnson, New Brunswick, N.J.
S.C. Johnson & Son, Racine, Wis.
Leo Burnett, Chicago
Levi Strauss, San Francisco
Los Boot, Chicago
Lincoln National, Ft. Wayne, Ind.
3M, St. Paul, Minn.
McDonald's, Oak Brook, Ill.

Magazine Names 10 Firms Best for Working Mothers

NEW YORK (AP)—Apple Computer Inc. runs an in-house child-care center and gives $500 to each employee's new baby. International Business Machines Corp. grants new mothers leaves of as much as three years with benefits and guarantees their jobs. Merck & Co. has donated land and money for a child care facility and allows mothers to work at home.

They're among the top 10 of the 60 U.S. companies considered best for working mothers by Working Mother magazine in its October issue.

The magazine said companies were chosen based on salary, advancement opportunity, support for child care, and a benefits package that included maternity leave, parental leave, adoption aid, flexible schedules, part-time work, job sharing and support for care of elderly dependents.

More than half of all women with children younger than six years old work outside the home, compared with 12% in 1950, according to Labor Department figures. By the year 2000, the Labor Department estimates, 84% of all women of childbearing age will be working.

Here are the 10 companies, listed alphabetically: Apple, based in Cupertino, Calif.; Beth Israel Hospital, Boston; DuPont Co., Wilmington, Del.; Fel-Pro Inc., Skokie, Ill.; Hoffmann-La Roche Inc., Nutley, N.J.; IBM, Armonk, N.Y.; Merck & Co., Rahway, N.J.; Morrison & Foerster, San Francisco; SAS Institute, Cary, N.C.; and Syntex Corp., Palo Alto, Calif.

Employment Relations Programs

At Hoffmann-La Roche, child-care facilities are a model of commitment to—and service for—employees' families.

REGION REPORT

Roche study grants to 3 teachers

NUTLEY — An Irvington High School teacher is one of three New Jersey instructors selected to participate in the 1987 Roche Biomedical Summer Grants Program at the Roche Institute of Molecular Biology, a branch of research at Hoffmann-LaRoche Inc.

...da Rosenblum was chosen to study with Roche scientists this ...

... from the state were David Strife, a resident of Cresskill, ...nafly High School, and Deborah Thorn Mango, an ...ny Park High School and a resident of Belleville.

Corporate Initiatives for a *Drug Free Workplace*

no way Out

Roche Joins Fight Against Teenage Suicide

Corporate Child Care:

PLAYPENS IN THE BOARDROOM OR PRODUCTIVITY INVESTMENT?

"Child care has become a necessity for men as well as women, white- and blue-collar workers alike, and both top-level manager and employees just entering the workforce."

By Leonard Silve...

...ding to child-care needs
...nother magazine

October 19...

La Roche's corporate child care is a blessing

By JUDY GIAMMETTINO
Associated Press Writer

Chicago Tribune Friday, September 22, 1989   Section 3

The choice of working moms

Family benefits plan makes Fel-Pro top 10 employer

By Carol Kleiman

Providing child care benefits, flexible hours, job sharing and other family benefits for working mothers means less turnover, reduced absenteeism, higher productivity and employee loyalty, according to Kenneth Lehman, president of Fel-Pro Inc., a gaskets manufacturer in Skokie.

It's just in recent years that these programs have become fashionable, but in our view, they've always been good business," said Lehman, whose company also makes sealing products and specialized lubricants. "Business can always do more. I see it happening."

Fel-Pro has a subsidized on-site day-care center considered a model for quality child care. It has a summer day camp, job-protected maternity leave, emergency home care, in-home tutoring for children, tuition and adoption aid, scholarships for employee's children, gifts for newlyweds and new babies and a referral service for child and elder care.

Not surprisingly, Fel-Pro was among the top 10 of the 60 U.S. companies judged best for working

mothers by Working Mother magazine in its October issue. Of Fel-Pro's 1,796 employees, 689 are female.

Family benefits have become increasingly important to businesses because more than half of U.S. women with children younger than 6 work outside the home. Employer response to this is the basis of the magazine's annual selections.

Among the local companies also credited with good programs, but not named in the top 10, were Arthur Andersen & Co., a Chicago-based professional business services firm; Hewitt & Associates, a benefits consulting firm based in Lincolnshire; Leo Burnett Co., a Chicago advertising agency; and Official Airline Guides of Oak Brook, a publishing firm owned by Maxwell Communications Corp.

The companies do well by doing good. "Cost benefit analyses are hard to come by, but you know there's a benefit involved in flexible policies, which cost little, and an on-site child care, the most expensive," said David J. Wille, Hewitt's director of human resources.

Arthur Andersen's policies "help

us in recruiting," said Peter Pesce, director of human resources. At Official Airline Guides, whose work force is 72 percent female, its on-site day-care center is credited with retaining working mothers and the company's investment in their training.

"In 1981, when we opened the center, we had a high turnover of women with children," said Susan Doctors, general manager of human resources. "Now our turnover is low."

Assisting working mothers also helps the company's image. "We're particularly pleased that some very aggressive benefit plans have enhanced the quality of life for our working mothers," said John C. Kraft, Leo Burnett's vice chairman of administration and finance.

Besides Fel-Pro, the top 10 includes Apple Computer Inc., Cupertino, Calif.; Beth Israel Hospital, Boston; E.I. du Pont de Nemours & Co., Wilmington, Del.; Hoffmann-La Roche Inc., Nutley, N.J.; Morrison & Foerster, San Francisco; SAS Institute, Cary, N.C.; and Syntex Corp., Palo Alto, Calif.

Employee Assistance Programs:

Roche Receives NJSNA President's Award

Roche President and Chief Executive Of... Irwin Lerner was recently presented ...th the New Jersey State Nurses Asso...on's (NJSNA) President's Aw... ...anding contributions to ...fessional educati... ...New Jersey...

The National Report on WORK & FAMILY

...through its employee assistance program, Hoffmann-LaRoche has devoted considerable resources to educating employees about—dealing with—ent substance abuse.

Parent Questionnaire

Thank you for your help in making the care center the best it can be. The
  information you provide here will be held in strict confidence.

Name (optional):

Number of children in the center:

Number of children under six years old not using the center:

Overall, how do you rate your child's experience at the care center?

What do you like most about the center? (Feel free to specify more than one
  thing.)

What do you like least about the center? (Feel free to specify more than one
  thing.)

What could we do to make the center better for your child?

What could we do to make the center more convenient or useful to you?

Comments:

If your child-care center wants to be accredited by an organization such as the National Academy of Early Childhood Programs,
parents using the center will be asked to fill out the kind of
questionnaire shown in Table 7–1.

TABLE 7–1
**Parent Questionnaire: Prepared by the National Academy of
Early Childhood Programs**

Dear Parents:

_____ is working
                          (Name of program)
toward being accredited by the National Academy of Early Childhood
Programs. The accreditation system identifies high-quality child-care centers
and preschool programs.

TABLE 7–1 (*continued*)

The academy feels that parents can provide valuable information about the quality of their children's center. As part of the accreditation process, all parents are being asked to fill out the questionnaire that is attached to this letter. The questions on it are related to the standards for accreditation.

You may want to say more about the program, so feel free to write any comments on the form. You do not need to sign your name. We would be grateful if you would return the completed questionnaire to the center by

_____ .

(Date)
Thank you very much for your help.

Sincerely yours,

Program Director

How long has your child (or children) been enrolled in this program? Check one.

☐ Less than six months   ☐ One to two years

☐ Six months to one year   ☐ More than two years

How old is your child (or children) who is enrolled in this program?

For each statement, circle "Yes" or "No" or "DK" for "don't know." If the statement does not apply to your child's program, write in "NA" for "not applicable."

			1. The center gives information to parents about
DK	No	Yes	a. The program's philosophy and goals for children.
DK	No	Yes	b. Payments and refunds.
DK	No	Yes	c. Hours the program is open and holidays and closings.
DK	No	Yes	d. Rules about attendance of sick children.
DK	No	Yes	e. Menus of meals and snacks given to children; or in the case of infants, times when babies are fed and what they eat.
DK	No	Yes	2. The center has a plan for helping new children to feel comfortable by including a visit before enrolling, having a parent meeting, or gradually bringing in new children.
DK	No	Yes	3. Teachers and parents talk about how the family and center handle different aspects of child-rearing, such as discipline, feeding, and toileting, and other important issues.

TABLE 7–1 (*concluded*)

DK No Yes 4. Parents are welcome visitors in the center at all times.

DK No Yes 5. There are many ways for parents to take part in the program, such as visiting and helping in the classroom, taking field trips, joining in at parties, or sharing a meal/snack.

DK No Yes 6. The center has a way of informing parents about day-to-day happenings that affect children (by notes or by teachers talking with parents when children are taken to or picked up from the center).

DK No Yes 7. Parents are informed about injuries and any changes in children's health or eating habits that teachers notice.

DK No Yes 8. Parent-teacher conferences are held to discuss children's progress at least once a year (hold conferences more often if parents want them).

DK No Yes 9. Parents are informed about the program through newsletters, bulletin boards, frequent notes, meetings, telephone calls (when needed), or other ways.

DK No Yes 10. At least once a year, parents are asked to evaluate how well the program is meeting their child's needs.

DK No Yes 11. Personally, I feel that the teachers have a good attitude toward me and my child.

DK No Yes 12. Personally, I am satisfied with the care and education my child receives in this program.

Please feel free to write any comments on what you like about the program or what you would like to see changed.

To evaluate the effects of company elder-care programs on working adult children and on the elders themselves, consider the following questions. Frequent yes answers to these questions are sure signs of a thriving elder-care program.

1. *Productivity.* Does the elder-care program contribute to a more productive work force? Have absenteeism, work interruptions, and disruptive personal phone calls been reduced because of the program? Has morale improved?

2. *Quality of Life.* Are employees less stressed by the demands of caring for elders? Do elders receive quality care? Can employees plan for such care without risking financial ruin?

3. *Recruitment and Retention.* Are employees more likely to join the company and stay with it because of the elder-care program?

4. *Company Image.* Has the elder-care program received media attention and community support? Do customers know of the program? Does the program predispose them to favor the company's products or services?

Questionnaires of this sort cannot be too long or too detailed. Even the most interested parent may not have the time to write out extended answers. In designing the questionnaire, therefore, get right to your main areas of inquiry. Be careful not to prejudge a response by the way you ask the question (*not:* "How much trouble have you experienced with the staff?").

And questionnaires have to *matter.* It's a good idea to report back to those who took the time to respond. For example, you could send out a brief report on the results of the survey. Indicate which matters will be pursued immediately, and which later.

THREE EXAMPLES OF SUCCESSFUL START-UPS

Start-Up Story No. 1: ABIG Child's Place

American Bankers Insurance Group (ABIG) has long been known for innovations in insurance. It is now a recognized leader in corporate child care and early childhood education as well. Here is the evolution of its corporate child-care programs, as told by an ABIG spokesperson.

The First Step.   In November 1975, the minister of the First Presbyterian Church of Miami approached ABIG for financial assistance in forming a day-care operation. He felt that a child-care center would be beneficial to the church and to both the residences and businesses in the neighborhood. One of these businesses was ABIG, which was located directly across the street from the church, on Brickell Avenue.

ABIG contributed $5,000 that month for remodeling existing church classrooms and for fencing a playground. Two senior managers were appointed to work with the church's day-care center committee. During the planning stages in 1976, ABIG made additional donations totaling $17,000. The Brickell Christian School opened for business on January 31, 1977. Six of the approximately 30 enrollees were children of ABIG employees. The school's enrollment grew to more than 60 by 1979.

ABIG contributed an additional $7,000 during the school's first two years. It also provided hot lunches for the children at a cost of $0.30, as well as warming ovens to transport the lunches to the church.

An Abrupt Change of Course.   A new minister assumed the pastoral duties of the church in 1979. He felt that church-oriented changes were necessary for the day-care center. The changes made no provision for the staff or for most of the children who were enrolled.

ABIG was again called on to help—this time by a group consisting of displaced parents and staff members. It owned a small, underutilized motel on its 600 Brickell Avenue property, whose premises it offered at an annual rate of $7 per square foot, with the provision that the group would form a nonprofit corporation to operate the day-care center.

The director and the parents accepted the offer and worked together to renovate the motel.

Greater Miami Children's Centers Is Formed.   A nonprofit corporation, Greater Miami Children's Centers, Inc., was established. Under its direction, Brickell Children's Center was opened in the renovated motel in July 1979, with an enrollment of approximately 30 children. By that time, ABIG's operations had outgrown its Brickell Avenue office building and a number of ABIG employees had been relocated to Koger Industrial Park.

The first-year income from the center's small enrollment was insufficient to meet expenses. Parents conducted fund-raising activities, but the director and program director sometimes received IOUs in lieu of salary and ABIG accepted notes instead of rent.

A concerted campaign was launched to obtain support from additional directors. Several business leaders responded to the campaign.

A Needed Transfusion.   Thirteen new directors from the Brickell Avenue and downtown Miami business community were
elected in 1980. With new backing and leadership, and with the
help of new directors who were added from time to time, a capital
fund drive was initiated. ABIG agreed to match the highest cash
gift pledged—which was $1,000.

By mid-1981, the Brickell Children's Center was out of debt.
Advertising and pavement pounding had increased its enrollment to a more realistic 45 to 48 students. At that time, ABIG was
planning a new building that would consolidate its international
headquarters under one roof.

Preliminary Planning for ABIG Child's Place.   When ABIG purchased land in south Dade County for an office park and its new
international headquarters, it considered several options for a
child-care program:

(1) Providing space for a franchised child-care center at
    the location.

(2) Reimbursing employees' child-care expenses.

(3) Entering into a partnership with an existing center.

(4) Establishing a company-operated child-care center in
    the new headquarters building.

A survey showed that about 40 ABIG employees were interested in child care. After visiting many child-care facilities locally
and in other parts of the country, a company manager narrowed
the options to two: establishing a company-operated center or
joining forces with an existing center in Cutler Ridge. He eliminated the latter option, on the advice of a county inspector. Planning then began in earnest for ABIG Child's Place.

The Making of ABIG Child's Place.   A ground floor location
with a contiguous playground was designated in the building
plan. The space allocated would enable the center to obtain licensing for 75 children. Child Care Consultants was employed to
assist with the interior design and furnishings, and a landscape
architect designed a "tot lot" for the playground.

About six months before completing its new office building, ABIG recruited and interviewed applicants for the position of center director. Employing a highly qualified, competent, and loving person as the director of the child-care center was paramount in the planning process.

The first director's responsibilities were completing the fulfillment of the licensing requirements; placing orders for furnishings, toys, and educational and playground equipment; and hiring a staff that could be phased in as enrollment increased. She communicated information and met with interested employees— but many had a "wait and see" attitude.

ABIG budgeted $40,000 for interior furnishings and equipment and $40,000 for design construction and equipment in the tot lot. The cost of the 3,500 square feet allocated for the center was $270,000, and additional finishing items came to $80,000.

ABIG Child's Place Opens.   The new center opened with 13 children in 1984. A county commissioner gave the principal address, and all of the local television network affiliates reported on the event.

Enrollment, open to employees' childrens aged six weeks through five years, grew to 62 within the first six months. A previously requested change in licensing to allow enrollment of children from outside the company was approved in January 1985. The change proved to be unnecessary, however, as by year-end enrollment stood at 68 and there was already a reservations list for infants.

Any remaining hesitation on the part of employee/parents was quickly dispelled as the caring attention and training the children received became apparent. The child-care center was already an important part of the new workplace and a valuable service to participating employees.

The First Two Years.   By 1986, expansion had become necessary. It was accomplished by converting an office to classroom space. Even so, with enrollment at 90, there was a waiting list. Philip J. Sharkey, senior vice president of human resources, attributes the center's overwhelming success and excellent reputation to senior management's commitment and to a highly qualified and caring staff of teachers and aides, including student volunteers from a local high school.

La Petite Academy Comes to American Bankers.   It became obvious within the first two years that demand would continue to exceed capacity at ABIG Child's Place. Negotiations with La Petite Academy, a nationally franchised child-care operation, resulted in its opening of a new child-care/preschool facility at American Bankers Office Park in 1987. Enrollment in the facility is open to the public, but since the facility is an adjunct to the ABIG child-care center, ABIG personnel receive priority.

ABIG Satellite Learning Center.   In 1987, ABIG became the first corporation in America with an on-site public school. The satellite school concept for grades K through 2 was proposed to the Miami business community at large by the superintendent of the Dade County public schools. ABIG viewed the idea as a logical extension of existing child-care/educational programs and an innovative opportunity.

The ABIG school, a satellite of Cutler Ridge Elementary School, was up and running in late August 1987—just three months after its first mention. Enrollment, limited to children of ABIG employees, was for kindergartners only in the first school year.

Classes were conducted during the 1987–88 term in a relocatable classroom building at Southridge Senior High School, adjacent to ABIG's property.

The temporary location was made possible, in part, by the relationship between ABIG and Southridge High. The two had been "Dade Partners" since 1981, and this was an example of the cooperation that can result from an active business and school partnership.

Use of the relocatable classroom building allowed the company time to design and construct the ABIG Satellite Learning Center at American Bankers Office Park. First grade was phased in when the center opened in August 1988.

Under a joint venture, ABIG provides the building, maintenance, utilities, and security; the school system supplies the teaching staff, administrative supervision, and educational materials. Before- and after-school supervision is contracted directly with Cutler Ridge Elementary School. (See Chapter 6 for a full description of this program.)

ABIG Satellite Learning Center, successful beyond anyone's expectation, has served as a model for additional satellite schools in Dade County. Widespread national publicity and interest may result in similar ventures in other parts of the country.

Participating parents view the child-care/preschool program as a primary benefit. Everyone enjoys having the youngsters on-site and looks forward especially to their annual Halloween costume parade and their Christmas caroling performances. The children of ABIG Child's Place have also taken stage center with their performance at meetings of the ABIG board of directors. They've been adopted, in fact, by one and all—including visitors who see them playing in the tot lot.

There are also many benefits to the company. Recruiting and personnel retention have been enhanced. Absenteeism and tardiness are almost nonexistent among participating employees.

Local and national publicity has established ABIG as a caring employer and as a front-runner in corporate child care. ABIG Child's Place has been featured on local and nationally syndicated television programs and in newspaper and magazine feature articles.

ABIG Child's Place has proven to be invaluable to both the company and its employees. Parents have the assurance that their children are receiving the best of care, the companionship of children of the same age, good nutrition, a solid preschool education, and the extra benefit of proximity—important to both parent and child.[9]

Start-Up Story No. 2: MCCARE—McDonnell Douglas–Sponsored Day Care

"Anybody can start a center, and anybody can make it work, but it's the quality that's behind the program that really makes it successful," says Steve Zwolak, director of MCCARE, the McDonnell Douglas day-care center. "We were committed to doing it right."

In mid-1984, the idea of a company-sponsored day-care center for McDonnell Douglas originated directly from employee input. By October of that year, management had appointed a task force

to analyze the need for such day care and to make recommendations. For the next six months, the task force considered the implications of demographics, alternative programs, siting requirements, and other matters. By July 1985, a business plan was
developed for the day-care center. At a well-received presenta-
tion of the plan to senior management, the task force delivered its
recommendation to proceed. McDonnell Douglas approved the
plan on July 31 on an experimental basis. Within a few months, it
formed MACARV, Inc., a wholly owned subsidiary to implement
a comprehensive, high-quality early childhood development program. "As a wholly owned subsidiary," Zwolak points out, "we
were able to gain lots of advantages—we were covered under
MAC's [McDonnell Douglas's] insurance umbrella, but I didn't
have to pay my maintenance people union wages. There was a
variety of reasons why it was definitely to our advantage to become a component in this way."

The site chosen for the day-care center was a nearby, unused
elementary school. By June 1986, the building had been renovated, staff hired, licensing arranged, and curriculum developed.
"The building was a fantastic, massive three-story brick elementary school no longer in use. It had 24 classrooms and a full library
area—ideal potential for a quality center," says Zwolak. A vigor-
ous marketing campaign was conducted to interest employees in
using the center. Part of that campaign was an employee contest
to *name* the center. The winning name turned out to be MCCARE.

On June 30, 1986, MCCARE opened for business with 28 children and 17 staff. Within four months, its enrollment had climbed
to 60 children. With the success of the center assured, McDonnell
Douglas reviewed business plans that had forecast a break-even
financial position for MCCARE by early 1988. A full year ahead of
schedule, in April 1987, the center generated its first month of
positive cash flow.

By September 1987, MCCARE's enrollment topped 100 children. In April 1988, responding to new federal programs, Mc-
Donnell Douglas implemented Flexible Spending Accounts for
pretax dependent care deductions. By April 30, 1988, with enrollment at 124 and staff at 39, MCCARE had achieved a break-even
cash flow position. "Initially, MAC wanted to know how and
when they were going to be financially committed . . . they
wanted to know how long we were going to be losing money.

The rule for all our subsidiaries is to have a break-even status. . . . We projected a two-year break-even, and we were able to do it with a quality program," says Zwolak.

Intense building took place at MCCARE in the fall of 1988. McDonnell Douglas furnished funds for the renovation of eight classrooms to accommodate a minimum of 150 additional children. Staffing underwent its own form of renovation and renewal with the implementation of the Missouri Parents as Teachers program at MCCARE.

At the end of 1990, MCCARE had an enrollment of more than 150 children and a dedicated staff of 49. It receives support and valuable input from its parent organization. As a media "star" for McDonnell Douglas, it attracts continuing widespread interest from the public and other companies. Most important, MCCARE continues to serve the children of McDonnell Douglas employees with expert care and kindness. Steve Zwolak comments, "The indication is that the parents want me to take the program through the third grade. . . . I don't think that's out of the realm of possibilities."[10]

Start-Up Story No. 3: Elder Care at IBM

IBM (International Business Machines Corporation), with 206,000 domestic employees in 50 states, "had absolutely no employee demand for an elder-care program," according to Ted Childs, program director of work/life programs, IBM United States.[11] IBM's decision makers, however, tried to prepare for coming social trends before these arrived in the form of employee problems. By 1984, their reading of data from the U.S. Census Bureau, the New York Business Group on Health, studies of The Travelers Companies, and their own internal investigations convinced them that a major social shift involving elder care would be under way.

In 1986, IBM conducted an Elder Care Feasibility Study in recognition of the aging of the U.S. population and its implications for the IBM work force. In the following year, IBM committed itself to the pioneering of a national program to assist employees and retirees with their elder-care responsibilities no matter where their elder relatives lived.

It contracted with Work/Family Elder Directions, Inc., a

Massachusetts consulting firm, to provide an assessment and impact report. The report demonstrated to IBM's satisfaction that community resources were up to the task of elder care—if only employees knew what was available. IBM committed itself, therefore, to a consultation and referral approach to elder-care assistance for its employees.

As recounted in the *Personnel Journal,* "Implementing the service was a five-month process. The service was preannounced on September 17, 1987, to allow Work/Family Elder Directions to put the program together without having to do it in secret. A meeting with the company's human resources staff followed shortly, and then all managers were briefed about the program. In late January of 1988, a 22-page brochure describing the program was mailed to employees and retirees. The brochure was also sent electronically to employees overseas, and offered on audiocassettes for the blind."[12] In February 1988, IBM implemented the Elder Care Referral Service (ECRS). The service includes consultation and individualized referrals to possible sources of support that meet a family's preferences.

Here's how an IBM employee—Jan, let's say—can use the ECRS. Selecting one of the phone numbers provided in a company brochure, Jan calls a trained counselor to discuss her elder-care situation. After helping Jan determine the full extent of her needs, the counselor refers her to specific services that are available in her community. The counselor then mails her a written confirmation of the recommended services along with a handbook for using community resources. About a month later, Jan receives a follow-up phone call from the counselor to see whether her needs are being met.

IBM prepays the cost of the consultation and referral service; employees pay the costs, if any, of the community service they use. IBM makes clear that its referrals are not recommendations and that employees should carefully assess the programs and expenses of any service they choose to use.

According to Sara Ann Gomez, program manager of work/life programs, "To date, over 13,000 IBMers have used the ECRS to find care for approximately 12,000 older relatives. Of those using the services, 72 percent are employees, 19 percent employee spouses, 9 percent retirees and retiree spouses. Many of the retirees are using the service for their parents."

Interesting trends are beginning to appear in the use patterns of the elder-care service. IBM work/life programs documented program success.

> "Regarding older relatives, 52 percent of the calls involved long-distance care-giving situations where the employee lived 100 miles or more from the older relative—20 percent lived more than 1,000 miles away. This reinforces our belief that this program minimizes employee distraction through the concept of "one-stop shopping"—saving the employee's time and enhancing IBM's productivity. Seventy percent of the older relatives are 75 to 89 years of age, and 9 percent are age 90 or older."

The program that was developed for IBM has been made available to other corporations. To date, 21 other national employers have offered the ECRS.

> "An important part of the ECRS program design included some funds for resource development to help increase the supply of elder-care services where shortages exist. This was to contribute to communities and, over time, better meet the needs of employees. With the help of ECRS Program Funds from IBM, more than 50 local resource development projects have been funded. Proposals are submitted by local ECRS network organizations to our national contractor—Work/ Family Elder Directions, Inc. Projects are diverse and include:
>
> - Caregiver support claims.
> - Medicare claims assistance.
> - Nursing home visitation program.
> - Volunteer respite care.
> - Expansion of home-delivered meals.
> - Shopping service.
> - Money management program."

Other parts of the start-up for elder-care programs included a nationwide seminar series and an Elder Care Project Development Fund. Gomez describes the programs:

> "Under our "A Plan for Life" Program, managed by Johnson & Johnson Health Management, Inc., we introduced a series

of seminars designed to help employees anticipating or already providing care for an older relative. *Caring for Elderly Relatives* consists of eight courses designed to help employees anticipating or already providing care for an older relative. Topics include:

- The normal aging process.
- Family decision making about care-giving.
- Approaches to care-giving.
- Community resources for older adults.
- Paying for care.
- Legal issues.
- Living arrangements.
- Balancing work and care-giving."

Participants learn how to sort through the maze of public and private health insurance, arrange discharge planning from hospitals, and assess nursing homes and other community services. In addition, participants develop a personal caregiver's guide and receive information to help them meet their older relative's varied needs. The courses offer a forum to discuss individual concerns, share ideas, and find mutual support among coworkers.

The IBM Elder Care Project Development Fund ($3 million) is intended to stimulate the development of new elder-care services and, where possible, the expansion of existing services. This support represents an expansion of community projects already funded by the company. Of the first dollars allocated under the fund, recipients included the Atlanta Regional Commission in support of in-home services for the elderly and the Jewish Family and Children's Services in Boca Raton, Florida, for respite care services."[13]

Chapter Eight
All the King's Men

GOVERNMENT PARTICIPATION IN KIN CARE

I n her 1990 Library of Congress report, *Child Day Care*, Anne C. Stewart, education and public welfare coordinator, competes for the "Understatement of the Year" award: "The broad range of federal programs supporting child care has been criticized as being uncoordinated and unfocused. The programs, it is argued, were developed on an ad hoc basis and do not reflect a unified, comprehensive federal policy in this area."

More than 40 federal programs provide "support" in one way or another for child-care services. None of these programs, says Stewart, "exclusively support child day care per se." It is important to understand the complexities, even the vagaries, of federal child-care programs as preparation for assessing the child-care legislation recently enacted by Congress.

FEDERAL SUPPORT FOR CHILD CARE

During 1988, the federal government spent about $6.9 billion on child care in some form (versus $350 billion for spending on elder care). The child-care programs with the largest budgets are in the control of the Senate Committee on Finance.

This powerful Senate committee gets its funds for child-care programs from two familiar provisions of the IRS code: (1) your right to take a child and dependent care tax credit, amounting in total to $4 billion (more than half of all the money earmarked for all child-care programs); and (2) the Flexible Spending Account, in which pretax dollars are taken out of your paycheck for certain forms of dependent care. The federal government considers that it "spends" these funds on child care because it does not collect them from you and me.

More traditional forms of spending can be found in the Title XX social services block grant (SSBG) program, child care provided as part of employment training for welfare recipients, and "income disregard" for child care for families with dependent children (the AFDC program).

Taken together, all of these programs account for about three

FIGURE 8–1

U.S. Expenditures on Children in Billions

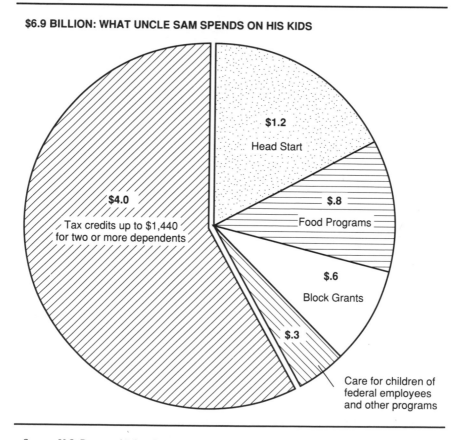

$6.9 BILLION: WHAT UNCLE SAM SPENDS ON HIS KIDS

$1.2
Head Start

$.8
Food Programs

$4.0
Tax credits up to $1,440
for two or more dependents

$.6
Block Grants

$.3

Care for children of
federal employees
and other programs

Source: U.S. Bureau of Labor Statistics, 1989 and U.S. Census data.

fourths of all federal expenditures for child care in 1988. The remaining quarter or so of federal expenditures—$1.6 billion— went for such programs as Head Start, the Child Care Food Program, and the Food Stamp Program and grants/research/pilot programs on child care.

The *Head Start* program provides local Head Start agencies with federal matching grants to help fund a variety of social, educational, nutritional, and medical services to low-income children before they begin their formal education. This program served more than 448,00 children in 1988.[1] That seemingly large number constitutes only 18 percent of the children whose parents' income qualifies them for the program.

The *Child Care Food Program* provides funds and foodstuffs to reimburse the states for the cost of meals served to children in public and private nonprofit day-care centers, family and group day-care homes, and Head Start programs. In 1988, approximately 1.2 million children were served daily under this program.

The *Food Stamp Program* allows child-care expenses relating to work or training of up to $160 per month per child to be deducted from household income in determining eligibility for food stamps and the value of the food stamps that a household may receive. It is estimated that only about 2 percent of food stamp households claimed deductions for child-care expenses. One analyst explains that food stamp households often qualify for full benefits without the deduction.

Current Child-Care Legislation

In late October 1990, Congress enacted the Child Care and Development Block Grant. (Since care-giving organizations and parents need to know the specific terms of this legislation to receive aid, its entire text appears in the appendix to this chapter.)

The highlights of this child-care legislation are as follows:

1. Congress appropriates $750 million in 1991, $825 million in 1992, and $925 million in 1993 for child-care grants to the states.
2. The states apply for these federal funds under guidelines ensuring that

- Of the funds received, 25 percent go toward improving "the quality of child care" and increasing "the availability of early childhood development and before and after-school care services."

- Parents can send their children to state-assisted programs or receive a certificate of equal value for their chosen provider. Children of working parents (or parents in job training) are eligible if they are under 13 and if the family income "does not exceed 75 percent of the state median income for a family of the same size."

- No funds are used "for the purchase or improvement of land, or for the purchase, construction, or permanent improvement (other than minor remodeling) of any building or facility."

- Priority in some forms of funding is given to "areas with concentrations of poverty" and "areas with very high or very low population densities."

3. Each state must develop a plan for the distribution of these funds. The legislation suggests typical projects and programs that the states might propose in such plans. These suggestions include efforts to upgrade health and safety requirements for child-care providers, to review state licensing procedures and standards, to develop consumer education programs for parents choosing child care, to subsidize the salaries of caregivers and the overhead expenses of child-care centers, to monitor compliance with licensing and regulatory requirements, to operate resource and referral programs for child care, to encourage public/private partnerships for child care, and to provide training in health, safety, and nutrition for child-care providers.

What to Expect from the Child Care and Development Block Grant Legislation

The impact of the Child Care and Development Block Grant legislation will depend on the states' wisdom in spending the money. As economist Robert J. Samuelson has pointed out, direct subsidies to all of the eligible children—some 16 million—would prove almost meaningless: about $45 per child per year. As Douglas Besharov of the American Enterprise Institute has said, either a smaller amount could be spent on each eligible child or a larger amount could be spent on each of a limited group of children.[2]

Because the legislation funds efforts to upgrade state standards for child care, the net cost of child care to parents may be more, not less, as a result of the grants to states. Rita Watson of the Bush Center in Child Development at Yale estimates that quality child care, with adequately trained staff and better child/caregiver ratios, would cost $7,800 a year for infants and $6,500 for toddlers.

Hank Brown, the ranking Republican on the House Ways and Means Committee, writes with congressional staffer Ron Haskins that "currently, about 4 million children, under age five and with working mothers, receive paid care, at an average cost of $42 per week.[3] Researchers at the University of North Carolina recently estimated that standards such as those sure to result from federal regulation will nearly double the cost of care. The cost of 'quality' care would average about $100 per week; if this increase is applied only to those 4 million children, the added cost is $12 billion, on top of the nearly $7 billion the government already spends on day care. With the S&L and nuclear cleanup crises, the government can't pick up that bill.

Economist Milton Friedman has said that the flaw in child-care legislation is that it penalizes the family in which the mother stays at home to provide child care. In effect, such families would be taxed to pay the child-care expenses of other families. We already have enough government policies that penalize the traditional family. We surely do not need any more."[4]

The argument is that Congress will never be able to afford substantive assistance to most of the families now crushed by child-care expenses. As Robert Samuelson wrote, "Current proposals are deceptive because they pretend to do something while actually doing little."[5] Samuelson's point can be made by considering what one child (one personal exemption) has been "worth" to Congress over the past 70 years in 1987 dollars. For a family of four, the relative amounts that Congress has spent on the family by means of allowable personal exemptions are:

1912	$45,977
1931	32,090
1940	22,764
1945	11,321
1984	4,376
1987	7,600

The message from even the most ardent advocates of federally supported child care is this: Don't expect more than a gesture for the time being, at least for the vast majority of American working parents and their children.

As a final note, it is interesting that the federal government has seen fit to provide for the children of its own employees. The United States operates about 70 day-care centers in federal buildings. And every morning, according to *Fortune,* "some 96,000 children at more than 400 U.S. military bases around the world march off to federally subsidized day-care centers."[6]

STATE, COUNTY, AND CITY CHILD-CARE PROGRAMS

Because of cutbacks in funds formerly available to low-income families under Title XX of the Social Security Act, the states may be witnessing what Carol Polsgrove called "a two-tiered system of child care, with low-income families excluded from the market of adequate care."[7]

She had in mind the gross mismatch between what states say they offer and the numbers of children they actually serve. In Georgia, for example, subsidies available by law to 76,000 children were received by only 8,000 children in 1990. Florida had a waiting list of 30,000 children for subsidized day care authorized under state legislation. In 1990, 22 states were helping fewer children than they helped six years earlier.

The classic study of this phenomenon is *Child Care: Facing Hard Choices,* by Alfred J. Kahn and Sheila B. Kamerman. "By the mid-1980s," they write, "the only children who were assured of access to a subsidized place in care were children in need of protection against neglect and abuse. Indeed, in several states, there was a basis for suspicion that this group had grown, in part, because some parents were prepared to label themselves neglectful or potentially abusive to qualify for affordable care."[8]

From 1985 to 1990, reports the National Conference on State Legislation, child-care issues were increasingly important to the states. The NCSL tracked 112 pieces of state child-care legislation enacted in 1987, compared to only 21 pieces enacted in 1984.

Arizona, California, Connecticut, Florida, Maryland, New Mexico, Oregon, and Rhode Island have corporate tax incentives for employers willing to establish care centers and subsidize care. Oregon gives an employer a tax credit of 50 percent, to a maximum of $2,500 (per employee), for "financial assistance for any kind of dependent care over and above compensation."

In California, the Employer-Assisted Child Care Tax Credit provides a similar 50 percent tax credit for employers who make ongoing contributions on behalf of employees to a child-care program, covering up to $600 for full-time care and up to $300 for part-time care.

Some states have mandated space reservations for child care in new developments. Maryland and California, for example, will not approve new state buildings unless they allocate space for on-site child care.

In 1988, Minnesota created a child-care unit to award grants from $200 to $30,000 to individuals and companies starting day-care centers. In Illinois, the Department of Children and Family Services is creating an extensive resource and referral network to be used by citizens with no charge or at nominal charges.

Other states distribute aid for child care through loan programs. Maryland has both a direct loan fund and a guaranteed loan fund for developers, employers, and private citizens who want to create or expand day-care facilities. The Massachusetts Industrial Finance Agency works directly with employers, giving them below-market loans for the start-up costs of developing child-care centers.

Perhaps the most ambitious of state efforts to date, however, is the California Child Care Initiative. In 1986, 24 corporations joined with 10 federal, state, and local agencies to launch the program. Its mission: to train and license individuals who care for children in their homes. According to Jan Brown, project specialist, by late 1989 the program had trained 1,200 new day-care providers, opening up places for up to 6,000 additional children in home-based day care. This one state effort is estimated to have expanded California's home-based resources for child care by 20 percent.

County and City Initiatives for Kin Care

At the county and city level, the move toward better kin care is also apparent. Since 1988, Montgomery County, Maryland has not approved plans for shopping malls and office complexes unless the developer has arranged for on-site day care. Fairfax County, Virginia, has appointed an Employer Child Care Council. Through its efforts, the number of on-site centers increased from a single center in 1986 to nine in 1990, with more planned. The council extended the number of child-care benefit programs available to employers from 5 in 1986 to 632 in 1990.

Nassau County and Suffolk County in New York each have a task force on child care. Formed in 1987, the Nassau County Task Force identified the need to stabilize the existing child-care centers through better recruitment and retention of staff. The county appropriated $600,000 for direct salary enhancement. In 1989, each assistant was to receive $1,500 and each teacher was to receive $2,500 at the 30 centers contracting with the county for subsidized care. The Suffolk County Task Force, organized more recently, has recommended that three child-care centers for county employees be built and that excess school facilities be used for child care.

Cities have started to wield their power on behalf of child care. In San Francisco, developers of hotels and office space exceeding 50,000 square feet must do one of the following:

- Devote 2,000 square feet or 1 percent of their floor space, whichever is less, to on-site child care.

- Provide an equivalent area for child care at a nearby site.

- Contribute $1 per square foot of office space to the San Francisco Affordable Child care Fund.[9]

In Philadelphia, the demand for child care has far outstripped the local supply of care. According to the Delaware Valley Child Care Council, "There is a shortage of licensed and registered child care in Philadelphia County. It is estimated that the demand for child day care in the county exceeds the supply of regulated care by at least 7,270 spaces for children ages zero through five whose mothers are in the labor force. For all children ages 0 through 12 . . . the adjusted, calculated shortfall then becomes 56,829 spaces."

Philadelphia has responded by passing an ordinance that reduces an employer's after-tax cost of child-care services by granting a credit against the amount of city business income tax due. In this way, reported the *Real Estate Finance Journal*, Philadelphia has given employers "an economic incentive to grant their employees greater access to child-care services."[10]

THE ELDER-CARE PERSPECTIVE

A not dissimilar story could be told of elder-care programs: seemingly immense amounts of federal money coming down to less than adequate assistance, and that for only a portion of the elderly; creative state programs offset by draconian measures to control medicaid spending; county and city initiatives long on goodwill and usually short on funding.

But within the limits of this chapter, it may be most helpful to define the major federal and state programs beyond social security payments that are now available to the elderly.

Medicare is a federal health program that provides hospital and medical insurance for people 65 years of age and over, as well as disabled individuals. The program consists of two parts:

- *Part A, Hospital Insurance.* This part of the Medicare program pays for certain kinds and levels of hospital, hospice, or skilled nursing facility care and, to a lesser degree, for qualifying home care.

- *Part B, Medical Insurance.* This part of the Medicare program covers some types of outpatient care, including visits to a physician, laboratory fees, and some prescription drugs.

The great majority of Americans over 65 have medicare coverage. For those who have worked long enough to qualify for social security, Part A of the Medicare program comes automatically as a matter of course. Spouses of eligible workers are also eligible, as are certain widows, widowers, divorced persons, and dependents. A disabled person, even before the age of 65, may also qualify for Part A. There is no fee for eligible Part A participants.

For Part B coverage, however, a premium must be paid. At present, it is deducted automatically from a participant's social security check. In general, application should be made for both parts of the Medicare program about three months before a person's 65th birthday.

So is the elderly person well covered? No, says Johnson & Johnson's elder-care booklet for employees:

It is important to know what Medicare leaves uncovered. These gaps include deductibles, co-payments, limits on reimbursement for certain services as well as lack of coverage for some services.

For example, while Medicare pays for an unlimited number of days of hospitalization, the Medicare beneficiary who has been hospitalized must pay an annual hospital deductible. This amount is set once a year and is equal to the national average cost of one day of hospitalization. In 1988, the Medicare Part A deductible was $540. For 1989, the Medicare Part A deductible was set at $564 per year.

There is also a Medicare deductible for outpatient care which is set for each calendar year by the federal government. In 1988, the Medicare Part B outpatient deductible was $75 and remained unchanged for 1989. Older persons are required to pay out of their own pockets the first $75 of their annual outpatient doctor bills unless they have other insurance to cover such charges.

If an elderly person's doctor accepts Medicare-approved charge limitations, then that person must pay 20 percent of the charge. (For a $40 doctor visit, Medicare would pay $32 and the patient $8.) If the health provider does not accept Medicare limitations, the person would co-pay the difference between what the doctor charges and the Medicare payment. (For an $80 doctor visit, Medicare would pay $32 and the patient $48.)

Medicare payment of prescription drugs was being phased out in 1990. Beginning in 1991, only prescription drugs in excess of a $600 deductible were to be paid, and then only with a 50 percent co-payment.

Late in 1990, the administration proposed significant additional cuts in Medicare benefits. Whether the administration's plan was able to withstand the flood of protest from elderly Americans and others will be known by the time this book is published.

Medigap Insurance

Though you would never guess it from conversation with elderly people, "medigap" is not a federal, state, or local program. Private insurers have profited grandly over the last decade with insurance claiming to "fill the gaps" left by Medicare. Some of this insurance duplicated Medicare benefits. In response, federal legislation enacted in July 1988 prohibited the policies of private insurance companies from overlapping with Medicare provisions.

But medigap policies can leave the elderly person partially unprotected. Policies claiming to pay Medicare deductibles often *themselves* involve deductibles. Often excluded from coverage are certain medical services, routine medical exams, eye exams, podiatric care, and dental care. Some medigap policies require a substantial waiting period before the insurance becomes effective. Others self-destruct after the policyholder files a certain number of claims. The key is to examine the policy with care, preferably with the aid of a knowledgeable benefits counselor.

Health Maintenance Organizations (HMOs)

One type of HMO that is increasingly popular with the elderly is the HMO-Medicare partnership. In this arrangement, the HMO contracts with Medicare to provide covered services to participants in Medicare. In return, Medicare pays the HMO a monthly fee to furnish this care. Virtually all out-of-pocket expenses are eliminated for the member, except for a monthly premium paid to the HMO by the elderly person. The only disadvantage of this plan lies in choice: in general, the HMO member must use only HMO doctors and hospitals.

Medicaid

This program, intended primarily for the destitute, pays for health care and nursing home care, even for extended periods. Medicaid is funded by both the federal and state government, and hence is subject to regulation by both.

As a general rule, the best way to qualify for medicaid is to spend all your money. That route to health coverage has proven so attractive that many states have enacted co-payment regulations to tap the estates of the children once the assets of the elderly person have been exhausted.

This sad travesty is euphemistically called "spending down." Because nursing home expenses are great, elderly people have found that they "spend down" their life savings quickly. States have stepped in, of course, to insist on *formulas* that are to be obeyed when spending down. An elderly person guilty of going on the dole too quickly may not be admitted to eligibility at all.

The statistics in this regard are both frightening and shameful for a society facing the Age Wave. In 1988 Claude Pepper, the late chair of the House Select Committee on Aging, said, "One million Americans, two thirds of them elderly, will fall into poverty this year trying to meet the costs of long-term care." In 1989, the same committee found that "the vast majority of the chronically ill elderly exhaust all their life savings within 13 weeks of nursing home admission."

The grisly tug-of-war, then, is between the elderly who are trying to get onto medicaid and the federal and state administrators and legislators who are trying to keep them off as long as possible. The implicit hope of the latter, I suppose, is that the elderly will die trying.

Long-Term Care Insurance

One of the newest and most popular benefits available in the cafeteria approach to benefit selection is long-term care insurance providing for nursing home care, home care, and some community-provided services. As America ages, we will see whether such insurance can remain both actuarially sound and affordable for the company and its employees.

FINAL NOTES

The tea leaves are not propitious for child-care and elder-care support from government in the near term. Despite the courage of some initiatives at the federal, state, county, and city levels, the forecast for kin care in the next five years is unremittingly stormy for most American families. Barring a major shift in public attitudes toward government funding of human services programs, we can probably look forward to individually paying more for scarcer kin care services.

In that case, corporations will be faced with the challenge of becoming a partner to government kin care efforts—and probably the lead partner as well.

Appendix

Below is the Child Care and Development Grant enacted in October 1990. It is included in its entirety since organizations and parents may need to know its specific terms and potential benefits.

SUBTITLE F—CHILD CARE AND DEVELOPMENT BLOCK GRANT[11]

SEC. 6501. CHILD CARE AND DEVELOPMENT BLOCK GRANT.

Chapter 8 of subtitle A of title IV of the Omnibus Budget Reconciliation Act of 1981 (Public Law 97–35) is amended—

    (1) by redesignating subchapters C, D, and E, as subchapters D, E, and F, respectively; and

    (2) by inserting after subchapter B the following new subchapter:

"Subchapter C—Child Care and Development Block Grant

"SEC. 658A. SHORT TITLE.

"This subchapter may be cited as the 'Child Care and Development Block Grant Act of 1990'.

"SEC. 658B. AUTHORIZATION OF APPROPRIATIONS.

"There are authorized to be appropriated to carry out this subchapter, $750,000,000 for fiscal year 1991, $825,000,000 for fiscal year 1992, $925,000,000 for fiscal year 1993, and such sums as may be necessary for each of the fiscal years 1994 and 1995.

"SEC. 658C. ESTABLISHMENT OF BLOCK GRANT PROGRAM.

"The Secretary is authorized to make grants to States in accordance with the provisions of this subchapter.

"SEC. 658D. LEAD AGENCY.

"(a) DESIGNATION.—The chief executive officer of a State desiring to receive a grant under this subchapter shall designate, in an application submitted to the Secretary under section 658E, an

---

appropriate State agency that complies with the requirements of
subsection (b) to act as the lead agency.

 "(b) Duties.—

  "(1) In general.—The lead agency shall—

  "(A) administer, directly or through other State agencies,
the financial assistance received under this subchapter by the
State;

  "(B) develop the State plan to be submitted to the Secretary under section 658E(a);

  "(C) in conjunction with the development of the State
plan as required under subparagraph (B), hold at least one
hearing in the State to provide to the public an opportunity to
comment on the provision of child care services under the
State plan; and

  "(D) coordinate the provision of services under this subchapter with other Federal, State and local child care and early
childhood development programs.

  "(2) Development of plan.—In the development of the
State plan described in paragraph (1)(B), the lead agency shall
consult with appropriate representatives of units of general purpose local government. Such consultations may include consideration of local child care needs and resources, the effectiveness
of existing child care and early childhood development services,
and the methods by which funds made available under this subchapter can be used to effectively address local shortages.

"SEC. 658E. APPLICATION AND PLAN.

 "(a) Application.—To be eligible to receive assistance under
this subchapter, a State shall prepare and submit to the Secretary
an application at such time, in such manner, and containing such
information as the Secretary shall by rule require, including—

  "(1) an assurance that the State will comply with the requirements of this subchapter; and

  "(2) a State plan that meets the requirements of subsection (c).

 "(b) Period Covered by Plan.—The State plan contained in
the application under subsection (a) shall be designed to be implemented—

  "(1) during a 3-year period for the initial State plan; and

  "(2) during a 2-year period for subsequent State plans.

 "(c) Requirements of a Plan.—

"(1) LEAD AGENCY.—The State plan shall identify the lead agency designated under section 658D.

"(2) POLICIES AND PROCEDURES.—The State plan shall:

"(A) PARENTAL CHOICE OF PROVIDERS.—Provide assurances that—

"(i) the parent or parents of each eligible child within the State who receives or is offered child care services for which financial assistance is provided under this subchapter, other than through assistance provided under paragraph (3)(C), are given the option either—

"(I) to enroll such child with a child care provider that has a grant or contract for the provision of such services; or

"(II) to receive a child care certificate as defined in section 658P(2);

"(ii) in cases in which the parent selects the option described in clause (i)(I), the child will be enrolled with the eligible provider selected by the parent to the maximum extent practicable; and

"(iii) child care certificates offered to parents selecting the option described in clause (i)(II) shall be of a value commensurate with the subsidy value of child care services provided under the option described in clause (i)(I);

except that nothing in this subparagraph shall require a State to have a child care certificate program in operation prior to October 1, 1992.

"(B) UNLIMITED PARENTAL ACCESS.—Provide assurances that procedures are in effect within the State to ensure that child care providers who provide services for which assistance is made available under this subchapter afford parents unlimited access to their children and to the providers caring for their children, during the normal hours of operation of such providers and whenever such children are in the care of such providers.

"(C) PARENTAL COMPLAINTS.—Provide assurances that the State maintains a record of substantiated parental complaints and makes information regarding such parental complaints available to the public on request.

"(D) CONSUMER EDUCATION.—Provide assurances that consumer education information will be made available to parents and the general public within the State concerning licensing and regulatory requirements, complaint procedures, and policies and practices relative to child care services within the State.

"(E) COMPLIANCE WITH STATE AND LOCAL REGULATORY RE-QUIREMENTS.—Provide assurances that—

"(i) all providers of child care services within the State for which assistance is provided under this subchapter comply with all licensing or regulatory requirements (including registration requirements) applicable under State and local law; and

"(ii) providers within the State that are not required to be licensed or regulated under State or local law are required to be registered with the State prior to payment being made under this subchapter, in accordance with procedures designed to facilitate appropriate payment to such providers, and to permit the State to furnish information to such providers, including information on the availability of health and safety training, technical assistance, and any relevant information pertaining to regulatory requirements in the State, and that such providers shall be permitted to register with the State after selection by the parents of eligible children and before such payment is made.

This subparagraph shall not be construed to prohibit a State from imposing more stringent standards and licensing or regulatory requirements on child care providers within the State that provide services for which assistance is provided under this subchapter than the standards or requirements imposed on other child care providers in the State.

"(F) ESTABLISHMENT OF HEALTH AND SAFETY REQUIRE-MENTS.—Provide assurances that there are in effect within the State, under State or local law, requirements designed to protect the health and safety of children that are applicable to child care providers that provide services for which assistance is made available under this subchapter. Such requirements shall include—

"(i) the prevention and control of infectious diseases (including immunization);

"(ii) building and physical premises safety; and

"(iii) minimum health and safety training appropriate to the provider setting.

Nothing in this subparagraph shall be construed to require the establishment of additional health and safety requirements for child care providers that are subject to health and safety requirements in the categories described in this subparagraph on the date of enactment of this subchapter under State or local law.

"(G) COMPLIANCE WITH STATE AND LOCAL HEALTH AND SAFETY REQUIREMENTS.—Provide assurances that procedures are in effect to ensure that child care providers within the State that provide services for which assistance is provided under this subchapter comply with all applicable State or local health and safety requirements as described in subparagraph (F).

"(H) REDUCTION IN STANDARDS.—Provide assurances that if the State reduces the level of standards applicable to child care services provided in the State on the date of enactment of this subchapter, the State shall inform the Secretary of the rationale for such reduction in the annual report of the State described in section 658K.

"(I) REVIEW OF STATE LICENSING AND REGULATORY REQUIRE-MENTS.—Provide assurances that not later than 18 months after the date of the submission of the application under section 658E, the State will complete a full review of the law applicable to, and the licensing and regulatory requirements and policies of, each licensing agency that regulates child care services and programs in the State unless the State has reviewed such law, requirements, and policies in the 3-year period ending on the date of the enactment of this subchapter.

"(J) SUPPLEMENTATION.—Provide assurances that funds received under this subchapter by the State will be used only to supplement, not to supplant, the amount of Federal, State, and local funds otherwise expended for the support of child care services and related programs in the State.

"(3) USE OF BLOCK GRANT FUNDS.—

"(A) GENERAL REQUIREMENT.—The State plan shall provide that the State will use the amounts provided to the State for each fiscal year under this subchapter as required under subparagraphs (B) and (C).

"(B) CHILD CARE SERVICES.—Subject to the reservation contained in subparagraph (C), the State shall use amounts provided to the State for each fiscal year under this subchapter for—

"(i) child care services, that meet the requirements of this subchapter, that are provided to eligible children in the State on a sliding fee scale basis using funding methods provided for in section 658E(c)(2)(A), with priority being given for services provided to children of families with very low family incomes (taking into consideration family size) and to children with special needs; and

"(ii) activities designed to improve the availability and quality of child care.

"(C) ACTIVITIES TO IMPROVE THE QUALITY OF CHILD CARE AND TO INCREASE THE AVAILABILITY OF EARLY CHILDHOOD DEVELOPMENT AND BEFORE- AND AFTER-SCHOOL CARE SERVICES.— The State shall reserve 25 percent of the amounts provided to the State for each fiscal year under this subchapter to carry out activities designed to improve the quality of child care (as described in section 658G) and to provide before- and after-school and early childhood development services (as described in section 658H).

"(4) PAYMENT RATES.—

"(A) IN GENERAL.—The State plan shall provide assurances that payment rates for the provision of child care services for which assistance is provided under this subchapter are sufficient to ensure equal access for eligible children to comparable child care services in the State or substate area that are provided to children whose parents are not eligible to receive assistance under this subchapter or for child care assistance under any other Federal or State programs. Such payment rates shall take into account the variations in the costs of providing child care in different settings and to children of different age groups, and the additional costs of providing child care for children with special needs.

"(B) CONSTRUCTION.—Nothing in this paragraph shall be construed to create a private right of action.

"(5) SLIDING FEE SCALE.—The State plan shall provide that the State will establish and periodically revise, by rule, a sliding fee scale that provides for cost sharing by the families that receive child care services for which assistance is provided under this subchapter.

"(d) APPROVAL OF APPLICATION.—The Secretary shall approve an application that satisfies the requirements of this section.

"SEC. 658F. LIMITATIONS ON STATE ALLOTMENTS.

"(a) No Entitlement to Contract or Grant.—Nothing in this subchapter shall be construed—

"(1) to entitle any child care provider or recipient of a child care certificate to any contract, grant or benefit; or

"(2) to limit the right of any State to impose additional limitations or conditions on contracts or grants funded under this subchapter.

"(b) Construction of Facilities.—

"(1) In general.—No funds made available under this subchapter shall be expended for the purchase or improvement of land, or for the purchase, construction, or permanent improvement (other than minor remodeling) of any building or facility.

"(2) Sectarian agency or organization.—In the case of a sectarian agency or organization, no funds made available under this subchapter may be used for the purposes described in paragraph (1) except to the extent that renovation or repair is necessary to bring the facility of such agency or organization into compliance with health and safety requirements referred to in section 658E(c)(2)(F).

"SEC. 658G. ACTIVITIES TO IMPROVE THE QUALITY OF CHILD CARE.

"A State that receives financial assistance under this subchapter shall use not less than 20 percent of the amounts reserved by such State under section 658E(c)(3)(C) for each fiscal year for one or more of the following:

"(1) Resource and referral programs.—Operating directly or providing financial assistance to private nonprofit organizations or public organizations (including units of general purpose local government) for the development, establishment, expansion, operation, and coordination of resource and referral programs specifically related to child care.

"(2) Grants or loans to assist in meeting State and local standards.—Making grants or providing loans to child care providers to assist such providers in meeting applicable State and local child care standards.

"(3) Monitoring of compliance with licensing and regulatory requirements.—Improving the monitoring of compliance with, and enforcement of, State and local licensing and regulatory requirements (including registration requirements).

"(4) TRAINING.—Providing training and technical assistance in areas appropriate to the provision of child care services, such as training in health and safety, nutrition, first aid, the recognition of communicable diseases, child abuse detection and prevention, and the care of children with special needs.

"(5) COMPENSATION.—Improving salaries and other compensation paid to full- and part-time staff who provide child care services for which assistance is provided under this subchapter.

"SEC. 658H. EARLY CHILDHOOD DEVELOPMENT AND BEFORE- AND AFTER-SCHOOL SERVICES.

"(a) IN GENERAL.—A State that receives financial assistance under this subchapter shall use not less than 75 percent of the amounts reserved by such State under section 658E(c)(3)(C) for each fiscal year to establish or expand and conduct, through the provision of grants or contracts, early childhood development or before- and after-school child care programs, or both.

"(b) PROGRAM DESCRIPTION. Programs that receive assistance under this section shall—

"(1) in the case of early childhood development programs, consist of services that are not intended to serve as a substitute for compulsory academic programs but that are intended to provide an environment that enhances the educational, social, cultural, emotional, and recreational development of children; and

"(2) in the case of before- and after-school child care programs—

"(A) be provided Monday through Friday, including school holidays and vacation periods other than legal public holidays, to children attending early childhood development programs, kindergarten, or elementary or secondary school classes during such times of the day and on such days that regular instructional services are not in session; and

"(B) not be intended to extend or replace the regular academic program.

"(c) PRIORITY FOR ASSISTANCE.—In awarding grants and contracts under this section, the State shall give the highest priority to geographic areas within the State that are eligible to receive grants under section 1006 of the Elementary and Secondary Education Act of 1965, and shall then give priority to—

"(1) any other areas with concentrations of poverty; and

"(2) any areas with very high or very low population densities.

"SEC. 658I. ADMINISTRATION AND ENFORCEMENT.

"(a) ADMINISTRATION.—The Secretary shall—

"(1) coordinate all activities of the Department of Health and Human Services relating to child care, and, to the maximum extent practicable, coordinate such activities with similar activities of other Federal entities;

"(2) collect, publish and make available to the public a listing of State child care standards at least once every 3 years; and

"(3) provide technical assistance to assist States to carry out this subchapter, including assistance on a reimbursable basis.

"(b) ENFORCEMENT.—

"(1) REVIEW OF COMPLIANCE WITH STATE PLAN.—The Secretary shall review and monitor State compliance with this subchapter and the plan approved under section 658E(c) for the State, and shall have the power to terminate payments to the State in accordance with paragraph (2).

"(2) NONCOMPLIANCE.—

"(A) IN GENERAL.—If the Secretary, after reasonable notice to a State and opportunity for a hearing, finds that—

"(i) there has been a failure by the State to comply substantially with any provision or requirement set forth in the plan approved under section 658E(c) for the State; or

"(ii) in the operation of any program for which assistance is provided under this subchapter there is a failure by the State to comply substantially with any provision of this subchapter;

the Secretary shall notify the State of the finding and that no further payments may be made to such State under this subchapter (or, in the case of noncompliance in the operation of a program or activity, that no further payments to the State will be made with respect to such program or activity) until the Secretary is satisfied that there is no longer any such failure to comply or that the noncompliance will be promptly corrected.

"(B) ADDITIONAL SANCTIONS.—In the case of a finding of noncompliance made pursuant to subparagraph (A), the Secretary may, in addition to imposing the sanctions described in such subparagraph, impose other appropriate sanctions, including recoupment of money improperly expended for purposes prohibited or not authorized by this subchapter, and disqualification from the receipt of financial assistance under this subchapter.

"(C) NOTICE.—The notice required under subparagraph (A) shall include a specific identification of any additional sanction being imposed under subparagraph (B).

"(3) ISSUANCE OF RULES.—The Secretary shall establish by rule procedures for—

"(A) receiving, processing, and determining the validity of complaints concerning any failure of a State to comply with the State plan or any requirement of this subchapter; and

"(B) imposing sanctions under this section.

"SEC. 658J. PAYMENTS.

"(a) IN GENERAL.—Subject to the availability of appropriations, a State that has an application approved by the Secretary under section 658E(d) shall be entitled to a payment under this section for each fiscal year in an amount equal to its allotment under section 658O for such fiscal year.

"(b) METHOD OF PAYMENT.—

"(1) IN GENERAL.—Subject to paragraph (2), the Secretary may make payments to a State in installments, and in advance or by way of reimbursement, with necessary adjustments on account of overpayments or underpayments, as the Secretary may determine.

"(2) LIMITATION.—The Secretary may not make such payments in a manner that prevents the State from complying with the requirement specified in section 658E(c)(3).

"(c) SPENDING OF FUNDS BY STATE.—Payments to a State from the allotment under section 658O for any fiscal year may be expended by the State in that fiscal year or in the succeeding fiscal year.

"SEC. 658K. ANNUAL REPORT AND AUDITS.

"(a) ANNUAL REPORT.—Not later than December 31, 1992, and annually thereafter, a State that receives assistance under this subchapter shall prepare and submit to the Secretary a report—

"(1) specifying the uses for which the State expended funds specified under paragraph (3) of section 658E(c) and the amount of funds expended for such uses;

"(2) containing available data on the manner in which the child care needs of families in the State are being fulfilled, including information concerning—

"(A) the number of children being assisted with funds provided under this subchapter, and under other Federal child care and pre-school programs;

"(B) the type and number of child care programs, child care providers, caregivers, and support personnel located in the State;

"(C) salaries and other compensation paid to full- and part-time staff who provide child care services; and

"(D) activities in the State to encourage public-private partnerships that promote business involvement in meeting child care needs;

"(3) describing the extent to which the affordability and availability of child care services has increased;

"(4) if applicable, describing, in either the first or second such report, the findings of the review of State licensing and regulatory requirements and policies described in section 658E(c), including a description of actions taken by the State in response to such reviews;

"(5) containing an explanation of any State action, in accordance with section 658E, to reduce the level of child care standards in the State, if applicable; and

"(6) describing the standards and health and safety requirements applicable to child care providers in the State, including a description of State efforts to improve the quality of child care; during the period for which such report is required to be submitted.

"(b) AUDITS.—

"(1) REQUIREMENT.—A State shall, after the close of each program period covered by an application approved under section 658E(d), audit its expenditures during such program period from amounts received under this subchapter.

"(2) INDEPENDENT AUDITOR.—Audits under this subsection shall be conducted by an entity that is independent of any agency administering activities that receive assistance under this subchapter and be in accordance with generally accepted auditing principles.

"(3) Submission.—Not later than 30 days after the completion of an audit under this subsection, the State shall submit a copy of the audit to the legislature of the State and to the Secretary.

"(4) Repayment of amounts.—Each State shall repay to the United States any amounts determined through an audit under this subsection not to have been expended in accordance with this subchapter, or the Secretary may offset such amounts against any other amount to which the State is or may be entitled under this subchapter.

"SEC. 658L. REPORT BY SECRETARY.

"Not later than July 31, 1993, and annually thereafter, the Secretary shall prepare and submit to the Committee on Education and Labor of the House of Representatives and the Committee on Labor and Human Resources of the Senate a report that contains a summary and analysis of the data and information provided to the Secretary in the State reports submitted under section 658K. Such report shall include an assessment, and where appropriate, recommendations for the Congress concerning efforts that should be undertaken to improve the access of the public to quality and affordable child care in the United States.

"SEC. 658M. LIMITATIONS ON USE OF FINANCIAL ASSISTANCE FOR CERTAIN PURPOSES.

"(a) Sectarian Purposes and Activities.—No financial assistance provided under this subchapter, pursuant to the choice of a parent under section 658E(c)(2)(A)(i)(I) or through any other grant or contract under the State plan, shall be expended for any sectarian purpose or activity, including sectarian worship or instruction.

"(b) Tuition.—With regard to services provided to students enrolled in grades 1 through 12, no financial assistance provided under this subchapter shall be expended for—

"(1) any services provided to such students during the regular school day;

"(2) any services for which such students receive academic credit toward graduation; or

"(3) any instructional services which supplant or duplicate the academic program of any public or private school.

"SEC. 658N. NONDISCRIMINATION.

"(a) RELIGIOUS NONDISCRIMINATION.—

"(1) CONSTRUCTION.—

"(A) IN GENERAL.—Except as provided in subparagraph (B), nothing in this section shall be construed to modify or affect the provisions of any other Federal law or regulation that relates to discrimination in employment on the basis of religion.

"(B) EXCEPTION.—A sectarian organization may require that employees adhere to the religious tenets and teachings of such organization, and such organization may require that employees adhere to rules forbidding the use of drugs or alcohol.

"(2) DISCRIMINATION AGAINST CHILD.—

"(A) IN GENERAL.—A child care provider (other than a family child care provider) that receives assistance under this subchapter shall not discriminate against any child on the basis of religion in providing child care services.

"(B) NON-FUNDED CHILD CARE SLOTS.—Nothing in this section shall prohibit a child care provider from selecting children for child care slots that are not funded directly with assistance provided under this subchapter because such children or their family members participate on a regular basis in other activities of the organization that owns or operates such provider.

"(3) EMPLOYMENT IN GENERAL.—

"(A) PROHIBITION.—A child care provider that receives assistance under this subchapter shall not discriminate in employment on the basis of the religion of the prospective employee if such employee's primary responsibility is or will be working directly with children in the provision of child care services.

"(B) QUALIFIED APPLICANTS.—If two or more prospective employees are qualified for any position with a child care provider receiving assistance under this subchapter, nothing in this section shall prohibit such child care provider from employing a prospective employee who is already participating on a regular basis in other activities of the organization that owns or operates such provider.

"(C) PRESENT EMPLOYEES.—This paragraph shall not apply to employees of child care providers receiving assistance under this subchapter if such employees are employed with the provider on the date of enactment of this subchapter.

"(4) EMPLOYMENT AND ADMISSION PRACTICES.—Notwithstanding paragraphs (1)(B), (2), and (3), if assistance provided under this subchapter, and any other Federal or State program, amounts to 80 percent or more of the operating budget of a child care provider that receives such assistance, the Secretary shall not permit such provider to receive any further assistance under this subchapter unless the grant or contract relating to the financial assistance, or the employment and admissions policies of the provider, specifically provides that no person with responsibilities in the operation of the child care program, project, or activity of the provider will discriminate against any individual in employment, if such employee's primary responsibility is or will be working directly with children in the provision of child care, or admissions because of the religion of such individual.

"(b) EFFECT ON STATE LAW.—Nothing in this subchapter shall be construed to supersede or modify any provision of a State constitution or State law that prohibits the expenditure of public funds in or by sectarian institutions, except that no provision of a State constitution or State law shall be construed to prohibit the expenditure in or by sectarian institutions of any Federal funds provided under this subchapter.

"SEC. 658O. AMOUNTS RESERVED; ALLOTMENTS.

"(a) AMOUNTS RESERVED.—

"(1) TERRITORIES AND POSSESSIONS.—The Secretary shall reserve not to exceed one half of 1 percent of the amount appropriated under this subchapter in each fiscal year for payments to Guam, American Samoa, the Virgin Islands of the United States, the Commonwealth of the Northern Mariana Islands, and the Trust Territory of the Pacific Islands to be allotted in accordance with their respective needs.

"(2) INDIAN TRIBES.—The Secretary shall reserve not more than 3 percent of the amount appropriated under section 658B in each fiscal year for payments to Indian tribes and tribal organizations with applications approved under subsection (c).

"(b) STATE ALLOTMENT.—

"(1) GENERAL RULE.—From the amounts appropriated under section 658B for each fiscal year remaining after reservations under subsection (a), the Secretary shall allot to each State an amount equal to the sum of—

"(A) an amount that bears the same ratio to 50 percent of such remainder as the product of the young child factor of the State and the allotment percentage of the State bears to the sum of the corresponding products for all States; and

"(B) an amount that bears the same ratio to 50 percent of such remainder as the product of the school lunch factor of the State and the allotment percentage of the State bears to the sum of the corresponding products for all States.

"(2) YOUNG CHILD FACTOR.—The term 'young child factor' means the ratio of the number of children in the State under 5 years of age to the number of such children in all States as provided by the most recent annual estimates of population in the States by the Census Bureau of the Department of Commerce.

"(3) SCHOOL LUNCH FACTOR.—The term 'school lunch factor' means the ratio of the number of children in the State who are receiving free or reduced price lunches under the school lunch program established under the National School Lunch Act (42 U.S.C. 1751 et seq.) to the number of such children in all the States as determined annually by the Department of Agriculture.

"(4) ALLOTMENT PERCENTAGE.—

"(A) IN GENERAL.—The allotment percentage for a State is determined by dividing the per capita income of all individuals in the United States, by the per capita income of all individuals in the State.

"(B) LIMITATIONS.—If an allotment percentage determined under subparagraph (A)—

"(i) exceeds 1.2 percent, then the allotment percentage of that State shall be considered to be 1.2 percent; and

"(ii) is less than 0.8 percent, then the allotment percentage of the State shall be considered to be 0.8 percent.

"(C) PER CAPITA INCOME.—For purposes of subparagraph (A), per capita income shall be—

"(i) determined at 2-year intervals;

"(ii) applied for the 2-year period beginning on October

1 of the first fiscal year beginning on the date such determination is made; and

"(iii) equal to the average of the annual per capita incomes for the most recent period of 3 consecutive years for which satisfactory data are available from the Department of Commerce at the time such determination is made.

"(c) PAYMENTS FOR THE BENEFIT OF INDIAN CHILDREN.—

"(1) GENERAL AUTHORITY.—From amounts reserved under subsection (a)(2), the Secretary may make grants to or enter into contracts with Indian tribes or tribal organizations that submit applications under this section, for the planning and carrying out of programs or activities consistent with the purposes of this subchapter.

"(2) APPLICATIONS AND REQUIREMENTS.—An application for a grant or contract under this section shall provide that:

"(A) COORDINATION.—The applicant will coordinate, to the maximum extent feasible, with the lead agency in the State or States in which the applicant will carry out programs or activities under this section.

"(B) SERVICES ON RESERVATIONS.—In the case of an applicant located in a State other than Alaska, California, or Oklahoma, programs and activities under this section will be carried out on the Indian reservation for the benefit of Indian children.

"(C) REPORTS AND AUDITS.—The applicant will make such reports on, and conduct such audits of, programs and activities under a grant or contract under this section as the Secretary may require.

"(3) CONSIDERATION OF SECRETARIAL APPROVAL.—In determining whether to approve an application for a grant or contract under this section, the Secretary shall take into consideration—

"(A) the availability of child care services provided in accordance with this subchapter by the State or States in which the applicant proposes to carry out a program to provide child care services; and

"(B) whether the applicant has the ability (including skills, personnel, resources, community support, and other necessary components) to satisfactorily carry out the proposed program or activity.

"(4) THREE-YEAR LIMIT.—Grants or contracts under this section shall be for periods not to exceed 3 years.

"(5) DUAL ELIGIBILITY OF INDIAN CHILDREN.—The awarding of a grant or contract under this section for programs or activities to be conducted in a State or States shall not affect the eligibility of any Indian child to receive services provided or to participate in programs and activities carried out under a grant to the State or States under this subchapter.

"(d) DATA AND INFORMATION.—The Secretary shall obtain from each appropriate Federal agency, the most recent data and information necessary to determine the allotments provided for in subsection (b).

"(e) REALLOTMENTS.—

"(1) IN GENERAL.—Any portion of the allotment under subsection (b) to a State that the Secretary determines is not required to carry out a State plan approved under section 658E(d), in the period for which the allotment is made available, shall be reallotted by the Secretary to other States in proportion to the original allotments to the other States.

"(2) LIMITATIONS.—

"(A) REDUCTION.—The amount of any reallotment to which a State is entitled to under paragraph (1) shall be reduced to the extent that it exceeds the amount that the Secretary estimates will be used in the State to carry out a State plan approved under section 658E(d).

"(B) REALLOTMENTS.—The amount of such reduction shall be similarly reallotted among States for which no reduction in an allotment or reallotment is required by this subsection.

"(3) AMOUNTS REALLOTTED.—For purposes of any other section of this subchapter, any amount reallotted to a State under this subsection shall be considered to be part of the allotment made under subsection (b) to the State.

"(f) DEFINITION.—For the purposes of this section, the term 'State' includes only the 50 States, the District of Columbia, and the Commonwealth of Puerto Rico.

"SEC. 658P. DEFINITIONS.

"As used in this subchapter:

"(1) CAREGIVER.—The term 'caregiver' means an individual

who provides a service directly to an eligible child on a person-to-person basis.

"(2) CHILD CARE CERTIFICATE.—The term 'child care certificate' means a certificate (that may be a check or other disbursement) that is issued by a State or local government under this subchapter directly to a parent who may use such a certificate only as payment for child care services. Nothing in this subchapter shall preclude the use of such certificates for sectarian child care services if freely chosen by the parent. For purposes of this subchapter, child care certificates shall not be considered to be grants or contracts.

"(3) ELEMENTARY SCHOOL.—The term 'elementary school' means a day or residential school that provides elementary education, as determined under State law.

"(4) ELIGIBLE CHILD.—The term 'eligible child' means an individual—

"(A) who is less than 13 years of age;

"(B) whose family income does not exceed 75 percent of the State median income for a family of the same size; and

"(C) who—

"(i) resides with a parent or parents who are working or attending a job training or educational program; or

"(ii) is receiving, or needs to receive, protective services and resides with a parent or parents not described in clause (i).

"(5) ELIGIBLE CHILD CARE PROVIDER.—The term 'eligible child care provider' means—

"(A) a center-based child care provider, a group home child care provider, a family child care provider, or other provider of child care services for compensation that—

"(i) is licensed, regulated, or registered under State law as described in section 658E(c)(2)(E); and

"(ii) satisfies the State and local requirements, including those referred to in section 658E(c)(2)(F); applicable to the child care services it provides; or

"(B) a child care provider that is 18 years of age or older who provides child care services only to eligible children who are, by affinity or consanguinity, or by court decree, the grandchild, niece, or nephew of such provider, if such provider is registered and complies with any State requirements that govern child care provided by the relative involved.

"(6) FAMILY CHILD CARE PROVIDER.—The term 'family child care provider' means one individual who provides child care services for fewer than 24 hours per day, as the sole caregiver, and in a private residence.

"(7) INDIAN TRIBE.—The term 'Indian tribe' has the meaning given it in section 4(b) of the Indian Self-Determination and Education Assistance Act (25 U.S.C. 450b(b)).

"(8) LEAD AGENCY.—The term 'lead agency' means the agency designated under section 658B(a).

"(9) PARENT.—The term 'parent' includes a legal guardian or other person standing in loco parentis.

"(10) SECONDARY SCHOOL.—The term 'secondary school' means a day or residential school which provides secondary education, as determined under State law.

"(11) SECRETARY.—The term 'Secretary' means the Secretary of Health and Human Services unless the context specifies otherwise.

"(12) SLIDING FEE SCALE.—The term 'sliding fee scale' means a system of cost sharing by a family based on income and size of the family.

"(13) STATE.—The term 'State' means any of the several States, the District of Columbia, the Virgin Islands of the United States, the Commonwealth of Puerto Rico, Guam, American Samoa, and Commonwealth of the Northern Mariana Islands, and the Trust Territory of the Pacific Islands.

"(14) TRIBAL ORGANIZATION.—The term 'tribal organization' has the meaning given it in section 4(c) of the Indian Self-Determination and Education Assistance Act (25 U.S.C. 450b(c)).

"SEC. 658Q. PARENTAL RIGHTS AND RESPONSIBILITIES.

"Nothing in this subchapter shall be construed or applied in any manner to infringe on or usurp the moral and legal rights and responsibilities of parents or legal guardians.

"SEC. 658R. SEVERABILITY.

"If any provision of this subchapter or the application thereof to any person or circumstance is held invalid, the invalidity shall not affect other provisions or applications of this subchapter which can be given effect without regard to the invalid provision or application, and to this end the provisions of this subchapter shall be severable".

Chapter Nine

See How They Run!

A GUIDE TO KIN CARE IN OVER 100 CORPORATIONS[1]

In 1978, only 110 U.S. employers offered their employees some form of child-care assistance. In 1990, 5,400 U.S. employers offered such assistance. The number of employers offering elder-care assistance was considerably smaller. These numbers represent a small percentage of the more than 6 million employers in the United States, yet they clearly demonstrate that American companies have been responding to demographic shifts in the labor force, to the need for kin care benefits, and to a recognition of their social responsibility for kin care. That response may, in fact, benefit the company as well as its employees.

This chapter presents an alphabetized guide to what over 100 companies have been doing to help employees balance their work and family life. All of the companies recognized by *Working Mother* magazine as the best companies for working mothers in the past few years were surveyed. Other companies were randomly selected from the Fortune 500 and the Service 500, listed by *Fortune* magazine. The companies covered include publicly and privately held large corporations and small firms across all industries. Information about the kin care programs of these companies was compiled through personal interviews and from surveys, company-provided materials, and media accounts.

Some companies have very proactive kin care policies. Others have just begun to explore kin care alternatives. Their programs may suggest viable options for kin care.

Aetna Life & Casualty

Aetna Life & Casualty, one of the nation's largest insurance companies, is located in Hartford, Connecticut, and has 44,258 employees. This company, recognized in *Working Mother* magazine as a top company for working mothers, supports kin care needs in a variety of ways. It offers a family leave policy, financial aid for adoptions, a child-care and elder-care referral service, flexible work arrangements including job sharing, and an Employee Assistance Program (EAP).

American Airlines, Inc.

American Airlines, Inc., with corporate headquarters in Dallas/Fort Worth, Texas has become more active with regard to its employees' work/family concerns. In January 1988, it started First Class Academy, a child-care center located near its corporate headquarters. Having the center was a direct result of an idea suggested by a reservation sales representative. American provided the start-up capital and agreed to subsidize enrollment to ensure the center's survival. The center is owned by Wilks & McCormick, a child-care consulting firm, and is open only to employees of American. The company subsidy has ended as enrollment is currently at 205 children. Families are anxious to use the center.

American also provides day-care assistance through a Dependent Care Reimbursement Account offered through the company's flexible benefits program. Veronica Zollo, a senior analyst with the company, says that this program offers employees an opportunity to pay for day care with pretax dollars, thus saving money. Approximately 1,000 participants used the account in the first year of its implementation. A higher number of employees are expected to use it in future years.

American Bankers Insurance Group (ABIG)

American Bankers Insurance Group (ABIG), headquartered in Miami, Florida, writes insurance policies that are sold primarily through banks, savings and loan associations, finance companies, and retailers. Over 1,400 ABIG employees work in the Miami area. ABIG support programs include on-site care, part-time work, and maternity leave.

An on-site center called ABIG Child's Place serves children of employees aged six weeks to five years. Enrollment of 90 children and large waiting lists resulted in ABIG's negotiations with a wholly owned and operated child-care center—La Petite Academy. This child-care center and preschool opened in 1987 in the American Bankers Office Park. Enrollment is open to the public, but employees receive priority.

A unique component of the ABIG child-care program and a demonstration of ABIG's leadership in the kin care field is an on-site public school and after-school programs. A satellite learning center with kindergarten through grade two operates in the office park. ABIG provides the maintenance and building, while the county provides teachers and educational materials.

According to the company, "absenteeism and tardiness are almost nonexistent among participating employees." The child-care programs and the school help recruiting efforts and hold turnover at low levels.

ABIG was noted as one of the top 75 companies for working mothers in *Working Mother* magazine.

American Express Company

American Express Company, one of the world's largest travel and financial services companies, is headquartered in New York City. It has 77,000 employees and was chosen as one of *Working Mother* magazine's top 60 companies for working mothers. The company has a resource and referral service for child care and elder care, and in its New York City offices it began lunchtime seminars on work and family issues. The company also provides a Dependent Care Assistance Plan (DCAP), maternity leave, and family leave.

American Express is committed to funding and strengthening its child-care programs. It sponsored a two-year child-care study with the French-American Foundation. The study produced a report detailing the findings of an interdisciplinary team of U.S. experts who examined the widely admired French system. The company is making the report, *A Welcome for Every Child*, available to policymakers, experts, and practitioners around the country.

American Express has spent over $2.2 million in grant money for community initiatives and national awareness campaigns. The money has been spent to improve the availability, affordability, and quality of child care, primarily in American Express communities. The company is also involved in advocacy efforts to make the country aware of the need for child care and is committed to securing additional funding for this purpose.

America West Airlines, Inc.

America West Airlines, Inc. provides airline service to 60 destinations throughout the United States, Hawaii, and Canada. Based in Phoenix, America West has more than 12,000 employees. Its most significant kin care benefit is its child-care program, comprising both home-based and center-based care.

The home-based program consists of a network of family homes throughout Phoenix and Las Vegas that provide child care 24 hours a day, seven days a week. America West provides specialists who visit these homes, acting as support people and introducing creative activities for the children.

The airline provides a child-care center, accredited by the National Association for the Education of Young Children (NAEYC), and recently expanded its existing program by contract with Sunrise Preschools. Employees can choose from 12 Sunrise facilities located in the Phoenix area and use these facilities for both full-time and "drop-off" care. Michael J. Conway, president and chief operating officer of America West, says of the program: "The development of America West's child-care program is consistent with our company's overall effort to provide a high-quality working environment for our employees. . . . We anticipate that our expanded program will help alleviate the existing waiting list for child care among our employees."

The company subsidizes 25–50 percent of the cost of child care, depending on the employee's income level and on the size of the employees's family.

Other America West programs responsive to kin care needs include an Employee Assistance Program (EAP), a family leave policy, and flexible working arrangements.

Congress has recognized the quality of the America West programs by presenting the company with a Pioneer Award for its innovative employer-sponsored child-care program. The real winners of this program, however, are kids and parents. "This is the first time I've felt good about leaving my children," says Kathy Bollinger, a flight attendant and customer service representative. "The company is concerned about you and the children." America West was also noted as one of the top 75 companies for working mothers in *Working Mother* magazine.

Ameritech

Ameritech, a provider of information technologies based in Chicago, has just issued a complete Work and Family policy in an effort to increase flexibility for employees with dependent care responsibilities. Support programs include a leave of absence of up to one year for child care or the care of a seriously ill family member with a job guarantee upon return, Flexible Spending Accounts for child- and/or elder-care expenses, adoption assistance, wellness programs, a teen hot line, resource and referral services, and seminars addressing numerous issues for families.

Arthur Andersen & Co.

Arthur Andersen & Co., the world's largest accounting and management consulting firm, has headquarters in Chicago and offices around the country. The firm employs about 25,000. It has adopted a work/family program providing such benefits as maternity leave, family leave, adoption assistance (up to $2,500), part-time work for returning mothers, child- and elder-care resource and referral services, and a Dependent Care Assistance Plan (DCAP). In the tax season, it also operates a child-care center on Saturdays so that parents can work during this busy time. The idea has worked so well that six other offices, in addition to headquarters, are implementing it. Arthur Andersen was recognized as one of the top 60 companies for working mothers in *Working Mother* magazine.

Anheuser-Busch Companies, Inc.

Anheuser-Busch Companies, Inc., a diversified corporation whose subsidiaries include the world's largest brewer, is headquartered in St. Louis, Missouri. Concerned about work and family issues, the company surveyed its St. Louis employees in the early 1980s regarding their child-care needs. In 1984, Anheuser-Busch started a child-care referral service for all of its employees in the St. Louis area. The company also surveyed its other brewery locations. In 1990 a study on establishing a national referral service resulted in a recommendation that all of its breweries establish a local referral service.

Recognizing the importance of flexibility, the company recently introduced job-sharing and flextime programs in St. Louis and its other brewery locations. Anheuser-Busch continues to monitor the needs for a child-care center and is considering the adoption of a Dependent Care Assistance Plan (DCAP) should this be warranted by employee interest.

Apple Computer, Inc.

Apple Computer, Inc., located in Cupertino, California, has 8,544 employees. Recognized by *Working Mother* magazine as a top company for working mothers, Apple has excellent child-care benefits. It offers an on-site child-care center that enrolls 70 children and has a long waiting list. It is involved in finding alternative child-care arrangements for those waiting. In addition to the center, the company provides a nationwide referral service, a Dependent Care Assistance Plan (DCAP), adoption aid (up to $3,000), a $500 gift to new babies, maternity leave, personal leave policies, flextime, part-time, job sharing, and an Employee Assistance Program (EAP).

Armstrong World Industries, Inc.

Armstrong World Industries, Inc., located in Lancaster, Pennsylvania, is best known as a manufacturer and marketer of interior furnishings, including floor coverings, building products, and furniture, as well as a wide variety of specialty products for other industries.

According to Eugene Moore, director of public relations, the most significant kin care problem the company faces is a need for emergency child and/or elder care. "One can readily find day care or make other arrangements for the care of both children and the elderly in this geographic area. But what about the occasional emergency? . . . A working parent finds that his or her child is ill with chicken pox and needs a special day-care arrangement . . . or an aging parent develops an illness and is temporarily unable to travel to the usual day-care center. . . . These are typical of the situations our employees face . . . and they are the types of problems we are attempting to help them solve."

Armstrong is currently working with Metro Day Care Systems to develop a convenient emergency and sick-child/elder-care resource and referral program for employees. The program will start at headquarters. After being tested locally, the company plans to extend it to other locations.

ARCO (Atlantic Richfield Company)

ARCO (Atlantic Richfield Company), one of the country's largest oil companies, is headquartered in Los Angeles. The company has 18,511 employees. It provides many benefits that address kin care needs, including maternity leave, family leaves of absence, flextime, job sharing, personal days, a Dependent Care Assistance Plan (DCAP), referral services for child and elder care in the Los Angeles area, and an Employee Assistance Program (EAP). ARCO has been recognized as one of the top 60 companies for working mothers in *Working Mother* magazine.

Baker Hughes Incorporated

Baker Hughes Incorporated, located in Houston, Texas, has over 21,000 employees worldwide in the oil field services and process equipment industries. The company provides employees with a cafeteria benefits plan in which employees can design their individual benefit package based on personal and family circumstances. Employees can choose to use the Reimbursement Account—a Dependent Care Assistance Plan (DCAP) to pay for dependent care expenses with pretax dollars.

Bank of America

Bank of America, with corporate headquarters in San Francisco, provides a variety of family supportive programs. In October

1987, a new unit specializing in work/family issues was created within the human resources department in response to the fact that increasing numbers of employees are managing both work and dependent care responsibilities.

Among the family supportive programs provided by Bank of America are Flexible Spending Accounts to pay for dependent care expenses with pretax dollars, adoption assistance reimbursement of up to $2,000, and scholarship programs for older children. The company also provides resource and referral services for child and elder care. In addition to the standard service, employees have access to literature and videotapes relating to family health and safety as well as managing child- and elder-care responsibilities.

Bank of America is also helping improve basic community services in the child-care area through the California Child Care Initiative. Designed and launched by BankAmerica Foundation, this growing public-private partnership of scores of corporations, foundations, and governments focuses on increasing the supply of licensed, quality child care in California. It provides funds for community-based child-care resource and referral agencies to recruit and train new providers of family day care and to help them get licensed and operational. Between October 1985 and March 1990, the program generated over 2,350 new providers, making spaces available for more than 9,300 children in urban, suburban, and rural communities.

Baptist Hospital of Miami

Baptist Hospital, a major health care provider in the Miami area, operates a 513-bed hospital. It is perhaps best known, however, for its outstanding on-site child-care center, the Children's Center. "This facility provides a developmental child-care program, encouraging the growth of the child in the areas of motor skills, socioemotional growth, self-help skills, language development, audio and visual development, and cognitive skills," says director Corey Gold. Children from six weeks to six years of age are eligible. The center provides additional after-school care for older children.

The costs to employees vary from $28 per week for part-time use of the center to $66 per week for full-time use, with discounts for second children. The center also charges $2.25–2.50 per hour for day and evening baby-sitting.

Summer programs are available for school-age children. The director welcomes the participation of "surrogate grandparents" in the care-giving activities of the center.

As a sign of its commitment to the center, Baptist Hospital is currently investigating future opportunities for expansion, including intergenerational care and emergency sick care. The sick care program is being negotiated as a joint venture with ABIG in Miami and is expected to meet the emergency care needs of both organizations. Baptist Hospital was noted as one of the top 60 companies for working mothers in *Working Mother* magazine.

Barrios Technology

Barrios Technology, located in Houston, Texas, employs just 335 workers. Although small, this company was recognized by *Working Mother* magazine as one of the top 60 companies for working mothers. Part of the reason for this is that the company knows how important flexibility and concern for employees are. The firm offers a Dependent Care Assistance Plan (DCAP), maternity leave, a leave of absence policy, flextime, part-time work for returning mothers, job sharing, and a program with a local hospital to care for sick children.

Baxter Healthcare Corporation

Baxter Healthcare Corporation, located in Deerfield, Illinois, identified its employees's child-care needs through a Child Care Task Force convened in May 1989. After a thorough review of employee kin care needs, the company began implementation of the following programs in 1990: a national Child and Elder Resource and Referral Program with access to all of Baxter's 36,000 U.S. employees; an extensive family leave policy under which up to 12 weeks of leave are granted for the care of ill family members or after the birth or adoption of a child; and a sick pay policy under which employees can use their own sick days to care for sick family members.

In addition, Baxter has demonstrated its commitment to kin care by expanding other programs: adoption reimbursement up to $2,500; flexible work arrangements such as flextime, part-time, job sharing, and telecommuting; an Employee Assistance Program (EAP); and Flexible Spending Accounts.

Bell Atlantic

Bell Atlantic, headquartered in Philadelphia, employs 79,100. The company has many programs that assist employees in balancing their work and family responsibilities. These programs include a Dependent Care Assistance Plan (DCAP), a child-care resource and referral service which includes funding for the recruitment and training of child-care providers in the areas where employees work and live, a dependent care leave of absence (2–12 months), paid personal days, an Employee Assistance Program (EAP), a family care resource library (employees can call the library to have materials mailed to them), an elder-care consultation and referral service, and a joint union/management advisory committee on family care that evaluates initiatives, studies employee needs, and sponsors educational programs. In addition, Bell Atlantic conducted a company-wide family care survey during 1990 to determine how employees were currently managing the dual responsibilities of home and career. Results from the survey will be used to modify existing programs and identify other areas for family care initiatives.

Beth Israel Hospital

Beth Israel Hospital, located in Boston, is a major teaching hospital of Harvard Medical School and a constituent agency of Combined Jewish Philanthropies. The hospital employs over 4,600 persons, over 70 percent of whom are women. Long committed to assisting employees with family concerns that may affect their ability to work, the hospital has initiated many programs and policies that address kin care needs.

These programs and policies include a Dependent Care Assistance Plan (DCAP); an earned time program in which traditional sick, vacation, and holiday hours are combined to provide employees with maximum flexibility in determining the use of their paid time-off benefits; parental leave policies; an Employee Assistance Center; a dependent care information and referral service that operates through the Harvard Medical Center Office of Parenting; a Breastfeeding Support Program; employee Lunch 'N Learn Seminars on working and parenting issues; flexible scheduling, job sharing, and part-time opportunities; and a work-at-home program for clerical and typing staff (currently being piloted).

In addition, the hospital purchased 12 child-care slots at the nearby Longwood Medical Child Care Center (which has 68 slots). Currently, 13 employee children are enrolled at the center. The Beth Israel Hospital Child Care Center, managed by Bright Horizons, will open in April 1991. The center will accommodate 120 children (24 infants, 46 toddlers, and 50 preschool children). Tuition will be subsidized for employees based on a sliding scale. The weekly rates will range from $50 to $200 for infants, from $49 to $165 for toddlers, and from $33 to $130 for preschoolers.

"Employees are very appreciative of the hospital's support in these areas," says Laura Avakian, vice president of human resources. "All programs are heavily utilized, and evaluations are consistently positive. We believe we could do more than we do, and have a number of plans for further enhancement of these programs."

The Bureau of National Affairs, Inc. (BNA)

The Bureau of National Affairs, Inc., located in Washington D.C., is America's largest private publisher of human resources information. The company has been recognized nationally for its concern for work/family needs of its employees, as well as for its publications on work/family issues.

BNA and The Newspaper Guild formed a joint committee to study issues pertaining to work and family and surveyed employees about their use of current benefits and needs. The company contracts out for a child-care referral service through two local agencies for all employees in the metropolitan Washington area, including those working in area subsidiaries (McArdle Printing Company and Pike & Fischer).

BNA offers maternity, paternity, and adoption leave, and employees can use their sick leave to care for their sick children and personal or annual leave to deal with other family illness. In addition, the company provides adoption reimbursement (up to $1,000); a dependent care spending account; an Employee Assistance Plan (COPE); parenting and elder care seminars; and a work and family library.

According to Emily M. Gilreath, manager of work/life issues, the company has no set policy on part-time work or flexible hours, but supervisors and employees are encouraged to explore different options. For example, she reports that the option of a compressed four-day workweek in the Indexing Services Division, and a new pilot job-sharing program in the Editorial Department have been successful. A number of women who return from maternity leave work part-time as well.

The company is committed to improving family/work issues in the company and throughout the nation. Besides the monthly *Special Report Series on Work & Family*, the company provides a variety of information services on the subject. BNA also sponsors an annual conference on work/family issues each fall, drawing several hundred corporate human resources officials from across the company to hear speakers on policy issues and employer options.

Burlington Northern Railroad

Burlington Northern Railroad, which is spread out over 25,000 miles, 25 states, and two Canadian provinces, has over 32,000 employees who are equally spread out. According to Don Scott, vice president of human resources, among the difficulties in addressing kin care problems are the 24-hour operation of the railroad, the vast area it covers, national union contracts, and the demographics of employees. One of the ways in which the railroad helps its employees is by assisting them in negotiating group discounts at specific kin care centers.

Scott believes that "addressing child-care concerns is good business philosophy to both attract and retain quality employees." As Burlington Northern plans a new campus-style headquarters complex, facilities for child care and for possible elder care are being included in the designs. These facilities will be the railroad's first in-house test in dealing with kin care issues.

Leo Burnett U.S.A.

Leo Burnett U.S.A., an advertising firm headquartered in Chicago, employs 2,207. In addition to a leave policy, financial aid for adoption, an Employee Assistance Program (EAP), and flexible work arrangements, the firm offers three major programs that help employees better manage their work and family lives.

It has contracted with Work/Family Directions to offer the *ChildCare Resource and Referral* program and the *Elder Care Consultation and Referral* Program. Both of these comprehensive programs offer a wide range of services. Employees work with trained specialists to find the child care and/or elder care that best meets the individual's needs.

In addition, Burnett implemented *SickKid Care* in March 1990. Under this program, the firm reimburses 80 percent of the cost of care for an employee's mildly ill child (up to an annual maximum reimbursement of $500 per employee). Parents select any licensed care provider. Burnett has compiled a list of local hospital-based sick care centers and services that provide in-home care.

According to Sue Holsinger, who manages Burnett's work and family programs, "Response has been tremendous. . . . Over 350 employees have taken advantage of the services provided by the programs."

Calvert Group

The Calvert Group, a small consulting firm located in Bethesda, Maryland, recently initiated a comprehensive dependent care policy in an effort to be more responsive to the changing work force and the needs of working mothers.

Cindy Chin, employee and community relations manager, explains that the Calvert Group is committed to conducting business in a socially responsible way. To that end, it has developed a Statement of Shared Values describing the principles to which it adheres.

The provisions of the dependent care policy include five days of parental leave, a $500 baby bonus to assist in the education or care of the child, a resource library on caring for children and the elderly, brown bag informational sessions with experts in the dependent care field, and 10 dependent care "flex days" to accommodate dependent care needs through flexible working hours. These provisions supplement the company's six weeks of paid maternity leave, adoption leave, and adoption reimbursement (up to $2,000). The Calvert Group was recognized as a leader in family care policies in the August 1990 issue of *Good Housekeeping*.

Campbell Soup Company

Campbell Soup Company, headquartered in Camden, New Jersey, has 32,000 employees. The company's strong commitment to meeting work/family needs is demonstrated in a wide variety of kin care programs. These include an on-site child-care center that enrolls 110 children from infancy through kindergarten. Campbell subsidizes the costs of the center, with the parents paying $53–80 a week, depending on the age of the child. The company offers maternity leave and leave for child or elder care as well as adoption aid (up to $2,000), flextime, and job sharing. Campbell was recognized as one of the top 60 companies for working mothers in *Working Mother* magazine.

Champion International Corporation

Champion International Corporation, one of the nation's largest producers of paper and wood products, is headquartered in Stamford, Connecticut. Since 1981, it has recognized the need to assist its 21,600 employees in care-giving by providing access to licensed psychiatrists or psychologists at no cost to the employee through an Employee Assistance Program (EAP). According to Sarah Mullady, director of the program, the EAP has been very successful in "dealing with matters relating to the mental and emotional pain of dealing with aging relatives as well as other kin. . . . Family-related problems are the primary problems [brought to] the EAP."

In addition to the EAP, Champion has an on-site child-care center for children aged three months to five years. The center enrolls both the children of its employees and the children of employees at other companies. Champion subsidizes the center costs of its employees based on need. It also provides sick-child day care through *Wee Care,* a program coordinated with the EAP in the company's Hamilton, Ohio, office and Fort Hamilton–Hughes Memorial Hospital. Both mill and office employees can use this program around the clock at a cost of $3 per hour.

Champion is considering the installation of other child-care facilities on or near mill sites as needed. Other company programs supportive of kin care include a family leave policy and flexible work arrangements. Champion was noted as one of the top 60 companies for working mothers in *Working Mother* magazine.

Chevron Corporation

Chevron Corporation, headquartered in San Francisco, is one of the largest oil companies in the United States. It comprises many operating companies. Chevron currently offers several kin care programs, including a family leave policy that provides up to six months of leave to care for a newborn, a newly adopted child, or a seriously ill family member; a dependent care program that allows employees to pay for dependent care expenses on a pretax basis; and a long-term care program for retirees. (The long-term care program is private insurance that provides coverage for home health care, adult day care, and nursing home care.)

Chevron is committed to investigating additional programs, such as alternatives for sick care, to further assist its employees in family care. Adjustable work schedules (flextime) are being tried as part of a pilot program at Chevron Information Technology Company.

Chrysler Corporation

Chrysler Corporation provides several flexible benefits for kin care in addition to a child-care effort coordinated with the United Automobile Workers (UAW) union. Throughout the company, Chrysler policy provides for personal leave of absence due to serious illness in an employee's immediate family. In 1990, the company was in the process of updating its parental leave policy. It has introduced a Flexible Spending Account for paying the dependent care expenses of nonunion employees with pretax dollars.

In 1985, negotiations between Chrysler and the UAW resulted in the installation of resource and referral services at two plants, with more such services to come on board as assessments of child-care needs are completed at other company facilities.

In addition to these services, the UAW and Chrysler are jointly launching an on-site Child Care Center at the Huntsville Electronics Plant in Huntsville, Alabama, a location where serious child-care problems exist. "Not only will the center provide high-quality child care for UAW families and other Chrysler employees at the plant; it also reaffirms our role in blazing new trails to meet the changing needs of our members," said former UAW vice president Marc Stepp when he headed the union's Chrysler department. Anthony St. John, vice president of employee relations at Chrysler, notes that "[we] have worked very hard to meet employee concerns that go beyond the usual issues of wages and benefits. . . . We feel this pilot program addresses one such concern among the Huntsville work force: adequate affordable child care for working parents." The center will be open from 5 A.M. to 1 A.M., Monday through Friday. Enrollment is anticipated at 100–200 children per shift.

Citicorp-Citibank

Citicorp-Citibank, headquartered in New York, has over 89,000 employees. Corporate-wide, Citicorp addresses its employees' kin care needs by means of an extensive child-care resource and referral service and an elder-care consultation and referral service, both of which are managed and networked countrywide by Work/Family Directions in Watertown, Massachusetts.

Citicorp-Citibank also serves families through a leave policy, flexible work arrangements, and an Employee Assistance Program (EAP). In addition, the company has sponsored day-care centers at two of its major offices—the Sioux Falls, South Dakota office and the Hagerstown, Maryland office. Beginning in January 1990, Citibankers could use sick days to care for sick dependents. Citicorp-Citibank is keeping track of the reasons employees use these days to determine how it can best meet employee needs in the future.

Consolidated Edison Company of New York (Con Edison)

Consolidated Edison Company of New York (Con Edison), located in New York City, provides gas, electricity, and steam in New York City and Westchester County. It has 19,768 employees. Named one of the top 75 companies for working mothers in *Working Mother* magazine, it offers many work/family benefits.

Con Edison offers a child-care resource and referral service, provided by Child Care, Inc.; adoption benefits (up to $2,000); an emergency child-care plan that provides professional in-home care on an emergency basis when normal arrangements have fallen through (the company subsidizes 90 percent of the costs for the first 10 hours and 75 percent of the costs for additional hours); maternity leave and parental leave; a Dependent Care Assistance Plan (DCAP) for both child care and elder care; and *Eldercare*, a comprehensive handbook that includes information on how to find the best resources for meeting the needs of the elderly. It is also exploring the possibility of offering an elder-care resource and referral service in 1991.

Con Edison, along with several other New York City employers, has funded a feasibility study on vacation and holiday care for school-age children.

Corning, Inc.

Corning, Inc., located in Corning, New York, has 11,000 employees. It manufactures glass and ceramic products and also provides laboratory testing services. Corning offers its employees many kin care benefits, including maternity leave, family leaves of absence, financial aid for adoption, resource and referral services for child and elder care, a Dependent Care Assistance Plan (DCAP), and flexible working arrangements (flextime, part-time, job sharing, and telecommuting). It also funds the Children's Center, a day-care facility, and offers an Employee Assistance Program (EAP). Corning was recognized as one of the top 60 companies for working mothers in *Working Mother* magazine.

Digital Equipment Corporation

Digital Equipment Corporation, the second-largest company in the computer industry, is headquartered in Maynard, Massachusetts. It employs 125,500 worldwide. Recognized as one of the top 60 companies for working mothers in *Working Mother* magazine, Digital provides many kin care benefits. These include a resource and referral service, maternity leave, parental leave, adoption aid (up to $1,500), flextime, part-time, job sharing, and an Employee Assistance Program (EAP). In 1989, Digital surveyed its employees to determine their kin care needs. It is committed to implementing new kin care programs as warranted.

Dominion Bankshares Corporation

Dominion Bankshares Corporation, a bank holding company operating more than 300 offices in Virginia, Maryland, Tennessee, and the District of Columbia, has over 6,134 employees, 78 percent of whom are female. Dominion was the second bank in the country to offer an on-site day-care center and the first to offer infant care. Accredited by the National Association for the Education of Young Children and subsidized by the company, the day-care center, located at corporate headquarters in Roanoke, Virginia, serves 70 children aged six weeks to five years. To cover their share of the costs, parents pay weekly fees ranging from $45 to $90 with pretax dollars. The center has served as a model for other centers around the country. Warner Dalhouse, chief executive officer, says that the decision to initiate the center had no "altruistic motivation. We know, after five years of research, analysis, and wonder, that it [the day-care center] will enhance our profitability. . . . We're going to ease minds. We're going to help. And we're going to end up making more money."

In addition to the day-care center, Dominion offers a wide range of policies to support family needs, including maternity leave, adoption leave, paternity leave, illness-in-family leave, personal days, parenting seminars with videos available to assure access in all bank locations, flexible work schedules, and Flexible Spending Accounts. Dominion was noted as one of the top 60 companies for working mothers in *Working Mother* magazine.

Dow Chemical Company

Dow Chemical Company, headquartered in Midland, Michigan, employs 29,600 and is the nation's second-largest chemical company. It was recognized as one of the top 60 companies for working mothers in *Working Mother* magazine. In 1989, the company demonstrated its ongoing commitment to kin care by hiring a full-time family issues coordinator. To support families, Dow Chemical provides a resource and referral service, before- and after-school programs, a Dependent Care Assistance Plan (DCAP), maternity leave, parental leave, flextime, job sharing, and an Employee Assistance Program (EAP).

Du Pont

Du Pont, the largest U.S. chemical company, is headquartered in Wilmington, Delaware. Employing over 100,000 workers in the United States, the company has earned a reputation for supporting kin care. Their commitment is spelled out in a Work and Family statement that says, ". . . the company is committed to making changes in the workplace, and fostering changes in the community that are sensitive to the changing family unit and the increasingly diverse work force."

Du Pont has invested over $1 million in funding child care facilities over the past three years and has contributed more than $250,000 to the *Child Care Connection*, a Delaware statewide referral service started with Du Pont seed money. In July of 1990, a nationwide child care and elder care referral service was implemented. The company has surveyed and continues to survey employees to determine the greatest benefit needs and implement responsive programs. Du Pont provided the start up money for two child care facilities in addition to providing the seed money for *Sniffles 'N Sneezes* sick child care center. A 50% discount at the *Sniffles 'N Sneezes* is offered to employees for first time use. A Girl Scout's summer camp for school age children was funded by the company as well.

The company offers a six-month family leave policy for maternity, paternity, adoption, and/or serious illnesses. An option for part-time work with full benefits is offered to employees during this family leave as well as flextime and job sharing opportunities. A study on flexible work practices is currently underway with Du Pont also looking at telecommuting options and compressed work weeks. The company provides training and educational materials for managers on work/family issues through its Work Force Partnering Division. The Division is currently networking with over 35 active Work/Family committees located throughout the company. These committees assess site needs and respond with a variety of resources—parent/caregiver support groups, flexible work arrangements, and special events that encourage safety for the family. The company has been recognized as one of the top 10 companies for working mothers in *Working Mother* magazine as well as *Good Housekeeping*.

Eastman Kodak Company

Eastman Kodak Company, in Rochester, New York, has over 83,000 employees. Former chairman and chief executive officer Colby H. Chandler summed up his commitment to kin care in these words: "If we are to be numbered among the top 25 companies, we must be recognized as a superior place for women and minorities to work."

In 1986, Kodak established a task force to make recommendations on the work and family needs of its employees. The following programs were implemented as a result of this effort: family leave of up to 17 weeks for birth, adoption, or serious illness of a family member; alternative work schedules such as flextime, part-time positions, and job sharing; a nationwide child-care resource and referral program; and adoption assistance up to $2,000. In addition, Kodak has a dependent care assistance program (DCAP), a maternity leave program, and a spouse assistance program.

Through corporate funding, Kodak has helped add more than 1,000 family day-care homes to the nationwide child-care provider system. A summer camp program was pilot tested during the summer of 1990. A pilot noon-hour parenting seminar program was being conducted between November 1990 and the spring of 1991.

Kodak was noted as one of the top 60 companies for working mothers in *Working Mother* magazine.

EG & G

EG & G, a research and development manufacturing and services company headquartered in Wellesley, Massachusetts, employs 25,000. It has addressed the child-care and elder-care concerns of its employees through a resource and referral program for child care and elder care that is included in a comprehensive Employee Assistance Program (EAP). Employees can work with counselors of the EAP on family problems and with resource specialists in finding care providers to meet their needs. Offices of the EAP have been sited throughout New England and the rest of the country so that employees can choose a conveniently located EAP office.

Electronic Data Systems Corporation (EDS)

Electronic Data Systems Corporation (EDS), a leader in the information technology services industry, is headquartered in Plano, Texas, a suburb of Dallas, and has operations in 27 countries. The firm recently addressed the need for kin care in its new *ChildCare Program.*

The program consists of two phases. The first phase, managed by the Partnership Group, Inc., is called the *ChildCare Solution.* This service provides a national network of specialists who, coordinating with local agencies, help EDS employees around the country find child-care providers.

The second phase, *The ChildCare Voucher Program,* allows pretax payroll contributions to be set aside for child-care expenses. Employees then receive four vouchers per month to give to their child-care providers as payment. Child-care providers may accept the vouchers, or parents can redeem the vouchers through the Voucher Corporation and pay the providers directly.

In addition to these programs, EDS has an active Education Outreach program. Seminars, educational pamphlets, and such books as *The Power of Positive Students,* by Dr. William Mitchell, are available to parents. Working with the community, EDS also contributes funds to Practical Parenting Education, a support program offering seminars on parenting and family problems. Says Cindy Canevaro, manager of the program, "We want our employees to take an active role in their children's education, and we want to give them the tools to make their participation positive."

Exxon Company, U.S.A.

Exxon Company, U.S.A., headquartered in Houston, Texas, has implemented a number of programs to help meet the work and family needs of its employees.

In addition to a nationwide resource and referral program managed by Work/Family Directions, the company has provided funds for the development of quality child-care services in the areas where its employees are located. It also provides educational seminars on child-care issues for its employees. Exxon has recognized the needs of mildly ill children. In certain areas, it has worked with local hospitals and caregivers to provide sick care.

Other Exxon kin care policies include six-month pregnancy leaves, part-time work, adjustable work hours, and pretax dependent care Reimbursement Accounts. In a recent survey, half of the respondents indicated that their opinion of Exxon as a place to work had improved as a result of its kin care programs and policies. Over 90 percent of the users of the resource and referral program evaluated it as helpful and would use it again if needed. One single parent needed day care for his nine-year-old son, who spent the summer with him. "In addition to getting referrals, the counselor also sent me a checklist for use in making evaluations during my search. . . . Happily, I found the center I was looking for, and my son was happy with it too."

Fannie Mae

Fannie Mae, located in Washington, D.C., is the major underwriter for Federal Housing Administration (FHA) home loans. It has approximately 1,400 employees.

The company initiated a unique program for providing emergency child care when an employee's regular child-care arrangements break down. Housed on the lobby level of the building Fannie Mae occupies, a child-care center is available Monday through Friday for children aged six months through 10 years. According to Julie Goldstein, the center's full-time manager, employees are very pleased with the service. "We have had an average of 10 children per day and have only had two days without children since opening in May 1990." The center is licensed for 20 children and emergency care only. Employees understand that the fundamental rule on the use of the center is that the center can succeed if it is used only when an employee's regular child-care arrangements are unavailable.

Federal Express

Federal Express, headquartered in Memphis, Tennessee, has over 90,000 employees nationwide. The company's commitment to kin care is perhaps best demonstrated by the existence of its corporate Taskforce on Work/Family Issues, which meets regularly to identify issues important to employees. Janice Frazier-Scott, senior personnel administration adviser, says that "through this type of employee participation, we hope to provide proactive and relevant programs for our employees and their families."

Employees of Federal Express can use their Flexible Spending Accounts to pay for dependent care expenses with pretax dollars. In addition, Federal Express has secured national discounts from a day-care provider with locations throughout the United States. The company also offers excellent health benefits and paid disability, flexible working arrangements, an Employee Assistance Program (EAP), MedQuest (a personal counseling program for families regarding any medical or health questions), and extensive part-time work schedules.

Fel-Pro, Inc.

Fel-Pro, Inc. is one of the world's largest manufacturers and marketers of automotive and industrial gaskets. Over 2,000 employees work in the company's manufacturing and office complex in Skokie, Illinois. Cochairmen emeriti Elliot Lehman and Lewis C. Weinberg believe that "it's good business to work closely with your people, pay them well, and make desirable benefits available to them. In return, you must obtain from your employees a high level of performance."

Fel-Pro's kin care benefits include maternity leave, a summer day camp for over 300 children, a subsidized day-care center accommodating over 45 children aged two to six, free psychological and family counseling, a referral service for elder care, scholarships, subsidized tutoring for children with learning problems, personal leaves of absence, up to $2,500 for adoption expenses, and a $1,000 Treasury security as a gift for having or adopting a new baby. (New parents also receive a pair of baby shoes engraved with the baby's name and date of birth.)

The Fel-Pro Day Care Center, opened in 1983, is a model for other corporate kin care centers around the country. Housed in its own building adjacent to the main plant, a visitor is struck by how special this center really is. (I was sorry my daughter wasn't with me as I toured the grounds—she would have had a wonderful time.) Scott Mies, director of the center, was given a free hand in designing, staffing, and outfitting the center. "We have rounded corners throughout to prevent children from hurting themselves. The architect and I worked closely together to do things like that." Parents pay $80 a week for day care, with the company subsidizing the remainder of the day-care costs.

Paul Lehman, Fel-Pro president, argues that chief executive officers "often hide behind the bottom line in choosing not to support family care. . . . [I feel] that companies need to take a risk—it's good for the family and good for the community! At Fel-Pro, it's also good for the company." Bob O'Keefe, vice president of human resources, notes that "our absenteeism is down, turnover low, and productivity up, thanks to our employee benefits." In 1989 and 1990, Fel-Pro was noted as one of the top 10 companies for working mothers in *Working Mother* magazine.

First Atlanta

First Atlanta, one of the top three commercial banks in Georgia, has 131 offices and 5,300 employees. The bank meets its employees' child-care needs with a subsidized on-site center that charges parents just $300 a month for infants and $250 a month for preschoolers. It also sponsors a downtown child-care center that is operated jointly by a consortium of Atlanta businesses. In addition to the centers, the bank offers its employees a resource and referral service, a Dependent Care Assistance Plan (DCAP), maternity leave, a leave of absence policy, and part-time work opportunities. First Atlanta was recognized as one of the top 60 companies for working mothers in *Working Mother* magazine.

Gannett Company

Gannett Company, headquartered in Arlington, Virginia, runs the nation's largest chain of newspapers and owns TV stations, radio stations, and an advertising firm. Kin care programs and policies such as resource and referral services, maternity leave, a leave of absence policy, a Dependent Care Assistance Plan (DCAP), adoption aid (up to $2,500), flextime, part-time, job sharing, and telecommuting led *Working Mother* magazine to recognize this company as one of the top 75 companies for working mothers in 1990. Gannett has also opened a near-site community child-care center near its Arlington headquarters.

Genentech, Inc.

Genentech, Inc., located in South San Francisco, California, develops drugs based on recombinant DNA technology. The company, which has 1,820 employees, was recognized by *Working Mother* magazine as one of the top 75 companies for working mothers in 1990. In 1989, Genentech opened its child-care center, *2nd Generation*, which enrolls more than 160 children of employees and has the capacity to enroll up to 225 children. The company subsidizes the center, with employees paying $390 for toddlers and $490 for infants monthly. In addition to the center, Genentech offers an Employee Assistance Program (EAP); resource and referral services for elder care; a Dependent Care Assistance Plan (DCAP); one share of stock as a gift to new babies; maternity leave; leaves of absence; and flextime, part-time, and job-sharing work arrangements.

General Mills, Inc.

General Mills, Inc., one of the nation's largest food companies, has over 95,000 employees. Its commitment to families is perhaps best noted by looking at its philanthropic contributions, which now top $10 million per year and include substantial amounts to train child-care providers for children with special needs (such as handicapped, disadvantaged, or abused children).

The kin care benefits that General Mills offers its employees include long-term care insurance for care received at home, adult day care, respite care, and nursing home care; a Dependent Care Assistance Plan (DCAP); a New Parents Support Group, which meets monthly to provide information and emotional support to new working parents; both child-care and elder-care resource and referral services; an information service on options for sick-child care; adoption assistance of up to $1,500; an Employee Assistance Program (EAP); maternity leave; and personal leaves of absence.

In addition, a Dependent Care Awareness Council made up of a group of General Mills employees meets regularly to increase awareness of work and family issues. General Mills was noted as one of the top 60 companies for working mothers in *Working Mother* magazine.

Grieco Brothers, Inc.

Grieco Brothers, Inc. makes clothing sold under the Southwick label. Located in Lawrence, Massachusetts, the firm employs 650. Grieco and another Lawrence company, Polo Clothing, provided start-up funds that, along with the contributions of union members, made it possible to open the *Merrimack River Community Child Care Center* in the Grieco factory. Grieco subsidizes this day-care center, which enrolls 85 children of its employees. Children from the community make up 50% of the enrollees. Parents pay from $107 to $141 a week. The state subsidizes these charges based on income. Grieco also offers a Dependent Care Assistance Plan (DCAP), maternity leave, family leaves, part-time opportunities, an Employee Assistance Program (EAP), and a resource and referral program. In 1990, it was recognized as one of the top 75 companies for working mothers in *Working Mother* magazine.

Group 243 Incorporated

Group 243 Incorporated, an advertising and design firm located in Ann Arbor, Michigan, was recognized as one of the top 75 companies for working mothers in *Working Mother* magazine. With just 96 employees, the firm is strongly committed to kin care. In considering the options for managing work and family, it decided to assume an active role and in 1983 opened its doors to *The Carriage House Nursery*. The center enrolls children from infancy through kindergarten, and the cost ($100–120 per week) is subsidized by Group 243 Incorporated. The firm also has a maternity leave, and its employees can negotiate for leaves of absence. Parent seminars and programs are conducted regularly, and alternative work options are available.

According to the firm, the child-care center is making good business sense as well as helping employees meet their work/family needs. "Employee satisfaction and morale have been positively influenced. Productivity, while often difficult to measure, is higher, recruitment is easier, and every department reports that turnover and absenteeism are down."

Grumman Corporation

Grumman Corporation, headquartered in Bethpage, New York, is a member of a consortium of Long Island companies that are combining their resources to expand the availability of affordable, accessible, high-quality child and elder care in the Long Island area.

In 1988, Grumman, along with the other companies in the consortium, launched the *Corporate Initiative for Child Care/Elder Care on Long Island.* These companies focused on four critical needs of their employees and the community: more trained providers of family day care; emergency day care; "one stop" sources for elder-care information and case management; and expanded infant and toddler day-care centers.

The advisory board of the *Corporate Initiative for Child Care/Elder Care* on Long Island, chaired by Judith Sanders of Grumman Corporation, has funded training programs for providers of family day care that will result in direct openings for children. "The board recommended the family day-care training program for initial funding because we believe it will improve the quantity and quality of day care (80 slots) on Long Island and improve the status of family day-care providers." The board has also recommended funding for programs meeting the other needs noted above.

The initiative is an ongoing effort; future funding will incorporate families and the community. In addition to Grumman, members of the consortium include AIL System, Inc.; Ariel Graphics; Bank of Smithtown; CMP; General Instruments, Inc.; Hazeltine; IBM; Lilco; Lloyd Creative Temps, Inc.; Long Island Employment

Assistance Programs (EAP's); Long Island Savings Bank; Lumex; N/A-Com Microwave Power Devices, Inc.; National Westminster Bank, USA; Newsday; Nikon; Northstar Bank; Olympus Corporation; and Record Newspapers.

G.T. Water Products, Inc.

G.T. Water Products, Inc., located in Moorpark, California, makes drain-cleaning devices for the plumbing industry. Employing only 29, this small firm is strongly committed to kin care. Recognized as one of the top 60 companies for working mothers in *Working Mother* magazine, it offers a primary school licensed by the state of California. The one-room school has a student population of 14, including the two children of George Tash, founder and president of G.T. Water Products. The firm also gives maternity leave and allows part-time work for returning mothers. It is flexible in giving time off for emergencies or medical reasons.

Hallmark Corporation

Hallmark Corporation, the world's largest greeting card company, is located in Kansas City, Missouri, and has over 15,000 employees.

Family Care Choices is its primary kin care program, and according to Adrienne Lallo, in the Public Affairs and Communications Department, quarterly follow-up surveys of employees using the program suggest a 100 percent satisfaction rating. The program operates as a resource and referral service for both child care and elder care. For elder care, employees speak with geriatric specialists who assess employees' needs and provide referrals, options, and counseling.

In 1987, Hallmark opened the Family Resource Center at corporate headquarters. At this center, employees can meet, share family care experiences, and find brochures, books, and videos on a wide range of family care subjects. Lunchtime seminars are presented on related topics.

Corporate contributions and the Hall family foundations support community kin care efforts by contributing financially to programs that recruit and train quality caregivers. Other Hallmark benefits to employees include a Dependent Care Assistance

Plan that is offered through the flexible benefits plan, parental leaves, flexible work arrangements, a Personal Assistance Program (a counseling service similar to an Employee Assistance Program), and job sharing.

The Work and Family Services Department coordinates a Job Share Clearinghouse that an employee can use to research the possibility of sharing a single full-time position with another employee on a part-time basis. This program also supports and assists employees and managers in creating job share arrangements.

In 1990, for the fifth consecutive year, Hallmark Corporation was noted as being one of the best companies for working mothers in *Working Mother* magazine.

John Hancock Mutual Life Insurance Company

John Hancock Mutual Life Insurance Company, headquartered in Boston, is strongly committed to kin care, as evidenced in its recently implemented corporate statement on family care issues. An excerpt from this statement demonstrates the high level of its commitment: "Recognizing that employees have responsibilities to their families as well as to their jobs, John Hancock will endeavor to provide an environment and policies that are supportive to our employees for achieving their own necessary balance between work and family issues."

The company has a variety of programs and policies that address kin care needs. For flexibility, it offers flextime, family care days, family emergency time, and personal leave.

In the area of child care, John Hancock offers a resource and referral service through an arrangement with The Child Care Resource Center (CCRC); *Kids-to-Go,* a program that provides activities for school-age children on school holidays and vacations; Summer Care Fair, which parents can attend to learn about children's summer programs, camps, and so on; *WarmLine,* a program through which employees can call home to check on their children; and the *John Hancock Child Care Center,* a day-care center enrolling 100 children. The center plans to expand to 200 slots over time. Children are eligible for enrollment from infancy through kindergarten. John Hancock also provides financial support to two local nonprofit child-care centers and helps maintain a sliding fee scale for families unable to afford the full cost of care. John Hancock employees are accommodated whenever possible.

In the area of elder care, John Hancock in partnership with the nonprofit Family Service of Greater Boston Agency and its Service for Older People, established the *Elder Care Access Program.* This program provides counseling, resources, and referrals to employees who are managing elder-care concerns.

In addition to these programs, John Hancock offers a Flexible Spending Account, a Dependent Care Assistance Plan (DCAP), an Employee Assistance Program (EAP), a Psychological Services Program, reimbursements for family care expenses when business needs dictate travel, leaves of absence, adoption benefits (up to $2,000), and manager training workshops on how to be supportive in dealing with employees on family care issues. The company has hired a family care consultant to coordinate programs, research family care activities, and act as an advocate on family issues.

As Diane Capstaff, senior vice president of human resources, says, "Even though we personally may not feel the burden of child care or elder parents, we work with people each day who do. We want to work with the best-qualified and most productive people that we can. To the extent that we can put some policies and programs in place that will assist our employees in being more productive, we are all winners."

Hasbro, Inc.

Hasbro, Inc., a leading toy manufacturer headquartered in Pawtucket, Rhode Island, recently implemented a child-care program called *Kid Care.* Alan Hassenfeld, chairman and chief executive officer, writes that he is "deeply committed to working side by side with Hasbro's parents for the best in child care at an affordable cost."

Kid Care, a network of over 35 child-care centers and in-home care providers throughout Rhode Island and nearby Massachusetts, provides quality care to the infant, preschool, and school-age children of Hasbro employees. The company subsidizes part of the costs of this care based on family income and the number of family members. Hasbro employees get priority for enrollment in the network. The centers and in-home care providers are affiliates of a network established by the YMCA of Pawtucket, Inc. and are fully licensed. Hasbro employees can use a voucher system to pay the subsidized portion of the costs.

In addition to regular day care, the *Kid Care* program includes after-school care for children aged 5–13, care on school holidays, and qualified summer day camp programs.

An advisory committee initiated by Hasbro monitors the *Kid Care* program on an ongoing basis and addresses the concerns of participants.

Hercules, Incorporated

Hercules, Incorporated, headquartered in Wilmington, Delaware, has a task force that is currently developing a work and family program designed to coordinate present programs and make recommendations for new ways of helping employees balance their work and family obligations.

Hercules has an ongoing Employee Assistance Program (EAP) that is managed by an outside provider, a child-care resource and referral program that is provided through *Child Care Connection*, and a Dependent Care Assistance Plan (DCAP) that Hercules offers through its flexible benefits program. Under the company's family leave policy, employees are given an extended leave of absence for personal needs whenever possible.

At the end of 1990, Hercules was developing the following programs and anticipating their implementation within the next three to four months: an adoption assistance program (up to $2,000), an emergency care program using approved providers to help working parents with sick children (the company would subsidize the cost), and an extended family leave policy applying to specific family concerns.

Hershey Foods Corporation

Hershey Foods Corporation, headquartered in Hershey, Pennsylvania, has over 11,000 employees. It has made "a concerted effort to monitor workplace trends and introduce work/family supportive programs," according to Eleanor S. Gathany, work force diversity director.

A near-site child-care center serves the children of both employees and nonemployees—infants, toddlers, and preschoolers.

The center is managed by an outside child-care provider, and Hershey provides in-kind services. In 1990, 33 children were being served. A larger day-care facility will provide child care near the new corporate facilities now under construction. The company expects to open the center in 1992. Gathany notes that "employees/parents have told us they have an enhanced comfort level knowing their child is nearby. The opportunity to share lunch or a walk with the child, as well as being in a position to deal with child emergencies, has improved morale and job satisfaction."

In addition to the center, Hershey offers employees an Employee Assistance Program (EAP), flexible working arrangements, a child-care referral system, and a Reimbursement Account for dependent care (a DCAP) through its flexible benefits package. Through ongoing dialogue and formal meetings with parent groups, the company and kin care providers help meet the needs of employees and their children.

Hewitt Associates

Hewitt Associates, headquartered in Lincolnshire, Illinois, designs compensation and benefit programs for companies around the country. The company has a full-time family resource consultant to help its 2,600 employees meet their kin care needs. The benefits include an on-site day-care center, reimbursement of baby-sitting costs for employees working late or traveling, financial aid for adoption (up to $2,500), maternity leave, parental leave, resource and referral services for elder and child care, a Dependent Care Assistance Plan (DCAP), flextime and part-time work, and an Employee Assistance Program (EAP). Hewitt Associates was recognized as one of the top 60 companies for working mothers in *Working Mother* magazine.

Hewlett-Packard Company

Hewlett-Packard Company, headquartered in Palo Alto, California, employs 59,456 around the country. It manufactures computers and other electronic equipment throughout the world. Recognized as one of the top 60 companies for working mothers in *Working Mother* magazine, Hewlett-Packard provides a wide variety of benefits. It offers local referral services and/or direct child-care benefits, depending on the locality; maternity leave; a leave of absence policy; flextime, part-time, and job sharing; and a Dependent Care Assistance Plan (DCAP).

Hill, Holliday, Conners, Cosmopulus

Hill, Holliday, Conners, Cosmopulus, one of the largest advertising agencies in the country, employs 411 in Boston. Recognized as one of the top 60 companies for working mothers in *Working Mother* magazine, it offers many kin care benefits. These include maternity leave, financial aid for adoption, flexible working arrangements, an Employee Assistance Program (EAP), and a near-site child-care center that enrolls 27 children of employees from infancy through the preschool years. The caregivers for these children are full-time teachers with teaching assistants.

Hoechst Celanese Corporation

Hoechst Celanese Corporation, a chemical company, is head-quartered in Somerville, New Jersey. Ernie Drew, president and chief executive officer, outlined the company's new dependent care programs in a letter to employees. "As part of our commitment to our employees' development, we need to provide a work environment that is more flexible in responding to family needs. By reducing the stress and pressures involved in balancing work and family responsibilities, these new programs will allow employees to be more productive and freer to pursue their career goals."

The programs include a dependent care leave policy, educational sessions for supervisors on the importance of being responsive to family issues, funding for programs that increase the quantity or improve the quality of day-care centers in the communities where employees live and work, and a resource and referral service for both child and elder care.

The programs were initiated after a corporate-wide dependent care quality action team (QAT) surveyed Hoechst employees about their needs and reviewed the programs and policies of other companies.

Hoffmann-La Roche, Inc.

Hoffmann-La Roche, Inc., maker of prescription drugs, vitamins, and diagnostic products, is headquartered in Nutley, New Jersey, and employs 14,300 around the country. This company opened its on-site child care center in 1980, enrolling 60 children, and is expanding the center to accommodate 120. It subsidizes part of the costs ($1,000 per child per year), with parents paying about $365 a month. The company also offers maternity leave, parental leaves, resource and referral services, personal leaves, flextime, part-time, and job sharing, as well as a women's support group. Hoffmann-La Roche was recognized as one of the top 60 companies for working mothers in *Working Mother* magazine.

Home Box Office, Inc. (HBO)

Home Box Office, Inc. (HBO), headquartered in New York City, has initiated its Work and Family Life Program to address kin care concerns. According to Nancy Platt, a human resources associate at the company, "Feedback from employees and managers alike has been very positive. . . . we continue to look at the development of new initiatives to further help all our employees balance their complicated lives."

Kin care programs at HBO include a resource and referral service for child and elder care, work and family lunchtime seminars, support groups, a Work & Family Life Resource Center, a Dependent Care Assistance Plan (DCAP), adoption assistance (up to $2,100), parental leave, flextime, part-time work, job sharing, and work-at-home opportunities. In addition to these programs, HBO provides an emergency child-care service that furnishes in-home child care for an employee's child when the child is mildly ill, regular care is unavailable, or the employee must make an unexpected business trip. The company is also one of a group of New York City employers that are working together to address employees' work and family concerns.

Honeywell, Inc.

Honeywell, Inc., headquartered in Minneapolis, Minnesota, offers a variety of work and family programs. These programs serve the more than 10,000 Honeywell employees in the Minneapolis area; several of the programs are offered to Honeywell's 9,000 employees in Phoenix, Arizona, and to the 2,000 employees in its Clearwater, Florida offices.

The programs include a flextime policy, job sharing, part-time employment, a Dependent Care Assistance Plan (DCAP), an adoption assistance program (up to $1,000), a spouse career assistance program that helps pay for unavoidable child-care expenses resulting from relocation, an Employee Assistance Program (EAP), a childbirth preparation class subsidy program, special parking for pregnant employees, a flexible unpaid family leave of absence policy, and a personal paid leave of absence (60 days) for the care of a seriously ill dependent.

In addition to these programs, Honeywell operates a Child Care Information network, a resource and referral service for child care, and a discount program for child care with 10 participating providers in Phoenix and 4 in Minneapolis. The Phoenix network also supplies elder-care referrals. A program subsidizing sick-child care gives employees the option of working when a child is mildly ill. Honeywell will subsidize 80 percent of the cost of sick-child care in the home or at a center. Honeywell's headquarters in Minneapolis are currently exploring the possibility of modeling an elder-care referral service, already available in Phoenix, after the successful child-care program.

Household International, Inc.

Household International, Inc., a $27 billion financial service company headquartered in Prospect Heights, Illinois, is committed to helping parents manage their work and family responsibilities. It is currently piloting a resource and referral service, *Child Care Connection*, to its employees in the Chicagoland area. The company decided to offer a resource and referral service after exploring a variety of alternatives that would provide child-care assistance to its employees and help it recruit potential employees. Given Household International's numerous worldwide locations, the resource & referral program was the most appropriate option, according to the employee assistance coordinator.

Employee response has been limited so far, yet employees are happy with the program. To maintain program awareness—a critical factor—a full-blown market campaign has been developed. Children enter a contest in which they draw their parents at work; fliers and brochures are distributed; and many in-house publications are disseminated.

The company is pleased with the results so far; staff costs are absent, the only real costs being the program coordinator's salary and incidental costs for in-house advertising.

IBM (International Business Machines Corporation)

IBM (International Business Machines Corporation), headquartered in Purchase, New York, employs over 206,000 nationwide. The company is known for its extensive employee benefits. An example of its commitment to kin care is its appropriation of $25 million for a Dependent Care Initiative that provides funds for elder-care and child-care projects in communities where IBM employees live and work.

IBM provides its employees with one of the most extensive child- and elder-care resource and referral services in the nation. The elder-care referral services, the first of its kind provided by an American company, is run through a network of 175 community-based agencies and administered by Work/Family Elder Directions, Inc. in Watertown, Massachusetts. Employees can contact the particular agency in the geographic area where the elder relative lives. Many employees find this critical since 54 percent of the callers live 100 miles away and 21 percent live 1,000 miles away from the elder relative. According to Jim Smith, an IBM spokesperson, the single most important benefit for those using the service is in-depth, personalized counseling about elder-care issues. By October 1990, 16,000 employees, retirees, and spouses had used the program to find care for 15,000 people. Of the employees surveyed, 91 percent reported the service as satisfactory.

The IBM Child Care Referral Service, administered by Work/Family Directions, uses a nationwide network of 250 community-based resource and referral offices and consultants. Since its inception, more than 43,000 employees have requested referrals for 50,000 children. Of the employees using the service, 85 percent said it was helpful or very helpful and 92 percent said they would use it again.

Among the other IBM programs that help meet kin care needs are up to three years of unpaid leaves of absence, with part-time work available; adoption aid (up to $2,500); flexible work arrangements that include flextime and work-at-home opportunities; work, family, and health education seminars; an Employee Assistance Program (EAP); and special care for children.

IBM's commitment to employee and family programs was recently recognized. On September 19, 1990, Walton E. Burdick, IBM senior vice president, was in Washington to receive one of the inaugural Lift America awards established by Elizabeth Dole, then secretary of labor, to recognize innovative and successful employee programs that improve the quality of the work force. Accepting the award from Secretary Dole, Burdick commented, "Our work/life programs represent an investment in the long-term economic and competitive health of our business. The payoff is a talented, dedicated work force that contributes significantly to our business objectives." IBM spokesperson Jim Smith declared that "we will continue to look for new ways to help our employees balance their work and family life. In 1990, IBM was also noted as being one of the top 10 companies for working mothers in *Working Mother* magazine, named one of *Good Housekeeping*'s top 69 companies for working mothers, and given the National Child Care Action Campaign's Corporate Caring award for its programs to help stimulate the supply and increase the quality of child care nationwide.

Johnson & Johnson

Johnson & Johnson, with corporate offices in New Brunswick, New Jersey, has over 33,000 employees. Along with its family of companies, subsidiaries in all facets of the health care industry, it is deeply committed to kin care. In recognizing this commitment, its corporate credo was expanded to include the words, "We must be mindful of ways to help our employees fulfill their family responsibilities."

In early 1989, Johnson & Johnson launched a Work and Family Initiative as a comprehensive effort consisting of new policies, programs, and services to help employees balance their work and family responsibilities.

The *Elder Care Consultation and Referral Service* is administered by Work/Family Elder Directions, Inc., which has contracted with 200 community-based organizations nationwide. The *Child Care*

Resource and Referral Service, administered by Work/Family Directions, contracts with community-based child-care resource and referral agencies to help parents find local child-care providers. Johnson & Johnson has also opened an on-site child-care center in New Brunswick and is committed to opening others at appropriate facilities.

In addition to these programs, other areas covered in the Work and Family Initiative are manager and supervisor training designed to increase sensitivity to work and family issues, family care leaves, family care absences for emergency care, alternative work arrangements, an Employee Assistance Program (EAP), a Dependent Care Assistance Account (DCAP) through the flexible benefits program, adoption benefits (up to $2,000), and a long-term care insurance plan covering nursing and custodial services for people unable to care for themselves.

Melvin L. Benjamin, director of work and family, indicates that Johnson & Johnson programs are just a beginning: "The Work and Family Initiative, coupled with our strong Live for Life Assistance and Wellness program, . . . is just the beginning of a cultural change that will create a new and innovative management/employee partnership—one that will enrich the lives of its employees while at the same time strengthening Johnson & Johnson's business."

The company was selected as one of the 60 best companies for working mothers in *Working Mother* magazine.

S. C. Johnson & Son, Inc.

S. C. Johnson & Son, Inc., better known as the S. C. Johnson Wax Company and for its household products (Pledge, Raid, and others), is located in Racine, Wisconsin. This firm has a reputation for supportive family policies. Its decision to sponsor a near-site day-care center was made as a result of a 1984 employee survey. The center offers full day care from 6:30 A.M. to 6 P.M. for children aged 2–6. Half-day programs are also available. The center includes before- and after-kindergarten care, after-school programs for grades 1–6, a full-day kindergarten program, and a summer day camp for children aged 7–12. The company's new day care facility will open in the summer of 1991. It will accommodate over 200 children including infants.

S. C. Johnson & Son has been recognized as a top company for working mothers in *Working Mother* magazine and has received awards from the Congressional Caucus for Women's Issues for its employer-sponsored programs.

Kellogg Company

Kellogg Company, with headquarters in Battle Creek, Michigan, is probably best known for its cereals and other food products. The Kellogg philosophy continues to be centered on "people," according to William E. LaMothe, chairman of the board and chief executive officer.

Programs responsive to employee kin care needs include maternity leave, parental leave, flextime, job sharing at corporate headquarters, and counseling and referral programs through an Employee Assistance Program (EAP). The EAP was recently expanded to include counseling services to ease the transition to child care by helping parents locate licensed facilities for family home care, group care, and temporary sick care and books/resource materials about child care.

In April 1988, Kellogg developed a workbook for working parents that contained a wealth of information on making child-care choices. In 1990, it completed an elder-care workbook that will help employees deal with issues facing their aging relatives. The company works with community groups to assess community resources and needs related to child care. It sent a dependent care survey to all of its employees to assess their kin care needs and assist the company in its future planning.

Lancaster Laboratories

Lancaster Laboratories, one of the nation's leading independent testing laboratories for the environmental, foods, and pharmaceuticals fields, employs 400 in Lancaster, Pennsylvania.

In 1986, an on-site child-care center with a capacity of 29 children was opened by the company's founder, Dr. Earl H. Hess. The need for a larger center grew, and the company built expanded facilities to care for 112 children. The center is on the company's premises but is operated by an independent contractor. Employees get discounts on the tuition that range from $51 per week for preschoolers to $72 per week for infants.

The benefits have been wonderful, comments Margaret Stoltzfus, human resources coordinator. "Since our program has been in place, only 3 new mothers from a total of 42 chose not to return to work. Having on-site care has helped us retain some of the finest scientific talent in the nation." One benefit that surprised the company has been the increased positive public relations that the center has brought. Stoltzfus reports that local and national media attention has been significant. Carol Miller, vice president of human resources, was named 1990 Working Mother of the Year by *Working Mother* magazine, and Lancaster Laboratories was noted as being one of the 60 best companies for working mothers by the same magazine.

The company is currently assessing the need for elder care. In October 1991, it distributed a questionnaire asking employees to assess their needs for the care of their older relatives. "If the results show a need, we will be starting the program-planning process all over again, this time for elder care," says Stoltzfus.

Levi Strauss & Co.

Levi Strauss & Co., with headquarters in San Francisco, employs 32,000 worldwide. The company's kin care philosophy is best summed up by Donna Goya, senior vice president of corporate personnel, in these words: "To give our employees more choices and more influence, we will focus on human needs and be empathetic, flexible, optimistic, and creative. 'Why not?' will be our most common phrase."

Levi Strauss programs responsive to employee needs include child-care leave following birth or adoption; sick leave to care for ill dependents (can be taken in hourly increments for doctor appointments, etc.); flextime, part-time, and job-sharing arrangements; a Dependent Care Assistance Plan (DCAP); and an Employee Assistance Program (EAP) that provides informal assistance in locating child care, noontime educational programs, and a parenting resource library of books, audiotapes, and videotapes.

The company has also supported community kin care efforts by providing grants to organizations that provide child care and/or programs in which employees are involved as volunteers.

Lincoln National Corporation

Lincoln National Corporation, a major insurance company with over 12,000 employees, 4,400 of whom work in the Fort Wayne, Indiana home office, began its Work/Family Programs with its in-house Child Care Resource and Referral Services. The programs have expanded significantly and are all run in-house by Madeline Baker, the company's full-time, professional child-care administrator (a working mom too).

Among the kin care programs recently adopted by Lincoln are elder-care services, which include monthly lunchtime support networks for elder-caring employees as well as quarterly seminars on aging issues, and a Family Resource Exchange Expo, at which a wide range of community resources is offered by vendor/organization participants that provide services and programs in the area of family issues.

Other Lincoln kin care programs include a lending resource library on elder-care and child-care issues; lunchtime support groups; a bimonthly newsletter; an annual Child Care Fair; a summer day camp (contracted with the local YMCA); recruitment, training, counseling, and other technical services for care providers; parental leave policies; financial aid for adoption; flexible work arrangements; and an Employee Assistance Program (EAP).

According to Baker, "We have received several national recognitions on our child-care resource-referral service, and it served as a foundation for expanding the components to include other work/family issues. . . . Lincoln is strongly committed to providing those 'family friendly' benefits which relate to sound business principles." For example, the company is currently exploring the following: addressing the "affordability" issue by providing direct subsidies, looking for ways to enhance resource and referral by exploring consortium care or partnership alternatives for sick-child care, and making the part-time position of assistant to Baker a full-time position so as to better meet employees' needs.

A unique benefit that points to the innovativeness of Lincoln's programs is help from a care provider who directs a "house sitting" program. A temporary in-home care provider comes into an employee's house while the employee travels for the company. This caregiver watches over the house, feeds pets, cares for children overnight, and so on. In addition, if an employee selects an in-home care provider to meet child-care needs, Baker works with the employee in writing the "customized classified ad," picks up the cost (to $75), and offers assistance in the interviewing process.

Lincoln National Corporation was recognized as a top company for working mothers in *Working Mother* magazine.

Lost Arrow Corporation

Lost Arrow Corporation, located in Ventura, California, makes mountain climbing gear and clothes under the Patagonia label. Employing 473, the company is committed to meeting its employees' work/family needs. Founder Yvon Chouinard funded the Great Pacific Child Development Center, which provides care for 82 children at two sites. The center also offers an accredited kindergarten and after-school programs for children to age 14. According to Chouinard, "The day-care center is a profit center in my mind. It keeps 5 to 10 people a year from having to quit. That saves us a lot of money."

Lost Arrow also offers maternity leave, flextime, and job sharing. It was recognized as one of the top 60 companies for working mothers in *Working Mother* magazine.

McDonnell Douglas Corporation

McDonnell Douglas Corporation, one of the major aerospace companies, is headquartered in St. Louis, Missouri, and is a major employer in the St. Louis area.

MCCARE, the company's child-care center, is organized to "provide a quality early childhood program with extended day care which addresses the needs of very young children of employees," says Steve Zwolak, director of the center. According to Zwolak, the MCCARE program emphasizes early childhood development, and quality is the number one concern. Zwolak works closely with the parents to develop the best possible atmosphere for the children. (Chapter 7 contains the MCCARE start-up story.)

MCCARE enrolls 233 children from six weeks of age through kindergarten. It also runs a school-age summer camp for children of employees from kindergarten through grade 6. Tuition is paid through payroll deduction. It ranges from $90 to $125 per week based on the child's age group.

McGraw-Hill, Inc.

McGraw-Hill, Inc., headquartered in New York City, is a major publishing and information services company. In an effort to meet the child- and elder-care needs of its employees, the company offers two resource and referral services. The first, *McGraw-Hill Childcare Referral Service,* was arranged with Work/Family Directions, Inc., which has contracted with community-based child-care resource and referral agencies throughout the country to provide the needed services. McGraw-Hill has also contracted with *Pathfinders/Eldercare* to offer employees a wide range of professional services (consultation, information, and resources related to benefits and services; consultation on legal, financial, and emotional concerns; aid with home care arrangements; and advice about institutional placement).

McGraw-Hill promotes both services by means of periodic reminders in the company newsletter, seminars in the company's larger locations, audiotapes, posters, brochures, and Rolodex cards.

Manville Sales Corporation

Manville Sales Corporation, headquartered in Denver, Colorado, is an international manufacturing and natural resources company employing 18,000 people at more than 50 plants and four mines worldwide.

The company currently offers *Child Care Resource and Referral* and *Adult Care Counselling and Referral* to its Denver-based employees. According to Cynthia Perez, chairperson of the Work/Family Advisory Board, these services have had consistent use and the feedback received so far has been very positive.

Manville also offers corporate discounts at local child-care centers, a series of work and family seminars, and individual counseling sessions on work and family options, and in June 1990 it hosted a Caregiver's Fair with a number of local providers of child-care and adult-care services.

As part of a corporate effort to make Manville a "great place to work," a team of employees met to draft a Work & Family mission statement. An excerpt from the statement demonstrates the company's commitment to kin care. "Balancing work and family is now a greater challenge than ever before. Manville believes that it is mutually beneficial to support employees as they face this challenge. By providing family support activities, we can help reduce the stress inherent in balancing these two important facets of life. At the same time, doing this enhances the corporation's ability to retain and attract quality individuals critical to the company's long-term success."

Marriott Corporation

Marriott Corporation, a diversified hospitality company, has approximately 230,000 employees worldwide and is one of the 10 largest employers in the United States. In January 1989, it established the Department of Work and Family, which is headed by Donna Klein.

An excerpt from the Statement of Philosophy on Working Families demonstrates the company's commitment to kin care. "The challenge to Marriott today is to provide employees with the environment they need to pursue and advance their careers while balancing the demands of their personal lives. . . . It is our belief that such accommodations (family care programs) will ensure the productivity and loyalty of our work force over the long term, thereby ensuring our competitive edge in the markets in which we do business."

Marriott's kin care efforts in 1990 included initiating *Child Care Choices*, a nationwide resource and referral service; instituting a child care discount program that provides all Marriott employees with a directory of day-care centers with which Marriott has negotiated discounts nationwide (both chains and independently run centers); holding parenting seminars; keeping employees informed through *The Balance*, a work and family newsletter; establishing dependent care spending accounts (DCAP's); and providing flexible work arrangements when possible.

On June 1, 1990, Marriott announced that an on-site child-care center for children aged six weeks to 36 months would open at its headquarters in Bethesda, Maryland. The center opened in the fall of 1990 with a planned capacity of 63 children. The center was developed and is operated for Marriott by Corporate Child Care, Inc., a Nashville-based firm specializing in employer-based child-care services.

Marriott plans to meet other kin care needs as well. "Our focus for 1991 will be in the areas of supervisory training, an executive education series, a pilot program on job sharing, and increased community involvement on the issue of quality child care," says Klein. The company will also begin to explore elder-care issues.

Merck & Company, Inc.

Merck & Company, Inc. is the largest pharmaceutical company in the world. Headquartered in Rahway, New Jersey, it has plants and laboratories throughout the United States and abroad. It has 17,000 employees in the United States.

For several years, Merck has been recognized by both *Working Woman* and *Working Mother* magazines as being one of the top companies for women. The company's many Work and Family Support programs and activities include maternity/paternity leave with approved leaves of absence (up to 18 months); a nationwide Child Care Resource and Referral program; a series of *Family Matters* workshops that deal with child- and elder-care issues as well as other family concerns; an Employee Assistance Program (EAP); workplace schedule flexibility through such means as flextime, part-time, and flexplace (telecommuting); stress reduction programs; supervisory training to sensitize managers to the fact that a quality worklife includes a personal life that must be managed; and near-site child-care centers.

The first child-care center was opened in 1980. Merck provided start-up funding and guidance, but the center is now self-supporting through tuition and fund-raising activities. The company provides "in kind" services and grants for staff development, and it is available for advice. Parents and professionals run the center through an independent board. Because of the waiting list, Merck gave a substantial sum to build a "state of the art" center for approximately 150 children, providing the land, site preparation, and architectural services. After extensive study, the company selected a child-care center in West Point, Pennsylvania, as the recipient of a sizable company grant in exchange for preferential admission of employees' children. The grant enabled the center to expand, and in 1988 another sizable grant enabled it to add rooms.

Merrill Lynch & Company, Inc.

In 1990 Merrill Lynch & Company, Inc., headquartered in New York City, implemented work-family policies as a direct result of the expressed needs of Merrill Lynch employees. According to Daniel P. Tully, president and chief operating officer, "These initiatives will enhance Merrill Lynch's position as a competitive and preferred employer, and provide tangible and significant benefits to a sizable portion of our employees."

The initiatives adopted include flexible work hours, unpaid illness- and/or maternity-related leave job guarantees, and a family leave policy. Lee Roselle, vice president of corporate staff and manager of employee relations, was responsible for developing and managing the work/family policies. He indicates that so far the feedback from employees has been positive. Merrill Lynch is also piloting programs for child-care resource and referral.

Mervyn's

Mervyn's, a department store chain of the Dayton Hudson Corporation, is headquartered in Hayward, California. It supports kin care issues through its *Family-to-Family Program*.

In the early 1980s, Mervyn's identified child care as an emerging priority in many of the communities where it had stores and facilities. Through grants to nonprofit organizations, it began funding local efforts to improve the quality and availability of child care. Every year, Mervyn's and the Dayton Hudson Foundation have committed funds to the support of family child care. For the four-year period 1988–91, the foundation targeted $3.7 million for this purpose. Mervyn's was a founding member of the California Child Care Initiative and helped launch the center-based accreditation program of the National Association for the Education of Young Children (NAEYC). The company has supported provider recruitment efforts in Atlanta, resource and referral services in Denver, provider support networks in Arizona, and a model accreditation and training program in Texas. In addition, the company's sick pay policy allows employees to use paid sick time for the care of sick children or other dependents. The company plans to implement a Dependent Care Assistance Plan (DCAP) for child and elder care in 1991.

Mervyn's views its *Family-to-Family Program* as "a major capital investment to develop an infrastructure which could impact the quality of family child care for years to come." In 1989, Mervyn's and Dayton Hudson were recognized as leaders in child-care issues and received the Presidential Citation for Private Sector Initiatives.

3M (Minnesota Mining & Manufacturing Company)

3M (Minnesota Mining & Manufacturing Company), headquartered in St. Paul, Minnesota, employs 48,860 and was recognized as one of the top 60 companies for working mothers in *Working Mother* magazine. The company has a full-time child-care administrator who is committed to meeting family needs. 3M offers a resource and referral service (it also holds a biannual working parent resource fair), a Dependent Care Assistance Plan (DCAP), maternity leave, parental leave, flextime, and part-time work opportunities. In addition, it is subsidizing a pilot program on sick-child care, and if that is successful, it will institute the program on a company-wide basis.

Mobil Oil Corporation

Mobil Oil Corporation, headquartered in Fairfax, Virginia, implemented a Work and Family Program in 1990. According to Rex Adams, vice president of administration, the company is committed to providing fully competitive work and family policies that will enable employees to fulfill both their job and family responsibilities. "Success depends upon open communication between managers and employees, and creativity in developing solutions to work and family conflicts. To that end, we are asking managers and employees to work together and to be flexible in striking a balance between family and business needs."

The variety of kin care programs offered by Mobil Oil include an Employee Assistance Program (EAP); a resource and referral service for both child and elder care, offered through Work/Family Directions, Inc.; work and family seminars; flexible working hours; discretionary time off; dependent care leaves of absence; dependent care reduced workweek provisions (temporary flexibility through part-time work); and maternity leave.

J. P. Morgan & Company, Inc.

J. P. Morgan & Company, Inc., headquartered in New York City, provides banking and other financial services to corporations, governments, institutions, and individuals throughout the world. The company has 8,500 employees.

Supportive of ways to help its employees better manage their work and family responsibilities, the company offers paid disability leave for childbirth, parental leaves for child-care needs, five consecutive paid "illness at home" days for caring for ill family members, personal leave in two-month increments, adoption assistance (up to $3,000), lunchtime seminars on family issues, and some flexible work arrangements (arranged individually).

The company also offers information and referral services for both child care and elder care. Child Care, Inc. manages the child-care information and referral services, and the elder-care information and referral services are provided by the Partnership for Eldercare.

J. P. Morgan participates with other major New York City employers in the Work/Family Consortium, which studies issues related to dependent care, such as emergency and sick-child care, holiday care, and vacation care.

Morrison & Foerster

Morrison & Foerster, the nation's 12th-largest law firm, is headquartered in San Francisco and employs 1,276. The firm offers a Dependent Care Assistance Plan (DCAP), paid sick leave to care for an ill child, maternity leave, parental leaves, flextime, part-time, job sharing, a negotiable work-at-home program, and a resource and referral service. Morrison & Foerster was recognized as one of the top 60 companies for working mothers in *Working Mother* magazine.

Motorola, Inc.

Motorola, Inc., headquartered in Schaumburg, Illinois, is very committed to addressing the work and family issues that confront its employees as they balance their roles as employees and parents. To meet the needs of its employees, the company introduced its *Child Care Resource and Referral Program*, which is maintained by Work/Family Directions, Inc. In addition to referrals nationwide, the service provides parents with information on the evaluation of child-care programs, state child-care regulations, and free publications on child-rearing.

According to Richard J. Dorazil, corporate director of benefits, Motorola will continually review additional work and family benefit programs to help meet family needs.

National Medical Enterprises, Inc. (NME)

National Medical Enterprises, Inc. (NME) currently provides on-site child care for the employees at its corporate headquarters in Santa Monica, California. The Learning Center (TLC) is managed by Cornerstone Child Care Centers, Inc. TLC is a high-quality development program for children from infancy through five years of age. NME subsidizes part of the tuition, making the center affordable for employees. Currently, the center is filled to capacity (60) and has a waiting list of 75.

NME's plans for the future include assessing the need for child care within the NME acute illness and psychiatric facilities and working toward the implementation of on-site child care at the large NME health campus facilities. An affiliate group, Hillhaven, has three adult day-care facilities and is expanding those to include child-care facilities.

According to Laura Peterston, director of operations at Cornerstone, "TLC has earned its keep, and the employees of NME definitely support the programs. Some of the specific benefits have been greater employee satisfaction and greater peace of mind knowing their child is in quality day care."

NCNB

NCNB, one of the nation's largest bank holding companies, is headquartered in Charlotte, North Carolina, and has over 30,000 employees throughout its system. Many kin care benefits are available to its employees, including maternity leave, family leave, part-time work, job sharing, child and elder resource and referral services, a Dependent Care Assistance Plan (DCAP), and an Employee Assistance Program (EAP). The company also meets child-care needs by providing a subsidized program for child care and an on-site child-care center. NCNB was recognized as one of the top 60 companies for working mothers in *Working Mother* magazine.

Northrop Corporation

Northrop Corporation, headquartered in Los Angeles, California, is a leader in the aerospace industry. In an effort to take a proactive stance on kin care issues, the company recently implemented a family care leave of absence policy in 1990 that allows its employees to take up to 12 months of unpaid leave. It also supports the use of part-time work assignments and offers a comprehensive Employee Assistance Program (EAP).

Official Airline Guides, Inc. (OAG)

Official Airline Guides, Inc. (OAG), the world's leading supplier of information on airline schedules and fares, employes 839 workers in its Oak Brook, Illinois office. It offers several programs to meet kin care needs.

Since 1973, OAG has had a full flextime policy whereby its employees work during core hours (10 A.M. to 3 P.M.), but beyond that time, their hours of work can be flexible. It also offers 10 weeks of paid maternity leave (which can be extended to three months), parental leave, and part-time work.

OAG opened an on-site child-care center in 1981, on the initiative of James Woodward, who was then the company's president. The center takes children aged three months to five years and has a capacity of 71 children. It is supported by tuition fees, which range from $75 to $121 per week based on the child's age. Expenses in excess of the tuition fees are underwritten by the company and recouped through savings in recruitment and training expense.

OAG was noted as being one of the 60 best companies for working mothers in *Working Mother* magazine.

Pacific Telesis Group

Pacific Telesis Group, headquartered in San Francisco, provides a variety of programs that help its employees balance their career and family responsibilities. These programs include family leave for the care of newborn (natural or adopted) children, adoption reimbursement (up to $2,000), a dependent care spending account (a DCAP), bereavement absence, floating holidays, personal days (which may be taken in two-hour increments), and an Employee Assistance Program (EAP).

In addition, the company has established a Company/Union Work and Family Life Committee. The committee consists of union members and corporate personnel who analyze specific work and family issues and make recommendations on new programs. A fund of $300,000 in seed money is available to test and implement approved programs.

J. C. Penney Company, Inc.

J. C. Penney Company, Inc., headquartered in Dallas, Texas, is one of the nation's largest employers of part-time workers, many of whom are parents. One of the company's goals is to offer its employees a flexible way to achieve harmony between home and work responsibilities. J. C. Penney's commitment to kin care is demonstrated by its major financial contributions to nonprofit community organizations that are searching for solutions to the problem of providing quality child care and family care. Working closely with the YMCA, the company has sought to expand after-school care networks across the country.

The *J. C. Penney Family Care Program* outlines other company programs that are responsive to kin care needs. These include personal holidays; emergency absences with pay; leaves of absence; *Healthy Beginnings,* a prenatal program whose participants receive a $100 gift certificate after the birth of a baby; a program through which tuition discounts can be obtained from national day-care chains (Kinder-Care, Children's World, and La Petite Academy); and a dependent care assistance account (DCAP) that enables employees to pay for child and elder care with pretax dollars.

J. C. Penney is committed to providing a supportive environment for balancing work and family obligations. Richard T.

Erickson, executive vice president, notes that "a manager's sensitivity training program [regarding family issues] in video will also be available to our managers nationwide."

PepsiCo, Inc.

PepsiCo, Inc., headquartered in Purchase, New York, employs 266,000 worldwide. Several programs of the company demonstrate its commitment to balancing family and work needs. A Choice Pay Reserve Account allows employees to set aside money from earnings before taxes to be used for child- and elder-care expenses (a DCAP).

The Center for the Study of Aging at the University of Bridgeport worked with PepsiCo in compiling an extensive *Resource Guide on Eldercare* for PepsiCo employees. This guide contains information about the normal aging process, physical and mental health, and how to find help with elder-care issues.

PepsiCo also provides elder-care lunchtime seminars, caregiver/health care fairs, and information and referral services for child care. Kathleen G. Cucchiarella, benefits administrator, indicates that PepsiCo is committed to considering enhancements in its child- and elder-care programs.

Phillips Petroleum Company

Phillips Petroleum Company, with headquarters in Bartlesville, Oklahoma, has 17,500 employees in the United States. It has contracted with The Partnership Group, Inc. to provide both a child-care resource and referral service and an elder-care referral service to its employees. Called *The ChildCare Solution* and *The ElderCare Connection*, these services provide families with counseling, referrals, educational materials, and workshops at various worksites. Both of the services are nationwide and can provide information to employees in all geographic areas.

According to Robert P. Nash, manager of compensation and benefits, the referral assistance has been well received by Phillips employees. "The vast majority of those who have used the service have found it helpful in addressing immediate needs and would use it again in the future."

Pitney Bowes

Pitney Bowes, headquartered in Stamford, Connecticut, makes business equipment and office supplies and has 22,369 employees worldwide. It has a Dependent Care Assistance Plan (DCAP), a maternity leave policy, a resource and referral service, adoption aid (up to $800), and flextime and part-time programs. It is determining the feasibility of establishing on-site child-care centers at its three biggest employment centers. Pitney Bowes was recognized as one of the top 60 companies for working mothers in *Working Mother* magazine.

Polaroid Corporation

Polaroid Corporation, located in Cambridge, Massachusetts, has 7,900 employees. Since 1971, it has recognized its employees' need to be satisfied that their dependents are receiving the best possible care while they are at work. Polaroid's first kin care program established day-care subsidies that subsidized from 10 percent to 80 percent of day-care costs based on total family income and number of family members.

The company also helps meet kin care needs through resource and referral services (Child Care Resource Center, Inc. in Cambridge and the Child Care Resource Exchange in New Bedford) and a dependent care spending account (a DCAP). Polaroid was noted as one of the 60 best companies for working mothers in *Working Mother* magazine.

The Procter & Gamble Co.

Procter & Gamble, with headquarters in Cincinnati, Ohio, employs 43,600 throughout the country. The company is best known for its variety of household products. Its kin care benefits include flextime, part-time work, financial assistance for adoption (up to $2,000), maternity leave, parental leave, and insurance for long-term care. It has funded two child-care centers and a community-based resource and referral service. More than 70 children are currently enrolled at the centers, and the children of Procter & Gamble employees have priority admission in return for the company's funding. Procter & Gamble was recognized as one of the top 60 companies for working mothers in *Working Mother* magazine.

SAS Institute, Inc.

SAS Institute, Inc., located in Cary, North Carolina, employs 1,246 in one of the nation's leading computer software businesses. It is no surprise that SAS was recognized as one of the top 60 companies for working mothers in *Working Mother* magazine. Two on-site child-care centers are housed on the company's grounds; one is for babies up to age 2½, and the other is for preschoolers up to age 5. There is no charge to parents using the centers—SAS picks up all of the fees. In 1990, 175 children were enrolled. In addition to this benefit, SAS provides maternity leave, parental leave, and flexible benefits.

Charles Schwab & Co., Inc.

Charles Schwab & Co., Inc., the largest discount broker in the country, is headquartered in San Francisco and employs 3,000 nationwide. The company offers several programs to address the kin care needs of its employees. First, Charles Schwab employees have the opportunity to set aside pretax dollars in a Dependent Care Assistance Plan (DCAP) to pay for dependent care expenses. Second, it has established nationwide agreements with two child-care centers (La Petite Academy and Kinder-Care) to provide discounts on tuition to employees using these centers.

The company has also developed a brochure that provides employees with a wealth of information regarding elder care. The brochure helps employees responsible for elder care to understand their unique care-giving responsibilities and the unique alternatives and resources available to givers of elder care.

Security Pacific Corporation

Security Pacific Corporation, a major banking and financial institution, is headquartered in Los Angeles. It offers a range of benefits that help employees better manage the balance between work and family responsibilities, and it has recently initiated several new kin care programs.

Among the kin care benefits offered by Security Pacific are Dependent Care Assistance Plans (DCAPs) for both child and elder care, adoption assistance (up to $1,500), an Employee Assistance Program (EAP) that provides guidance and community resource information on family care problems, a family leave policy, and flexible work schedules.

Security Pacific's recently initiated kin care programs include a unique Salary Continuation program. Jacqueline Hempstead, vice president of human resources, explains that this program "offers employees the use of up to five days of salary continuation each time a family care need arises." Security Pacific also provides discounts with Children's World and La Petite Academy day-care centers, a child-care resource and referral service provided through Working Solutions, Inc., and access to the Resource and Referral Agencies list, which includes child-care agencies located throughout California. A pilot sick care facility in downtown Seattle started in January 1991 and will be available to the mildly ill children of Security Pacific employees. The company will subsidize a significant portion of the cost.

Southeast Bank, N.A.

Southeast Bank, N.A., in Miami, Florida, feels that assisting its employees in balancing their work and family responsibilities requires flexibility. It therefore offers a flexible pretax benefits plan whereby employees can select the kin care benefits that best suit their needs. One of these benefits is the Dependent Day Care Reimbursement Account, which permits the use of pretax dollars to pay for dependent care (a DCAP). Other flexible benefits offered by Southeast include sick leave, excused absences, personal days, maternity or option leave, flextime, and part-time work. The company also provides job opportunities for the older children of its employees during the summer months.

In addition to these benefits, Southeast has an Employee Assistance Program (EAP) and a lunchtime lecture series covering a wide range of on- and off-the-job topics.

Sovran Financial Corporation

Sovran Financial Corporation, headquartered in Norfolk, Virginia, is strongly committed to family-supportive policies, programs, and services. As Mary D. Kramer, first vice president of the company, says, "We are extremely proud of our proactive approach to kin care issues."

Both full- and part-time employees (20 or more hours) can choose from the benefit options of Sovran's Flexible Benefits Plan. These options include a dependent care reimbursement spending account (a DCAP). They also include medical leaves of absence (which can be taken after the birth of a child with 50–100 percent of pay, depending on tenure and/or officer status), personal leave, and sick leave (which can be used to care for sick dependents).

Other kin care benefits offered by Sovran are long-term care insurance, preretirement planning seminars, an Employee Assistance Program (EAP), and family-oriented activities. The company provides a work and family education and information program that provides lists of the kin care resources available in a geographic area and information on choosing and evaluating child- and elder-care alternatives. It has also made arrangements that enable Sovran employees to obtain discounts and/or reserve spaces at particular day-care facilities, especially facilities near which there is a large concentration of these employees.

Sovran has demonstrated its continuing commitment to kin care by making grants and donations to community-based organizations to benefit child- and elder-care initiatives.

Steelcase

Steelcase, the world's largest manufacturer of office furniture, has 14,000 employees in Grand Rapids, Michigan. It is committed both to helping its employees meet their child-care needs and to improving the quality of child-care providers.

The company offers an extensive information and referral service that includes individual counseling, assessment of available child-care providers, referral and computer access to a network of child-care providers, library resources, and parent education seminars. The service helps Steelcase employees address their needs for information on part-time care, nighttime care, emergency care, and summer camps. For child-care providers, the company offers CPR training, education seminars, equipment, library resources, a newsletter, and individual technical assistance.

In addition to its child-care programs, which met the needs of 355 employees by serving 523 children, the company offers extended job sharing in its main office. In 1988, 70 people shared 35 jobs. It also offers a leave policy, an Employee Assistance Program (EAP), and financial aid for adoptions. Steelcase was noted as one of the 60 best companies for working mothers in *Working Mother* magazine.

Stride Rite Corporation

Stride Rite Corporation, headquartered in Cambridge, Massachusetts, is a leading producer of children's shoes and has over 4,000 employees. Its unique Intergenerational Center, which helps its employees meet their needs in both child and elder care, has received national publicity and has served as a national model.

The company set up its first kin care center in Roxbury, Massachusetts, in 1971. The center provided child care to children of Stride Rite employees and children in the community. In 1983, when Stride Rite moved its corporate headquarters to Cambridge, it opened a second child-care center in that city. At that time, its two child-care centers accommodated 90 children ranging in ages from two to six. In 1988, Stride Rite converted its Cambridge on-site child-care center into an intergenerational care center with 79 openings for children and elders—55 children aged 15 months to 6 years and 24 elders at least 60 years of age. The Intergenerational Center is a collaborative effort of Stride Rite, Somerville-Cambridge Elder Services, Inc. (SCES), and Wheelock College. Among the benefits of this program are the model of public/private partnership that it provides, the intergenerational understanding that it creates, the cost efficiency obtained by bringing elders and children together in a single day-care center, the resource efficiency obtained by uniting the unique services and expertise of multiple organizations, and research that will augment the limited body of available information on the social effects and policy implications of intergenerational caregiving.

Stride Rite subsidizes elder and child care based on family income, with a cap of $95 a week. In addition to on-site child and elder care, the company's kin care programs include maternity leave, family leave, and *ElderLink*, a resource and referral service that it offers through SCES. Stride Rite was noted as one of the 60 best companies for working mothers in *Working Mother* magazine.

Syntex Corporation

Syntex Corporation, headquartered in Palo Alto, California, makes prescription drugs, diagnostic systems, and veterinary products and has 5,363 employees. It is committed to meeting the work/family needs of its employees.

In 1984, Syntex opened the Children's Pre-School Center, located 3 miles from its headquarters. The center accommodates up to 150 children from six weeks of age through kindergarten. Syntex provided the funds for play equipment and initial renovation of the center site. It supports the center by providing funds for expansion and by subsidizing operating losses when necessary. In addition, each year it provides up to $40,000 in center scholarships based on family income and family size.

Syntex assisted parents in establishing a mutual benefit corporation that independently controls and operates the center. The center's fees range from $480 to $670 a month based on the child's age. A formal Dependent Care Assistance Plan (DCAP) allows Syntex employees to pay these fees with pretax dollars. Single parents with one or more children in the center and couples with more than one child in the center receive discounts.

In addition to the near-site child-care center, other Syntex benefits responsive to kin care needs include alternative working hours (job sharing, part-time work, flexible working hours), maternity leave, adoption benefits (up to $2,000), an Employee Assistance Program (EAP), college scholarships for the children of employees, and seminars and workshops on financial and health topics. Syntex Corporation was noted as one of the 60 best companies for working mothers in *Working Mother* magazine.

Tandem Computers, Inc.

Tandem Computers, Inc., headquartered in Cupertino, California, is committed to the use of employee input and involvement in developing its dependent care programs. It recently established an employee advisory committee that meets regularly, shares thoughts and ideas on kin care issues, and makes recommendations to management.

Tandem kin care programs currently in place include a Dependent Care Assistance Plan (DCAP); *CARE*, a program managed by Work/Family Directions, Inc., which provides a nationwide referral and information service and handbooks with a wealth of advice for parents choosing and evaluating child-care options; and parental leave.

In the summer of 1990, Tandem cosponsored in conjunction with the YMCA, a YMCA-Tandem Day Camp for children of Tandem employees in kindergarten through grade 9. According to Carla Mazotti, benefits administrator, "The program was successful and will be continued."

TIAA-CREF

TIAA-CREF, a pension and insurance organization serving the educational community, is located in New York City. It meets kin care needs by providing resource and referral services for both elder and child care. Contracting with The Partnership Group, Inc., TIAA-CREF offers its employees *The ChildCare Solution* and *The ElderCare Connection*.

Time Warner, Inc.

Time Warner, Inc., headquartered in New York City, is one of the world's largest communication conglomerates. It has a comprehensive Work & Family Program that provides many kin care benefits to its employees. Karol Rose, manager of the program, says that the objective is "to look at initiatives that would address our employee population's needs and to be responsive. The whole thrust is to provide support, information, and resources for our employees so they can manage their family lives and also be productive at work." The initiatives include child- and elder-care resource and referral services (*The ElderCare Connection* and *The ChildCare Solution*, which are managed by The Partnership Group, Inc.), a work and family booklet that provides a wealth of useful information about company policies and programs and a list of kin care resources, lunchtime workshops, employee-sponsored lunchtime discussion groups, a newsletter, an Employee Assistance Program (EAP), and an emergency child-care service.

Time Warner, Inc. also provides a Dependent Care Assistance Plan (DCAP), college scholarships, and adoption assistance (up to $2,100). Maternity leave, parental leaves, family leave, and emergency leave are available. Also available are a graduated return to work, part-time work, job sharing, and work at home.

The company also participates in a New York City employers' work and family group which addresses employees' work and family concerns. Time Warner, Inc. was noted as one of the 60 best companies for working mothers in *Working Mother* magazine.

Trammell Crow Company

Trammell Crow Company, headquartered in Dallas, Texas, is the nation's largest developer of commercial real estate. It has 3,000 employees. A near-site child-care center, opened in 1982, enrolls 60 children of its employees and will be expanded to enroll more. Trammell Crow subsidizes 33 percent of the costs, with parents paying between $67 and $85 per week. The firm also has a standard maternity leave policy and adoption aid of 28 paid days off. Trammell Crow was recognized as one of the top 60 companies for working mothers in *Working Mother* magazine.

The Travelers Companies

The Travelers Companies, headquartered in Hartford, Connecticut, is one of the largest insurance firms in the country. Its comprehensive program of kin care benefits, called *Family Care*, represents a "significant financial and philosophical commitment to the personal issues of employees."

Travelers kin care programs include a child-care resource and referral program and an elder-care consultation and referral program managed by Work/Family Directions, Inc. Travelers helps its employees pay their dependent care bills in two ways. First, it provides its employees with a dependent care spending account that enables them to pay their dependent care expenses with pretax dollars (a DCAP). Second, it adds a percentage subsidy to this account. Such subsidies range from 10 percent to 30 percent based on the annual income of the employee. The company also offers both paid and unpaid family leaves, maternity leave, personal holidays, and entitlement time for unexpected personal obligations.

In addition, alternative work arrangements (such as flextime, job sharing, telecommuting, part-time work, and compressed workweeks) and an Employee Assistance Program (EAP) are available.

Union Carbide Corporation

Union Carbide Corporation, headquartered in Danbury, Connecticut, has a strong commitment to addressing family/work issues. Among the family/work programs currently in place at the company are flexible work schedules (including permanent part-time and work-sharing opportunities), maternity leave, dependent care leave of absence, an Employee Assistance Program (EAP), a Dependent Care Assistance Plan (DCAP), and a resource and referral (R & R) service for child and elder care. The R & R is run through the EAP at headquarters (the EAPs at other company locations are being encouraged to do the same). The R & R headquarters uses the services of *Child Care Connections* of Western Connecticut, a community-based resource and referral organization that helps employees clarify their kin care needs and find providers to meet them.

Union Carbide also has a standing committee that reviews issues concerning elder care/long-term care and a Child Care Task Force that, according to R. V. Welty, vice president of human resources, did a great deal of work to address family/work issues in 1990. Another company task force is dedicated to promoting the upward mobility of women and minorities, focusing on such areas as the value of work force diversity, flexible management of human resources, and other "family friendly" benefits. A series of work and family seminars have come about as a result of task force efforts.

A unique company benefit is its Wellness Program, which provides information and assistance in many areas. The Wellness team sponsored two plays involving family/work issues that were performed by *Plays for Living*. Welty said that "the plays raise awareness and are followed immediately with opportunities for discussion and processing."

UNUM Life Insurance Company

UNUM Life Insurance Company, headquartered in Portland, Maine, is one of the nation's leading writers of group long-term disability insurance. It has 4,000 employees, and it is committed to balancing their work and family responsibilities.

UNUM has established flexible working hours (core hours 9:30 A.M.–3 P.M.) to help its employees meet their business and family needs. Part-time hours, job rotation, job sharing, evening or early morning hours, and telecommuting are other options offered by the company. UNUM's policies also include personal days, Flex Vacation (employees may buy up to one additional week of vacation time annually), dependent care leave, family leaves of absence, and a dependent care reimbursement account (a DCAP).

The company has created a child-care subsidy program that provides financial assistance to home office employees whose annual household income is $35,000 or less and to field office employees whose annual income is $40,000 or less. A graduated payout based on household income and number of children subsidizes up to $2,080 per year of the child-care costs for a single child and up to $3,120 per year of the child-care costs for two or more children. Information, resource, and referral services are provided through *Child Care Connections*.

The company also has an on-site day-care center operated by KoalaKare, a local chain of day-care centers. The center accommodates 84 children, including 12 infants, and UNUM employees receive a 10 percent discount from the regular KoalaKare rates.

For two years running, UNUM has been recognized as one of the nation's "60 best companies for working mothers." In 1989, it received an award for its "profamily policies and practices" from the University of Southern Maine's Child and Family Institute.

The Upjohn Company

The Upjohn Company, a major U.S. pharmaceutical company, has corporate headquarters in Kalamazoo, Michigan. In 1990, the company began an expanded Child/Family Care Program. Family care initiatives include child care information and referral, provided by a community agency, Child Care Resource & Referral (CCRR). The company also provided CCRR with a $75,000 grant to develop and conduct provider training programs to improve the quality of care and to recruit additional child-care providers. Additional money was given to develop an infant equipment lending program. According to Diane Sikora, manager of Child Care Programs, the company is committed to "continuing to direct a portion of our resources to programs aimed at improving child care in the community."

Upjohn has established a home care program that provides child care and care for mildly ill children, adults, or elders in the employee's home. Employees pay $3.25–3.50 an hour, with Upjohn subsidizing the rest. Upjohn has also reserved several child-care slots in local child-care facilities for employees to use as a backup to their primary provider arrangements. Other company kin care programs include a parent education program, a pretax spending account for dependent care, family leaves of absence, and adoption reimbursement.

US Sprint

US Sprint, headquartered in Kansas City, Missouri, has initiated the *FamilyCare Program* to help its employees manage their career and family responsibilities. The program was designed to enhance productivity, attract and retain talented employees, and improve the quality of work life at US Sprint.

The program includes flexible work schedules (flextime, part-time, job sharing, and compressed workweeks), personal and family counseling through an Employee Assistance Program (EAP), family care leaves of absence (up to one year with benefit continuation and job reinstatement), relocation and income assistance for working partners; adoption assistance (up to $1,000), a Dependent Care Assistance Plan (DCAP), a flex day (two or more hours used for family emergencies), and a dependent care resource and referral service (R & R). The R & R, managed by The Partnership Group, Inc., includes *The ChildCare Solution* and *The ElderCare Connection*, which provide consultation on parenting and adult care-giving issues, educational materials, workshops, and referrals to local caregivers. In addition, the R & R addresses the need for increased child-care resources in the communities where Sprint employees live and work.

According to William McCullough, vice president of human

resources, the FamilyCare Program, in place since August 1989, "has exceeded employee utilization projections. These results demonstrate program usefulness in assisting the majority of Sprint employees to resolve family needs and concerns while increasing productivity at the workplace."

US West

US West, headquartered in Englewood, Colorado, provides telephone service to 14 Western states and has 70,000 employees. It was recognized as one of the top 60 companies for working mothers in *Working Mother* magazine. A variety of company programs and policies help its employees meet their kin care needs. These programs and policies include flextime, a compressed workweek, job sharing, telecommuting, a Dependent Care Assistance Plan (DCAP), adoption assistance, maternity leave, family leave, an Employee Assistance Program (EAP), and a child and elder care resource and referral service. In addition, the Communications Workers of America, the employees' union, joined with the management of US West to pilot a child-care center in Tempe, Arizona, in cooperation with America West's child-care center programs. More than 30 children were enrolled, and the company is committed to expanding the program if the pilot is successful.

Warner-Lambert Company

Warner-Lambert Company makes prescription drugs and a wide array of over-the-counter health care and consumer products (for example, Lubriderm, Benadryl, Listerine, Dentyne and Trident gum, and Schick razors). It is headquartered in Morris Plains, New Jersey, and has 11,000 employees in the United States.

The company's child-care programs include a nationwide information and referral service (I & R), managed through Work/Family Directions, Inc.; funding for community child-care resources; an in-home caregiver program for mildly ill children, which premiered in the late fall of 1990; and a Dependent Care Assistance Plan (DCAP). Elder care is also served by the I & R and DCAP programs. According to Jane Cassi, in Human Resources, 98 percent of the users of the child-care I & R program would use the program again if needed. "Anecdotal reports from early users [of the elder-care I & R] indicate high satisfaction as well."

Other Warner-Lambert benefits that address kin care needs include family leave, sick days that can be used to care for ill family members, flextime in most departments, part-time work, job-sharing and telecommuting possibilities, seminars and workshops on family issues, and an Employee Assistance Program (EAP).

Warner-Lambert managers are trained in the *Managing a Diverse Workforce* program, which sensitizes them to family issues. In addition, the company has helped fund child-care centers near its major facilities, given marketing assistance to campaigns for recruiting providers of family day care, and joined with other area businesses to start a service that offers in-home care for mildly ill children. In 1989 and 1990, Warner-Lambert was recognized as one of the top 60 companies by *Working Mother*.

Xerox Corporation

Xerox Corporation, headquartered in Stamford, Connecticut, is the leading U.S. manufacturer of copying and duplicating equipment. It has over 66,000 employees throughout the country.

The company's kin care benefits include a Dependent Care Assistance Plan (DCAP), called the Salary Redirection Program; adoption assistance (up to $1,000); maternity leave; flextime, part-time, and job-sharing opportunities; and a child-care resource and referral program (R & R). The R & R is managed through Work/Family Directions, Inc., which contracts out with R & R agencies based in the communities where Xerox employees live. Thus, Xerox employees are able to speak with trained specialists who are familiar with the child-care providers in their community.

The company also offers a comprehensive Employee Assistance Program (EAP) and personal holidays that can be used to deal with concerns regarding child or elder care.

Zenith Electronics Corporation

Zenith Electronics Corporation, headquartered in Glenview, Illinois, offers a cafeteria benefits plan, called Z-flex, under which its employees can choose the benefits that best meet their individual needs. To address kin care needs, Zenith offers a Dependent Care Assistance Plan (DCAP). Under this plan, Zenith employees can put pretax dollars in a Reimbursement Account and then draw funds from that account to pay for dependent care expenses.

Afterword

A new wave is gathering force within corporate America and specifically within human resources functions and departments. That is to fundamentally redesign our companies to embrace a new value-added strategic focus. Rather than positioning a singular expense-centered image, the characteristics of value-added management reveal a more pragmatic and less administrative style of management that champions visioning, preparation, and action as critical to corporate success. Key to this new style of management is the notion that there must always be a value—rather than expense—orientation throughout the company. Decision makers and human resource professionals who champion this new vision position themselves as strategic business partners within their organizations in identifying and, more importantly, acting upon strategic business objectives. No human objective can exist that does not have human resource implications. Certainly increased competition for skilled employees and documented concerns about the availability of quality dependent care will compel future-oriented companies to position work and family management and dependent-care options as a clear business issue.

Significant changes in work force demographics, coupled with a myriad of environmental forces, caused the mushrooming of employer-provided dependent care assistance throughout the last decade. A 1989 study by the Conference Board indicated over 4,000 large U.S. employers provided child-care financial assistance (50 percent), information and referral (25 percent), and on- or near-site child-care (25 percent) support for their employees. Other, less notorious support took the form of increased leave time for family care, support of licensed family home care, flexible work arrangements such as flextime and part-time work, and flexible health care benefits.

Adoption of these support programs and benefit plans represents a growing trend in response to anticipated needs of a new and much more diverse work force. These programs are also in response to four new and emerging environmental forces: (1) increased competition for skilled workers, (2) changing employee expectations, (3) the negative impact of work-family conflict upon workplace productivity, and (4) the short supply of quality dependent care in this country.

The human resource professional will make the greatest contribution to his/her organization, and to the ever-expanding work-family issue, by serving as an informed counselor to management—anticipating alternative care options to meet different emerging needs and proposing action in response to these needs which ensures the economic return of human resource investments in solving the work and family dilemma.

A disciplined and factual approach to collecting relevant data that helps to quantify the costs and benefits of assistance—while at the same time viewing dependent care assistance as a necessary investment—will aid in planning for future policies and programs to ensure corporate effectiveness. The goal must be to empower management with valid and relevant data on the business impact of the work-family conflict in order to help shape management thinking and decision making beyond "quick fixes."

We know that the 21st century will be a time of intense global competition among complex multinational corporations struggling to continually increase market share in an era of unparalleled technological development and great social change. Continued survival will depend upon people who have the vision, energy, and courage to champion unpopular or complex issues so that tomorrow's results will satisfy the demands of the new, more active marketplace. Organizations that plan for and measure the impact of *Kin Care* assistance will be positioned to evaluate future costs/benefits of programs and the need for policy expansion and alteration as their own work force changes and diversifies.

WILLIAM J. McCULLOUGH
Senior Vice President-Human Resources
Sprint/United Management Company

Kin Care Resources

1. Organizations

Administration on Aging
c/o Department of Health and Human Services
200 Independence Avenue, SW
Washington, DC 20201
(202) 245-0724

Alzheimer's Disease and Related Disorders, Inc.
70 East Lake, Suite 600
Chicago, IL 60601
(800) 621-0379

American Association of Retired Persons (AARP)
1909 K Street, NW
Washington, DC 20049
(202) 872-4700

American Bar Association
Commission on Legal Problems of the Elderly
1800 M Street, NW
Washington, DC 20036

American Society on Aging
833 Market Street, Suite 512
San Francisco, CA 94103
(703) 543-2617

Children of Aging Parents
2761 Trenton Road
Levittown, PA 19056
(215) 945-6900

Family Survival Project
44 Page Street, Suite 600
San Francisco, CA 94102

Gray Panthers National Office
311 South Juniper Street, Suite 601
Philadelphia, PA 19107
(215) 545-6555

National Association of Area Agencies on Aging
600 Maryland Avenue, SW, Suite 208, West Wing
Washington, DC 20024
(202) 484-7520

National Council for Senior Citizens
1511 K Street, NW
Washington, DC 20005
(202) 783-6850

National Council on the Aging
600 Maryland Avenue, SW, Suite 100, West Wing
Washington, DC 20024
(202) 479-1200

National Institute on Aging
9000 Rockville Pike
Bethesda, MD 20205

National Self-Help Clearinghouse
City University of New York Graduate Center
33 West 42nd Street
New York, NY 10036
(212) 840-1259

National Senior Citizens Law Center
1302 18th Street, NW
Washington, DC 20036
(202) 887-5280

2. Helpful Books and Other Resources

Cadmus, Robert. *Caring for Your Aging Parents*. Englewood Cliffs, N.J.: Prentice-Hall, 1984.

Crichton, Jean. *The AgeCare Source Book: A Resource Guide for the Aging and Their Families*. New York: Simon & Schuster, 1987.

Davis, Richard H., ed. *Aging: Prospects and Issues*. 3rd ed. Los Angeles: University of Southern California Press, 1981.

Gold, Margaret. *The Older American's Guide to Housing and Living Arrangements*. Mount Vernon, N.Y.: Institute for Consumer Policy Research, 1984.

All about Home Care: A Consumer's Guide. Send $2 and write to: National Home-caring Council, Inc., 235 Park Avenue South, New York, NY 10003; (212) 674-4990.

Porcino, Jane. *Growing Older, Getting Better: A Handbook for Women in the Second Half of Life*. Menlo Park, Calif.: Addison–Wesley Publishing, 1983.

Springer, Diane, and Timothy Brubaker. *Family Caregiving and Dependent Elderly*. Beverly Hills, Calif.: Sage Publications, 1984.

3. State Agencies on Aging

State Agency	Telephone
Alabama Commission on Aging	(205) 261-5743
Older Alaskans Commission	(907) 465-3250
Arizona Office on Aging and Adult Administration	(602) 255-4446
Arkansas Department of Human Services	(501) 682-2441
California Department of Aging	(916) 322-5290
Colorado Aging and Adult Services Division	(303) 866-5905
Connecticut Department on Aging	(203) 566-4810
Delaware Division on Aging	(302) 421-6791
District of Columbia Office of Aging	(202) 724-5622
Florida Aging and Adult Services	(904) 488-8922
Georgia Office of Aging	(404) 894-5333
Hawaii Executive Office on Aging	(808) 548-2593
Idaho Office on Aging	(208) 334-3833
Illinois Department on Aging	(217) 785-3356
Indiana Department on Aging and Community Services	(317) 232-7006
Iowa Commission on Aging	(515) 281-5187

State Agency	Telephone
Kansas Department on Aging	(913) 296-4986
Kentucky Division for Aging Services	(502) 564-6930
Louisiana Governor's Office of Elderly Affairs	(504) 925-1700
Maine Bureau of Elderly	(207) 289-2561
Maryland Office of Aging	(301) 383-5064
Massachusetts Department of Elder Affairs	(617) 727-7750
Michigan Office of Services to the Aging	(517) 373-8230
Minnesota Board on Aging	(612) 296-2770
Mississippi Council on Aging	(601) 354-7011
Missouri Division of Aging	(314) 751-3082
Montana Community Services Division	(406) 444-3865
Nebraska Department on Aging	(402) 471-2307
Nevada Division for Aging Services	(702) 885-4210
New Hampshire State Council on Aging	(603) 271-2751
New Jersey Division on Aging	(609) 292-4833
New Mexico State Agency on Aging	(505) 827-7640
New York State Offices for the Aging	(518) 474-4425
North Carolina Division of Aging	(919) 733-3983
North Dakota Aging Services	(701) 224-2577
Ohio Commission on Aging	(614) 466-5500
Oklahoma Services for the Aging	(405) 521-2281
Oregon Senior Services Division	(503) 378-4728
Pennsylvania Department of Aging	(717) 783-1550
Puerto Rico Gericulture Commission	(809) 722-0225
Rhode Island Department of Elderly Affairs	(401) 277-2858
South Carolina Commission on Aging	(803) 758-2576
South Dakota Office of Adult Services and Aging	(605) 773-3666
Tennessee Commission on Aging	(615) 741-2056
Texas Department on Aging	(512) 475-2717
Utah Division of Aging and Adult Services	(801) 533-6422
Vermont Office on Aging	(802) 241-2400
Virginia Department for the Aging	(804) 225-2271
Virgin Islands Commission on Aging	(809) 774-5884
Washington Bureau of Aging and Adult Services	(206) 753-2502
West Virginia Commission on Aging	(304) 348-3317
Wisconsin Office on Aging	(608) 266-2536
Wyoming Commission on Aging	(307) 777-6111

CHILD CARE

1. Organizations

Administration for Children, Youth, and Families
Office of Human Development Services
U.S. Department of Health and Human Services
P.O. Box 1182
Washington, DC 20013
(202) 245-0354

Bank Street College of Education
Center for Children's Policy
610 West 112 Street
New York, NY 10025
(212) 222-6700

Bureau of National Affairs, Inc.
1231 25th Street, NW
Washington, DC 20037
(202) 452-4501

Center for Public Advocacy Research
12 West 37th Street
New York, NY 10018
(212) 546-9220

Child Care Action Campaign
99 Hudson Street, Room 1233
New York, NY 10013
(212) 334-9595

Child Care Employee Project
P.O. Box 5603
Berkeley, CA 94705
(415) 653-9889

Child Care Information Exchange
P.O. Box 2890
Redmond, WA 98073
(206) 883-9394

Children's Defense Fund
122 C Street, NW
Washington, DC 20001
(202) 628-8787

Child Welfare League of America
440 First Street, NW, Suite 310
Washington, DC 20001

The Conference Board
Work and Family Information Center
845 Third Avenue
New York, NY 10022
(212) 759-0900

Families and Work Institute
330 Seventh Avenue
New York, NY 10001
(212) 465-2044

Family Resource Coalition
230 North Michigan Avenue, Suite 1625
Chicago, IL 60601
(312) 726-4750

National Association for Child Care Resource and Referral
Agencies
2116 Campus Drive, SE
Rochester, MN 55904
(507) 287-2020

National Association for Family Day Care
815 15th Street, NW, Suite 928
Washington, DC 20005
(202) 347-3356

National Association for the Education of Young Children
1834 Connecticut Avenue, NW
Washington, DC 20009
(800) 424-2460

National Black Child Development Institute
1463 Rhode Island Avenue, NW
Washington, DC 20005

National Child Care Association
920 Green Street
Conyers, GA 30207
(800) 543-7161

National Coalition of Hispanic Mental Health and Human
Services Organizations
1030 15th Street, NW, Suite 1053
Washington, DC 20005

National Maternal and Child Health Clearinghouse
38th and R Streets, NW
Washington, DC 20201
(202) 625-8410

Resources for Child Caring
450 North Syndicate Avenue, Suite 5
St. Paul, MN 55104
(612) 641-0305
(800) 423-9309

Resources for Infant Educarers
1550 Murray Circle
Los Angeles, CA 90026
(213) 663-5330

School-Age Child Care Project
Wellesley College
Center for Research on Women
Wellesley, MA 02180
(617) 431-1453

School-Age NOTES
P.O. Box 120674
Nashville, TN 37212
(615) 292-4957

Work and Family Clearinghouse at the Women's Bureau
U.S. Department of Labor
200 Constitution Avenue, NW
Washington, DC 20210
(202) 523-6611

Many libraries carry state- and county-specific resource
directories for child-care professionals that list local,
regional, and state-coordinated agencies providing
resource and other information for caregivers, parents,
employers, and other professionals interested in the care
and education of children.

2. Helpful Books and Other Resources

Beers-Boguslawski, Dorothy. *Guide for Establishing and Operating Day Care Centers for Young Children*. New York: Child Welfare League of America, 1986.

Blank, Helen. *Child Care: The Time Is Now*. Washington, D.C.: Children's Defense Fund, 1986.

Bredekamp, Sue, ed. *Accreditation Criteria and Procedures of the National Academy of Early Childhood Programs and Possibilities*. Washington, D.C.: National Association for the Education of Young Children, 1984.

Comfort, Randy L., and Constance D. Williams. *The Child Care Catalog: A Handbook of Resources and Information on Child Care*. Littleton, Colo.: Libraries Inc., 1985.

Indenbaum, Valerie. *The Everything Book for Teachers of Young Children*. Livonia, Mich.: Partner Press, 1985.

Kingsbury, Daniel; Sally Vogler; and Christine Benero. *The Everyday Guide to Opening and Operating a Child Care Center*. Lakewood, Colo.: Vade Mecum Press, 1990.

Miller, Ann, and Susan Weissman. *The Parents' Guide to Daycare*. New York: Bantam Books, 1987.

Phillips, D. A. *Quality in Child Care: What Does Research Tell Us?* Washington, D.C.: National Association for the Education of Young Children, 1987.

Reaves, John, and James B. Austin. *How to Find Help for a Troubled Kid: A Parents' Guide to Programs and Services for Adolescents*. New York: Henry Holt, 1990.

Resources for Child Caring. St. Paul: Toys 'n Things Press, 1989.

Scarr, Sandra. *Mother Care/Other Care*. New York: Basic Books, 1988.

Wilson, Miriam J. *Help for Children: Hotlines, Helplines, and Other Resources*. Shepherdstown, W. Va.: Rocky River Publishers, 1987.

3. State Licensing Agencies for Child Care

Alabama
Department of Human Resources
Division of Day Care and Child Development
Administrative Building
64 North Union Street
Montgomery, AL 36130
(205) 261-5785

Alaska
Department of Health and Social Services
Division of Family and Youth Services
P.O. Box H–05
Juneau, AK 99811–0630
(907) 465-3206

Arizona
Arizona Department of
Health Services
Child Day Care Facilities
1824 East McKinley
Phoenix, AZ 85006
(602) 258-0551

Arkansas
Department of Social
Services
Child Development Unit
P.O. Box 1437
Little Rock, AR 72201
(501) 682-8456

California
Department of Social
Services
Community Care Facilities
Division
744 P Street, Mail
Section 17–17
Sacramento, CA 95814
(916) 322-8538

Colorado
Licensing Administrator
Department of Social
Services
1575 Sherman Street,
Room 420
Denver, CO 80203–1714
(303) 866-5958

Connecticut
State Department of
Human Resources
1179 Main Street
Hartford, CT 06115
(203) 556-8048/8056

Day Care Licensing
Department of Health
Services
Division of Maternal and
Child Health
150 Washington Street
Hartford, CT 06106
(203) 566-2575

Delaware
Department of Services for
Children, Youth, and Their
Families
Division of Program
Support
1825 Faulkland Road
Wilmington, DE 19805–1195
(302) 633-2700

District of Columbia
Department of Consumer
and Regulatory Affairs
614 H Street, NW,
Room 1031
Washington, DC 20001
(202) 727-7822

Florida
Department of Health and
Rehabilitative Services
Child Care Branch
1317 Winewood Boulevard
Tallahassee, FL 32301
(904) 488-1800

Georgia
Day Care Licensing
Office of Regulatory
Services
Georgia Department of
Human Resources
878 Peachtree Street,
Room 607

Atlanta, GA 30309
(404) 894-5688

Hawaii
Department of Social
Services and Housing
Public Welfare Division
Program Development
P.O. Box 339
Honolulu, HI 96809
(808) 548-2302

Idaho
Child Care Coordinator
Department of Health and
Welfare
Bureau of Social Services
450 West State Street
Boise, ID 83720
(208) 334-5700

Illinois
Department of Children
and Family Services
406 Monroe Street
Springfield, IL 62006
(217) 627-1498

Indiana
Department of Public
Welfare
Child Welfare/Social
Services Division
141 South Meridian Street,
6th Floor
Indianapolis, IN 46225
(317) 232-4521

Iowa
Bureau of Adult, Children,
and Family Services
Department of Human
Services

Hoover State Office
Building, Fifth Floor
Des Moines, IA 50319
(515) 281-6074

Kansas
Kansas Department of
Health and Environment
Bureau of Child Care
Licensing
900 Southwest Jackson,
Suite 1001
Topeka, KS 66612–1290
(913) 296-1270

Kentucky
Division for Licensing and
Regulation
275 East Main Street
CHR Building, 4th Floor
East
Frankfort, KY 40621
(502) 564-2800

Louisiana
Division of Licensing and
Certification
Department of Health and
Human Resources
P.O. Box 3767
Baton Rouge, LA
70821–3767

Maine
Licensing Unit for Day Care
Bureau of Social Services
221 State Street
State House, Station 11
Augusta, ME 04333
(207) 289-5060

Maryland
Department of Child Care
Licensing and Regulation
600 East Lombard Street
Baltimore, MD 21201
(301) 333-8049

Department of Health and
Mental Hygiene
Family Health
201 West Preston Street
Baltimore, MD 21201
(301) 225-6743

Massachusetts
Day Care Licensing
Office for Children
10 West Street
Boston, MA 02111
(617) 727-8900

Michigan
Michigan Department of
Social Services
Child Day Care Licensing
Division
300 South Capital
P.O. Box 30037
Lansing, MI 48909
(517) 373-8300

Minnesota
Division of Licensing
Department of Human
Services
444 Lafayette Road
Saint Paul, MN 55155–3842
(612) 296-3971

Mississippi
Child Care and Special
Licensing
Bureau of Personal Health
Services

State Board of Health
P.O. Box 1700
Jackson, MS 39205
(601) 960-7740

Missouri
Missouri Department of
Social Services
Division of Family Services
Broadway State Office
Building
P.O. Box 88
Jefferson City, MO 65103
(314) 751-2450

Montana
Department of Family
Services
P.O. Box 8005
Helena, MT 59604
(406) 444-5900

Nebraska
Department of Social
Services
P.O. Box 95026
Lincoln, NE 68509–5026
(402) 471-3121

Nevada
Nevada Bureau of Child
Care Services
Department of Human
Resources
Kindead Building, Suite 606
505 East King Street
Carson City, NV 89710
(702) 885-5911

New Hampshire
Bureau of Child Care
Standards and Licensing
Division of Public Health
Services

Health and Welfare
Building
Hazen Drive
Concord, NH 03301
(603) 271-4624

New Jersey
Division of Youth and
Family Services
Bureau of Licensing
New Jersey Department of
Social Services
One South Montgomery
Street
Trenton, NJ 08625–0717
(609) 292-1018

New Mexico
Public Health Division
Licensing Bureau and
Certification
Health and Environment
Department
1190 St. Francis Drive
Runnels Boulevard,
Suite 1350 N
Santa Fe, NM 87503
(505) 827-2444

New York
New York State
Department of Social
Services
Day Care Unit
40 North Pearl Street
Albany, NY 12243
(518) 473-1004

New York City
Bureau of Day Care
New York City Department
of Health

65 Worth Street, 4th Floor
New York, NY 10013
(212) 334-7712

North Carolina
Division of Facility Services
Child Day Care Section
701 Barbour
Raleigh, NC 27603
(919) 733-4801

North Dakota
North Dakota Department
of Human Services
Children and Family
Services
State Capitol
Bismarck, ND 58505
(701) 224-4809

Ohio
Ohio Department of
Human Services
Child Care Services
State Office Tower, 30th
Floor, Sections E and F
30 East Broad Street
Columbus, OH 43266–0423

Oklahoma
Department of Human
Services
P.O. Box 25352
Oklahoma City, OK 73125
(405) 521-3561

Oregon
Children's Services Division
Department of Human
Resources
198 Commercial Street, SE
Salem, OR 97310
(503) 378-3178

Pennsylvania
Day Care Division
Department of Public
Welfare
Office of Policy Planning
and Evaluation
P.O. Box 2675
Harrisburg, PA 17105
(717) 783-6196

Puerto Rico
Department of Social
Services
Services to Families with
Children
P.O. Box 11398
Santurce, PR 00910
(809) 724-0303

Rhode Island
Rhode Island Department
for Children and Their
Families
Licensing Day Care Services
610 Mount Pleasant Avenue
Providence, RI 02908
(401) 457-4536

South Carolina
South Carolina Department
of Social Services
DCD Regulatory Unit
P.O. Box 1520
Columbia, SC 29202–9988
(803) 734-5740

South Dakota
Department of Social
Services
Office of Child Protection
Services

Richard F. Kneip Building
700 Governor Drive
Pierre, SD 57501–2291
(605) 773-3227

Tennessee
Department of Human
Services
Licensing Unit
400 Deaderick Street
Nashville, TN 37219
(615) 741-7129

Texas
Texas Department of
Human Resources
Licensing Division
P.O. Box 15995
Austin, TX 78761
(512) 835-2350

Utah
Department of Social
Services
Day Care Licensing
120 North Temple "200
West"
Salt Lake City, UT 84103
(801) 538-4242

Vermont
Department of Social and
Rehabilitation Services
Division of Licensing and
Regulation—Day Care
103 South Main Street, 2nd
Floor Osgood Boulevard
Waterbury, VT 05676
(802) 241-2158

Virginia
Department of Social
Services
Division of Licensing
Programs
Blair Building
8007 Discovery Drive
Richmond, VA 23229–8699
(804) 281-9025

Virgin Islands
Bureau of Day Care Service
Department of Social
Welfare
P.O. Box 550
Charlotte Amalie
Saint Thomas, VI 00801
(809) 774-4570

Washington
Department of Social and
Health Services
Division of Children and
Family Services
OB–41 D
Olympia, WA 98504
(206) 753-0614

West Virginia
Department of Human
Services
Division of Social Services
1900 Washington Street,
East
Charleston, WV 25305
(304) 348-7980

Wisconsin
Wisconsin Department of
Health and Social Services
Office for Children, Youth,
and Families
Division of Community
Services
One West Wilson Street
P.O. Box 7851
Madison, WI 53707
(608) 266-8200

Wyoming
Division of Public
Assistance and Social
Services
Family Services
Hathaway Building
Cheyenne, WY 82002
(307) 777-6285

Bibliography

Adolph, B., and K. Rose. *Employer's Guide to Child Care: Developing Programs for Working Parents*. New York: Praeger Publishers, 1985.

————. "Perceiving the Need, Delivering the Options." *Personnel Journal*, June 1986, pages 57–65.

Adult Day Care in America: Summary of a National Survey. Washington, D.C.: National Council on the Aging, 1987.

After-School Partnership: Pulling Together for Houston's Children. Houston, Tex.: Houston Committee for Private Sector Initiatives, 1989.

"Aging of Nation Means Change at Work." *Washington Post*, December 12, 1986, page F1.

Alpert, D., and A. Culbertson. "Daily Hassles and Coping Strategies of Dual Earner and Non-Dual Earner Women." *Psychology of Women Quarterly*, September 1987, pages 59–66.

American Association for Retired Persons and the Traveler's Foundation. *A National Study of Caregivers: Final Report*. Washington, D.C.: AARP, 1988.

"America's Child-Care Crisis: The First Tiny Steps toward Solutions." *Business Week*, July 10, 1989, pages 64–65+.

Anastas, J. W.; J. L. Gibeau; and R. J. Larson. *Breadwinners and Caregivers: Supporting Workers Who Care for Elderly Family Members*. Final report submitted by the National Association of Area Agencies on Aging to the U.S. Administration on Aging, 1987.

Aravanis, S. C.; R. Levin; and T. T. Nixon, eds. *Private/Public Partnership in Aging: A Compendium*. Washington, D.C.: National Association of State Units on Aging and Washington Business Group on Health, November 1987.

300

Armbrust, Pauline H. "The Parental-Leave Debate: Should the Federal Government Get into the Act?" *Montgomery Journal*, April 3, 1990, page 31.

Auerbach, J. *In the Business of Child Care: Employee Initiatives and Working Women.* New York: Praeger Publishers, 1988.

"Baby Face-Off." *New Republic*, May 9, 1988, pages 8–10.

Background Information on Major Child Care Programs and Legislation under the Jurisdiction of the Committee on Finance. Washington, D.C.: Congressional Research Service, Library of Congress, April 1989.

Bailey, J. E. "Personnel Scheduling with Flexshift: A Win-Win Scenario." *Personnel*, September 1986, pages 62–67.

Bass, D. M., and G. T. Kiemling. "Family Caregivers and Their Support." *Benjamin Rose Bulletin*, First Quarter, 1988.

Beach, B. *Integrating Work and Family Life: The Home-Working Family.* Albany, N.Y.: State University of New York Free Press, 1989.

Becker, Gary S. "Sure, Spend More on Child Care, But Spend Wisely." *Business Week*, May 8, 1989, page 24.

Besharov, Douglas. "Suffer the Little Children." *Policy Review*, Winter 1987, pages 52–55.

Bloom, D. E., and T. P. Steen. "Why Child Care Is Good for Business." *American Demographics*, August 1988, pages 22–27.

Borrfield, P. K. "Working Solutions for Working Parents." *Management World*, February 1986, pages 8–10.

"Bringing Up Baby." *New Republic*, June 13, 1988, pages 4, 7.

Brookes, Warren T. "The Great Child Care Debate." *Washington Times*, February 7, 1990, Section F-3.

Brothers, J. *The Successful Woman: How You Can Have a Career, a Husband, and a Family—and Not Feel Guilty about It.* New York: Simon & Schuster, 1988.

Brown, Luther. "Congress Delivers a New Child Care Bill." *Black Enterprise*, September 1989, page 27.

Burud, S.; P. Aschbacher; and J. McCroskey. *Employer-Supported Child Care: Investing in Human Resources.* Boston: Auburn House, 1984.

Cadden, Vivian, and S. Kamerman. "Where in the World Is Child Care Better?" *Working Mother*, September 1990, pages 62–68.

California Child Care Initiative, Year-End Report. *California Child Care Resources and Referral Network.* San Francisco, 1989.

Campbell, T. A., and D. E. Campbell. "71 Percent of Employers Say They Could Be Part of the Child Care Solution." *Personnel Journal*, April 1988, pages 84–86.

Caregivers in the Workplace. Washington, D.C.: American Association of Retired Persons, 1989.

Caregiving: The Challenge of Elder Care. New York: Southwestern Bell Telephone, 1987.

Carter, John D., and Diane S. Piktialis. "What to Do about Mother in Milwaukee." *Business and Health*, April 1988, pages 19–21.

"Catching Up on Child Care." *Time*, October 16, 1989, page 36.

Cherlin, A., and F. Furstenberg. *The New American Grandparent: A Place in the Family, a Life Apart*. New York: Basic Books, 1986.

Child Care and Elder Care on Long Island. Report of the Corporate Initiative for Child Care/Elder Care on Long Island, March 31, 1989.

Child Care: The Time Is Now. Washington, D.C.: Children's Defense Fund, 1987.

"The Child Care Dilemma." *Time*, June 22, 1989, pages 54–59.

Child Day Care: Funding Under Selected Programs. Washington, D.C.: Congressional Research Service, Library of Congress, January 1990.

Child Day Care: Patterns of Use among Families with Preschool Children. Washington, D.C.: Congressional Research Service, Library of Congress, 1988.

A Children's Defense Budget: An Analysis of Our Nation's Investment in Children. Washington, D.C.: Children's Defense Fund, 1989.

Congressional Research Service. *Child Day Care: Funding Under Selected Programs*. Washington, D.C.: Library of Congress, Report 88–686EPW.

Conniff, Dorothy. "What's Best for the Child?" *Progressive*, November 1988, pages 21–23.

Cook, Alice H. "Public Policies to Help Dual-Earner Couples Meet the Demands of the Work World." *Industrial and Labor Relations Review*, January 1989, pages 201–215.

Corporate and Employee Response to Caring for the Elderly: A National Survey of U.S. Companies and the Workforce. Sponsored by *Fortune* magazine and John Hancock Financial Services, 1989.

"Corporate Nannies for a New Decade." *U.S. News & World Report*, December 25, 1989, page 70+.

Creedon, M. A. *Issues for an Aging America: Employees and Eldercare*. Southport, Conn.: Creative Services, 1988.

————, ed. *Issues for an Aging America: Employees and Eldercare—A Briefing Book*. Bridgeport, Conn.: University of Bridgeport, Center for the Study of the Aging, 1987.

Cutler, Blayne. "The Swedish Example." *American Demographics*, April 1989, page 70.

"Daycare: A Bottom-Line Issue." *Corporate Communications Report*, Fall 1988.

Day Care and the Law of Church and State: Constitutional Mandates and Policy Options. Washington, D.C.: Congressional Research Service, Library of Congress, 1989.

"Day Care, Child Care, Word Care." *New York Times*, May 29, 1985, page 8+.

"Daycare for the Elderly." *U.S. News & World Report*, September 12, 1988, page 73.

Demos, J. *Past, Present, and Personal: The Family and the Life Course in American History*. New York: Oxford University Press, 1986.

Dusky, Lorraine. "The Corporation vs. the Family: Can the Conflict Be Resolved?" *Working Woman*, September 1989, pages 125–139.

————. "Mommy Tracks That Lead Somewhere Good." *Working Woman*, November 1989, page 133.

"Eldercare: A Quicker Corporate Response to a Growing Problem?" *Management Review*, July 1987, pages 8–9.

Eldercare: A Resource Guide. Bridgeport, Conn.: PepsiCo, Inc., 1986.

Elder Care and the Work Place, Special Survey Report. Bulletin to Management, Bureau of National Affairs Policy and Practice Series, February 1989.

"The Emerging Child-Care Issue." *Time*, May 16, 1988, page 42.

Employers and Child Care: Tax and Liability Considerations. Bureau of National Affairs Special Report no. 7, July 1988.

Employers and Eldercare—A New Benefit Coming of Age: The National Report on Work and Family. Washington, D.C.: Bureau of National Affairs, 1988.

"Employers Begin to Adopt Day Care." *National Underwriter*, April 13, 1987, pages 74–75.

"Employers Help with Eldercare." *Personnel*, March 1988, pages 4–5.

Employer-Supported Child Care in Michigan. Lansing, Mich.: American Association of University Women, 1987.

Employer Support for Child Care. New York: National Council of Jewish Women, 1988.

Etzion, D. "The Experience of Burnout and Work/Non-Work Success in Male and Female Engineers: A Matched-Pairs Comparison." *Human Resource Management*, Summer 1988, pages 168–179.

"Executive Guilt: Who's Taking Care of the Children?" *Fortune*, February 16, 1987, pages 30–37.

Faludi, Susan. "Are the Kids Alright?" *Mother Jones*, November 1988, pages 15–19.

"Family Care Programs: Investing in a Company's Work Force." *HR Focus* (John Hancock Mutual Life Insurance Company), November 1989.

Fernandez, J. P. *Child Care and Corporate Productivity: Resolving Family and Work Conflicts.* Lexington, Mass.: Lexington Books, 1986.

————. *The Politics and Reality of Family Care in Corporate America.* Lexington, Mass.: Lexington Books, 1990.

Fierman, Jaclyn. "Child Care: What Works—and Doesn't." *Fortune*, November 21, 1988, pages 165–176.

Fortune magazine and John Hancock Financial Services, *Corporate and Employee Response to Caring for the Elderly: A National Survey of U.S. Companies and the Workforce.* New York: Fortune, 1989.

Frank, Meryl, and Mary E. Lang. "The Day Care Dilemma: From Infants to Pre-Teens." *USA Today*, May 1, 1987, pages 59–62.

Friedman, D. E. "Child Care for Employees' Kids." *Harvard Business Review*, March–April 1986, pages 28–34.

————. "Eldercare: The Employee Benefit of the 1990s?" *Across the Board*, June 1986, pages 45–51.

————. *Linking Work-Family Issues to the Bottom Line: A Summary of Research.* New York: Conference Board, 1991.

————. "The Productivity Effects of Workplace Centers." Prepared for the Conference on Child Care Centers at the Workplace, Chicago, June 7–8, 1989.

Friedman, Milton. "Day Care: The Problem." *National Review*, July 8, 1988, page 14.

Fulton, Luella H. "The Child-Care Patchwork." *Ladies' Home Journal*, November 1989, pages 199–200.

Fusco, Mary Ann Castronovo. "Employment Relations Programs." *Employment Relations Today*, Autumn 1988, pages 257–260.

Gallinsky, E., and J. David. *The Preschool Years.* New York: Time Books/Random House, 1988.

Gallinsky, E., and D. Hughes. *The Fortune Magazine Child Care Study.* New York: Bank Street College, 1987.

Gallinsky, E., and D. Phillips. "The Day Care Debate." *Parents*, November 1988, pages 114–115.

Googins, B., and D. Burden. "Vulnerability of Working Parents: Balancing Work and Home Roles." *Social Roles*, July–August 1987, pages 295–300.

Gould, G., and M. Smith. *Social Work in the Work Place: Practice and Principles.* New York: Springer, 1988.

Gress-Wright, Jessica. "ABC and Me." *Commentary*, January 1990, pages 29–35.

Grim, S. *Employers and Eldercare.* Washington, D.C.: Bureau of National Affairs, 1988.

Halcrow, Allan. "IBM Answers the Elder Care Need." *Personnel Journal*, September 1988, pages 67–69.

Haskins, Ron, and H. Brown. "The Day-Care Reform Juggernaut." *National Review*, March 10, 1989, pages 40–41.

Hayne, Howard V. "Employers and Child Care: What Roles Do They Play?" *Monthly Labor Review*, September 1988, pages 38–44.

Health Action Forum. *Employer Eldercaregiving Survey.* Boston: Health Action Forum of Greater Boston, 1989.

"Helping Employees Cope with Aging Relatives." *Personnel Advisory Bulletin*, February 25, 1990, Section 1, no. 1804.

Holosko, M., and M. Feit. *Evaluation of Employee Assistance Programs.* New York: Haworth Press, 1988.

"Home Away from Home." *American Health*, September 1988, pages 87–88.

"How to Size Up Day Care." *Changing Times*, July 1988, pages 69–72.

Horne, J. *Caregiving: Helping an Aging Loved One.* Washington, D.C.: American Association of Retired Persons, 1986.

Hughes, D., and E. Gallinsky. "Balancing Work and Family Life: Research and

Corporate Application." In *Maternal Employment and Children's Development: Longitudinal Research,* eds. A. E. Gottfried and A. W. Gottfried. New York: Plenum Press, 1988.

Kahn, A. J., and S. B. Kamerman. *Child Care: Facing the Hard Choices.* Dover, Mass.: Auburn House, 1987.

Kola, Lenore A., and R. E. Dunkle. "Eldercare in the Workplace." *Social Casework,* November 1988.

LaFarge, Phyllis. "A Day in Family Day Care." *Parents,* January 1990, pages 56–64.

LaFleur, Elizabeth K. "Opportunities for Child Care." *Personnel Administrator,* June 1988, pages 146–149.

Lehrman, Karen, and Jana Pace. "Day Care Regulation: Serving Children or Bureaucrats?" *USA Today,* May 6, 1987, pages 63–66.

Levine, H. Z. "Alternative Work Schedules: Do They Meet Workforce Needs?" *Personnel,* February 1987, pages 57–62.

Levine, Karen. "Children at Work." *Parents,* April 1988, pages 70–74.

———. "Should I Stay Home?" *Parents,* January 1988, pages 58–62, 66.

Longstreth, Thatcher. "Local Child-Care Initiatives: The Philadelphia Approach." *Real Estate Finance Journal,* Summer 1990, pages 76–79.

Lubeck, Sally, and P. Garrett. "Child Care 2000: Policy Options for the Future." *Social Policy,* Spring 1988, pages 31–36.

Lyman, Karen A. "Day Care for Persons with Dementia: The Impact of the Physical Environment on Staff Stress and Quality of Care." *Gerontologist* 29:4 1989, pages 557–560.

Magid, R. Y. *Child Care Initiatives for Working Parents: Why Employers Get Involved.* New York: American Management Association, 1983.

Magnus, Margaret. "Eldercare: Corporate Awareness, But Little Action." *Personnel Journal,* June 1988, pages 19, 23.

Managing Work and Family Life: A Honeywell Task Team Report. Minneapolis: Honeywell, Inc., 1987.

Marshner, Connaught. "Socialized Motherhood: As Easy as ABC." *National Review,* May 13, 1988, pages 28–31.

McKay-Rispoli, K. "Small Children: No Problem." *Management World,* March–April 1988, pages 15–16.

Meisels, Samuel J., and L. Steven Sternberg. "Proprietary Child-Care Givers: Is '18 and Warm' Enough?" *Education Week,* January 1990, pages 62–64.

A Model for Developing Public/Private Partnerships for Employer-Supported Child Care. Northridge, Calif.: Center for the Study of Leisure and Play Behavior, 1987.

Moen, P., and D. I. Demster McClain. "Employed Parents: Role Strain, Work Time, and Preferences for Working Less." *Journal of Marriage and the Family,* August 1987, pages 579–590.

Mothers in the Workplace. New York: National Council of Jewish Women, 1987.

Myers, J. E. *Adult Children and Aging Parents*. Dubuque, Iowa: Kendall/Hunt Publishing, 1989.

The National Report on Work and Family. Special Report no. 2. Washington, D.C.: Buraff Publications, a subsidiary of the Bureau of National Affairs, 1988.

A National Survey of Caregivers, Final Report. Opinion Research Corporation. Washington, D.C.: American Association of Retired Persons, 1988.

Nelton, Sharon. "Six Ways to Be Family-Friendly." *Nation's Business*, March 1989, pages 12–13.

Ness, Immanuel. "Elder Care Benefit Needs Cited." *National Underwriter*, March 29, 1989, pages 27–28.

New York Business Group on Health (NYBGH). *Employer Support for Employee Caregivers*. New York: NYBGH, 1986.

Nollen, Stanley D. "The Work-Family Dilemma: How HR Managers Can Help." *Personnel*, May 1989, pages 25–30.

O'Brien, P. *How to Select the Best Child Care Option for Your Employees*. Binghamton, N.Y.: Almar Press, 1987.

"Old Hands: Who's Minding the Kids?" *Life*, December 1989, pages 102–104+.

"100 of the Best Companies for Working Mothers," *Working Mother*, October 1990, pages 36–45.

Ostroff, J. *Successful Marketing to the 50+ Consumer: How to Capture One of the Biggest and Fastest-Growing Markets in America*. Englewood Cliffs, N.J.: Prentice-Hall, 1989.

Overman, Stephanie. "State Report." *Personnel Administrator*, April 1989, page 39.

Parker, Michael. "Vouchers for Day Care of Children: Evaluating a Model Program." *Child Welfare*, November–December 1989, pages 633–642.

Perry, K. S. *Employers and Child Care: Establishing Services through the Workplace*. Washington, D.C.: Women's Bureau, U.S. Department of Labor, 1982.

Peterson, Donald J., and D. Massengill. "Childcare Programs Benefit Employers, Too." *Personnel*, May 1988, pages 58–62.

Phillips, J. D. *Employee Turnover and the Bottom Line*. Rahway, N.J.: Merck & Co., Inc., 1989.

Pierce, Jon L. *Alternative Work Schedules*. Boston: Allyn & Bacon, 1988.

Pifer, A., and L. Bronte. *Our Aging Society: Paradox and Promise*. New York: W. W. Norton, 1986.

Polniaszek, S. *Long-Term Care: A Dollar and Sense Guide*. Washington, D.C.: United Seniors Health Cooperative, 1988.

Posgrove, Carol. "One Mother's Search for Child Care." *Progressive*, November 1988, pages 16–20.

Pratt, Clara C., and A. J. Kethley. "Aging and Family Caregiving in the Future: Implications for Education and Policy." *Educational Gerontology* 14 (1988), pages 567–576.

A Profile of Older Americans. Washington, D.C.: American Association of Retired Persons, 1988.

Ranson, C., and S. Burud. *Productivity Impact Study.* Conducted for Union Bank Child Care Center. Pasadena, Calif.: Burud & Assles, 1987.

Reisman, B., et al. *Child Care: The Bottom Line.* New York: Child Care Action Campaign, 1988.

Remington Elder Care Programs. Bridgeport, Conn.: Remington Products, Inc., 1988.

"Research Is Needed to Ease Elderly Care Tab." *Arizona Republic,* May 2, 1990, page A-8.

Resources for Older Residents. Washington, D.C.: Iona House, 1990.

Robbins, S. P. *Essentials of Organizational Behavior.* Englewood Cliffs, N.J.: Prentice-Hall, 1988.

Rodgers, Fran S., and C. Rodgers. "Business and the Facts of Family Life." *Harvard Business Review,* November–December 1989, pages 120–129.

Salk, Lee. "Women's Changing Roles: Helping Your Child Understand." *McCall's,* November 1988, page 51.

Samalin, Nancy. "Building Your Child's Support System." *Working Woman,* October 1988, pages 155–157.

Samuelson, Robert J. "The Debate over Day Care." *Newsweek,* June 27, 1988, page 45.

Sandroff, R. "Helping Your Company Become Family-Friendly." *Working Woman,* November 1989, page 136.

———. "Why Pro-Family Policies Are Good for Business and America." *Working Woman,* November 1989, page 127+.

Schappi, J. *Improving Job Attendance.* Washington, D.C.: Bureau of National Affairs, 1988.

Scharlach, Andrew E.; Beverly F. Lowe; and Edward Schneider. *Elder Care and the Work Force: Blueprint for Action.* Lexington, Mass.: Lexington Books, 1991.

Schiffres, Manuel. "Another Break for Working Parents." *Changing Times,* September 1988, pages 73–75.

Schifrin, Matthew. "The Little Nursery That Lost Its Way." *Forbes,* May 16, 1988, pages 34–35.

Schnur, Susan. "In New Jersey: Day Care with a Lot of Caring." *Time,* March 28, 1988, pages 8, 10.

Schwab, T. *Caring for an Aging World: International Models for Long-Term Care, Financing and Delivery.* New York: McGraw-Hill Information Services, 1989.

Shell, Ellen Ruppel. "Babes in Day Care: The Controversy over whether Nonmaternal Care Harms Infants." *Atlantic,* August 1988, pages 73–74.

Silverman, Leonard. "Corporate Child Care: Playpens in the Boardroom or Productivity Investment?" *USA Today,* May 6, 1987, pages 67–69.

Smith, D. "Is Family Care a Corporate Responsibility?" *South Florida Business Journal,* February 1990, page 10.

"Staff Turnover May Be Day Care's Biggest Problem." *U.S. News & World Report,* October 23, 1989, page 33.

The State of Children and Families on Long Island: Report of the Long Island Roundtable. Melville, N.Y.: December 12, 1988.

Stautberg, Susan S. "Status Report: The Corporation and Trends in Family Issues." *Human Resource Management,* Summer 1987, pages 277–290.

Stern, George G., M.D. "Finding the Right Day Care for Your Child!" *Good Housekeeping,* September 1988, pages 130–132.

Stipek, Deborah, and J. McCroskey. "Investing in Children: Government and Workplace Policies for Parents." *American Psychologist,* February 1989, pages 416–423.

Stone, R. E., and P. Kemper. *Spouses and Children of Disabled Elders: Potential and Actual Caregivers.* Washington, D.C.: U.S. Department of Health and Human Services, January 1989.

Straus, Hal. "The Day Care Dilemma." *American Health,* September 1989, pages 87–88.

————. "Home Away From Home." *American Health,* September 1988, page 87.

"The Superdad Juggling Act." *U.S. News & World Report,* June 20, 1988, pages 67–71.

"Take Care with Child Care." *America,* September 10, 1988, page 123.

Thomas-Cote, Nancy. "Make Room for the Children." *Nation's Business,* October 1989, page 13.

Thompson, Roger. "Caring for the Children." *Nation's Business,* May 1988, pages 18–20+.

Tkac, D. "Day Care: Why It Makes Sense for Your Employer." *Children,* February 1988, page 24+.

Tonnessen, Diana. "Day Care Redeemed." *Health,* July 1988, page 18.

Traver, Nancy. "The ABCs of Child Care." *Time,* July 3, 1989, page 17.

Trost, Cathy. "Marketing-Minded Child-Care Centers Become More than 9-to-5 Babysitters." *The Wall Street Journal,* June 18, 1990, Section B, page 1.

Trost, Cathy, and Carol Hymowitz. "Careers Start Giving in to Family." *The Wall Street Journal,* June 18, 1990, Section B, pages 1, 4.

U.S. Congress. *Child Care and Development Block Grant of 1990,* Subchapter of the 1990 Tax Bill.

U.S. Congress Select Committee on Aging, "Exploding the Myths: Caregiving in America." *Comm. Pub. 99–611,* Washington, D.C.: U.S. Government Printing Office.

U.S. Department of Health and Human Services. *Aging America: Trends and Projections.* Washington, D.C.: U.S. Government Printing Office, 1987–88.

U.S. Department of Labor, Report of the Secretary's Task Force on Child Care. *Child Care: A Work Force Issue.* Washington, D.C.: U.S. Government Printing Office, April 1988.

U.S. House Select Committee on Aging. *Long-Term Care and Person Impoverishment: Seven in Ten Elderly Living Alone at Risk.* Washington, D.C.: U.S. Government Printing Office, October 1987.

U.S. House Select Committee on Children, Youth, and Families. Hearings, May 3, 1988.

U.S. Senate Special Committee on Aging. *Aging America.* Washington, D.C.: U.S. Government Printing Office, 1988.

A Vision for America's Future: An Agenda for the 1990s: A Children's Defense Budget. Washington, D.C.: Children's Defense Fund, 1988.

Wagner, D. L.; M. B. Neal; J. L. Gibeau; A. E. Scharlach; and J. W. Anastas. *Eldercare and the Working Caregiver: An Analysis of Current Research,* unpublished manuscript. Bridgeport, Conn.: Center for Aging, University of Bridgeport, 1988.

"When Companies Play Nanny." *U.S. News & World Report,* September 19, 1988, pages 43–45.

"Who Cares about Day Care?" *Newsweek,* March 28, 1988, page 73.

"Who's Taking Care of the Kids?" U.S. Census Bureau pamphlet. Washington, D.C.: U.S. Census Bureau, 1989.

Winfield, E. "Workplace Solutions for Women under Eldercare Pressure." *Personnel,* July 1987, pages 31–39.

Wojahn, Ellen. "Bringing Up Baby: The Myths and Realities of Day Care." *INC.,* November 1988, pages 64–75.

Work and Family Resource Kit. Washington, D.C.: U.S. Department of Labor, Women's Bureau, 1989.

Workforce 2000: Work and Workers for the 21st Century. Washington, D.C.: Hudson Institute, for the U.S. Department of Labor, 1987.

"The Working Mom's Handbook." *Ladies' Home Journal,* August 1989, pages 55–76.

Zimmerman, S. L. "Adult Day Care: Correlates of Its Coping Effects for Families of an Elderly Disabled Member." *Family Relations* 35 (1986), pages 305–311.

Zinmeister, Karl. "Brave New World: How Day-Care Harms Children." *Policy Review,* Spring 1988, pages 40–47.

_____. "Hard Truths about Day Care." *Reader's Digest,* October 1988, pages 89–93.

Zola, I. K. "Aging and Disability: Toward a Unifying Agenda." *Educational Gerontology* 14 (1988), pages 365–387.

Endnotes

Chapter 1

1. Ellen Gallinsky and Diane Hughes, *The Fortune Magazine Child Care Study* (New York: Bank Street College, 1987), p. 6.

2. Gary S. Becker, "Sure, Spend More on Child Care, But Spend Wisely," *Business Week*, May 8, 1989, p. 24.

3. Patricia Schroeder quoted by *Working Woman*, November 1989, p. 129.

4. Vivian Cadden and Sheila Kamerman, "Where in the World Is Child Care Better?" *Working Mother*, September 1990, p. 63.

5. Ronni Sandroff, "Why Pro-Family Policies Are Good for Business and America," *Working Woman*, November 1989, p. 127.

6. "Who's Taking Care of the Kids?" U.S. Census Bureau pamphlet, 1989 report.

7. D. E. Bloom and T. P. Steen, "Why Child Care Is Good for Business," *American Demographics*, August 1988, p. 24.

8. Sandroff, p. 129.

9. Jaclyn Fierman, "Child Care: What Works—and Doesn't," *Fortune*, November 21, 1988, p. 166.

10. Sandroff, p. 129.

11. Fierman, p. 167.

12. Ronni Sandroff, "Helping Your Company Become Family-Friendly," *Working Woman*, November 1989, p. 136.

13. Fran Sussner Rodgers and Charles Rodgers, "Business and the Facts of Family Life," *Harvard Business Review*, November–December 1989, p. 125.

14. "The Superdad Juggling Act," *U.S. News & World Report*, June 20, 1988, p. 69.

Chapter 2

1. Dana Friedman, *Linking Work-Family Issues to the Bottom Line: A Summary of Research* (New York: Conference Board, 1991).

2. Kathryn S. Perry, *Employers and Child Care: Establishing Services through the Workplace* (Washington, D.C.: Women's Bureau, U.S. Department of Labor, 1982), p. 10.

3. Renee Y. Magid, *Child Care Initiatives for Working Parents: Why Employers Get Involved* (New York: American Management Association, 1983), p. 45.

4. Sandra Burud, Pamela R. Aschbacher, and Jacquelyn McCroskey, *Employer-Supported Child Care: Investing in Human Resources* (Boston: Auburn House, 1984), p. 67.

5. "Exploding the Myths: Caregiving in America," U.S. Congress Select Committee on Aging, Comm. Pub. 99–611 (Washington, D.C.: U.S. Government Printing Office), p. 8.

6. M. A. Creedon, *Issues for an Aging America: Employees and Eldercare—A Briefing Book* (Bridgeport, Connecticut: University of Bridgeport, Center for the Study of Aging, 1987), p. 5.

7. *Fortune* magazine and John Hancock Financial Services, *Corporate and Employee Response to Caring for the Elderly: A National Survey of U.S. Companies and the Workforce* (New York: *Fortune*, 1989), p. 4.

8. A. E. Scharlach, Beverly F. Lowe, and E. L. Schneider, *Elder Care and the Work Force: Blueprint for Action* (Lexington, Massachusetts: Lexington Books, 1991), p. 37.

9. Larry Taylor quoted by Ellen Wojahn, "Bringing Up Baby: The Myths and Realities of Day Care," *INC.*, November 1988, p. 64.

10. Howard V. Hayne, "Employers and Child Care: What Roles Do They Play?" *Monthly Labor Review*, September 1988, p. 42.

11. "100 of the Best Companies for Working Mothers," *Working Mother*, October 1990, p. 36.

12. Hayne, p. 40.

13. Wojahn, p. 42.

14. Interview with Jo Anne Brandes, December 14, 1990.

15. Dana Friedman quoted by D. Tkac, "Day Care: Why It Makes Sense for Your Employer," *Children*, February 1988, p. 24.

16. Stephen P. Robbins, *Essentials of Organizational Behavior* (Englewood Cliffs, New Jersey: Prentice-Hall, 1988), pp. 30–31.

17. Robbins, pp. 30–31.

18. Wojahn, p. 65.

Chapter 3

1. Interview with Cherie Kester, August 7, 1990.

2. Leonard Silverman, "Corporate Child Care: Playpens in the Boardroom or Productivity Investment?" *USA Today*, May 1987, p. 69.

3. Carol Posgrove, "One Mother's Search for Child Care," *Progressive*, November 1988, p. 16.

4. Hal Straus, "The Day Care Dilemma," *American Health*, September 1989, p. 88.

5. "How to Size Up Day Care," *Changing Times*, July 1988, p. 71.

6. "The Child Care Dilemma," *Time*, June 22, 1989, p. 57.

7. Elizabeth Walters quoted by Lorraine Dusky, "Mommy Tracks That Lead Somewhere Good," *Working Woman*, November 1989, p. 133.

8. Dusky, p. 134.

Chapter 4

1. Samuel J. Meisels and L. Steven Sternberg, "Proprietary Child-Care Givers: Is '18 and Warm' Enough?" *Education Week*, January 1990, p. 63.

2. Hal Straus, "Home Away From Home," *American Health*, September 1988, p. 87.

3. Dorothy Conniff, "What's Best for the Child?" *Progressive*, November 1988, p. 22.

4. Karl Zinmeister, "Brave New World: How Day-Care Harms Children," *Policy Review*, Spring 1988, p. 42.

5. Zinmeister, p. 43.

6. Ibid.

7. Zinmeister, p. 42.

8. Ibid.

9. Selma Deitch quoted by "The Working Mom's Handbook," *Ladies' Home Journal*, August 1989, p. 68.

10. Straus, "Home Away From Home," p. 87.

11. Ellen Gallinsky and Deborah Phillips, "The Day Care Debate," *Parents*, November 1988, p. 114.

12. Gallinsky and Phillips, p. 115.

13. Gallinsky and Phillips, p. 114.

14. Gallinsky and Phillips, p. 115.

15. "The Working Mom's Handbook," p. 68.

16. Meisels and Sternberg, p. 66.

17. Ibid.

18. Meisels and Sternberg, p. 64.

19. Ibid.

20. "America's Child-Care Crisis: The First Tiny Steps toward Solutions," *Business Week*, July 10, 1989, p. 65.

21. Meisels and Sternberg, p. 64.

22. Conniff, p. 24.

23. Correspondence with Kinder-Care Learning Centers, La Petite Academy, Children's World Learning Centers, Gerber Children's Centers, and Children's Discovery Centers, October–November 1990, and *Business Week*, July 10, 1989, p. 65.

24. Meisels and Sternberg, p. 67.

25. Ibid.

26. Linda Burton quoted by Karl Zinmeister, "Hard Truths about Day Care," *Reader's Digest*, October 1988, p. 90.

27. Zinmeister, "Hard Truths about Day Care," p. 93.

Chapter 5

1. Figures obtained July 1990 from the Social Security Administration and Health Care Financing Administration.

2. "Eldercare: A Quicker Corporate Response to a Growing Problem?" *Management Review*, July 1987, p. 8.

3. American Association for Retired Persons and the Traveler's Foundation, *A National Study of Caregivers: Final Report* (Washington, D.C.: AARP, 1988).

4. A. E. Scharlach, Beverly F. Lowe, and E. L. Schneider, *Elder Care and the Workforce: Blueprint for Action* (Lexington, Massachusetts: Lexington Books, 1991), p. 29.

5. Health Action Forum, *Employer Eldercaregiving Survey*, (Boston: Health Action Forum of Greater Boston, 1989) p. 6; D. L. Wagner, M. B. Neal, J. L. Gibeau, A. E. Scharlach, and J. W. Anastas, *Eldercare and the Working Caregiver: An Analysis of Current Research*, unpublished manuscript, Center for Aging (Bridgeport, Connecticut: University of Bridgeport, 1988).

6. Child Care and Elder Care on Long Island, Corporate Initiative for Child/Elder Care on Long Island (provided by Grumman Corporation) March 31, 1989, pp. 1–3.

7. Margaret Magnus, "Eldercare: Corporate Awareness, But Little Action," *Personnel Journal,* June 1988, p. 19.

8. J. W. Anastas, J. L. Gibeau, and R. J. Larson, *Breadwinners and Caregivers: Supporting Workers Who Care for Elderly Family Members* (Final report submitted by the National Association of Area Agencies on Aging to the U.S. Administration on Aging, 1987), Grant #90AM158.

9. New York Business Group on Health, *Employer Support for Employee Caregivers* (New York: NYBGH, 1986), pp. 8–11.

10. Scharlach, et al., p. 56.

11. Scharlach, et al., p. 57.

Chapter 6

1. Fel-Pro, located in Skokie, Illinois, manufactures gaskets and other automotive and aeronautical components.

2. Interviews with Scott Mies, May–June 1990.

3. Interview with Robert O'Keefe, May 5, 1990.

4. Interview with Paul Lehman, May 5, 1990.

5. Interview with Gail Bjorklund, October 2, 1990.

6. Interview with Play and Learn Services, October 6, 1990.

7. Interview with Roselyn Karll, October 15, 1990.

8. Interview with Beulah Richards, November 1990.

9. Interview with Julie Goldstein, October 24, 1990.

10. Personal correspondence, America West Airlines, September 1990.

11. Interviews with Carol Anne Rudolphe, September–October 1990.

12. Personal correspondence, Phillips Petroleum Company, August 1990.

13. Interviews with IBM employees Ted Childs, Sarah Ann Gomez, and Jim Smith, September–November 1990.

14. Interviews and personal correspondence, Marriott Corporation, September–October 1990.

Chapter 7

1. "The Child Care Dilemma," *Time*, June 22, 1989, p. 58.

2. A. J. Kahn and Sheila B. Kamerman, *Child Care: Facing the Hard Choices* (Dover, Massachusetts: Auburn House, 1987), p. 62.

3. Interviews with Margery Sher, October–November 1990.

4. Personal correspondence, American Airlines, November 10, 1990.

5. Interview with *The Partnership Group*, October 8, 1990.

6. Interviews with Corporate Child Care Inc. employees, Dave Gleason and Dianne Huggins, October 1990.

7. Interviews and personal correspondence with Margery Sher, October 1990.

8. Carey Ferchland quoted by Ellen Wojahn, "Bringing Up Baby: The Myths and Realities of Day Care," *INC.*, November 1988, p. 10.

9. Interviews and personal correspondence, American Bankers Insurance Group, October–November 1990.

10. Interviews and personal correspondence, Steve Zwolak, MCCARE, October 12, 1990.

11. Interviews and personal correspondence, Sarah Ann Gomez, IBM, October–November, 1990.

12. Allan Halcrow, "IBM Answers the Elder Care Need," *Personnel Journal*, September 1988, pp. 67–69.

13. Interviews and personal correspondence, Sarah Ann Gomez, IBM, October–November 1990.

Chapter 8

1. Congressional Research Service, *Child Day Care: Funding Under Selected Programs* (Library of Congress, Report #88–686 EPW), p. 6.

2. Robert J. Samuelson, "The Debate over Child Care," *Newsweek*, June 27, 1988, p. 45.

3. Ron Haskins and Hank Brown, "The Day-Care Reform Juggernaut," *National Review*, March 10, 1989, p. 41.

4. Milton Friedman, "Day Care: The Problem," *National Review*, July 8, 1988, p. 14.

5. Samuelson, p. 45.

6. Jaclyn Fierman, "Child Care: What Works—and Doesn't," *Fortune*, November 21, 1988, p. 170.

7. A. J. Kahn and S. B. Kamerman, *Child Care: Facing the Hard Choices* (Dover, Massachusetts: Auburn House, 1987), p. 18.

8. Stephanie Overman, "State Report," *Personnel Administrator*, April 1989, p. 39.

9. Thatcher Longstreth, "Local Child-Care Initiatives: The Philadelphia Approach," *Real Estate Finance Journal*, Summer 1990, p. 79.

10. U.S. Congress, *Child Care and Development Block Grant of 1990*, Subchapter of the 1990 Tax Bill (provided courtesy of Senator Christopher Dodd).

Chapter 9

1. Chapter 9 material is compiled from personal interviews, surveys, company literature, media accounts, and personal correspondence. Information is up-to-date as of December 1990. Any changes and/or additions to corporate programs were not made available to the author by date of publication.

Index